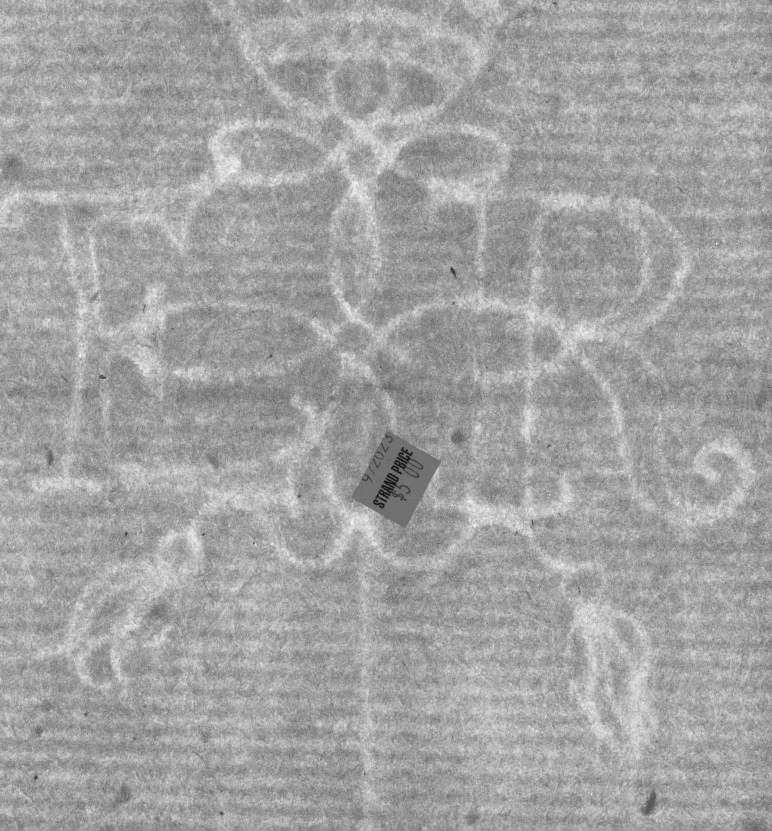

# Elizabeth I: Her Life in Letters

# Elizabeth I:

# Her Life in Letters

Felix Pryor

University of California Press

Berkeley Los Angeles

2003

For Sally

University of California Press
Berkeley and Los Angeles, California

Published by arrangement with
The British Library
First published in 2003



Cataloging-in-Publication data is on file with the Library of Congress

ISBN 0-520-24106-1 cloth

Designed and typeset by Peter and Alison Guy
Printed in Hong Kong by South Sea International Press

Frontispiece: Elizabeth *c.* 1574, the 'Pelican' portrait, attributed to Nicholas Hilliard
Postscript: Elizabeth *c.* 1600, the 'Rainbow' portrait, attributed to Isaac Oliver
Endpapers: Watermarks in paper manufactured for Queen Elizabeth
by John Spilman at his papermill in Dartford, Kent, *c.* 1590 (enlarged)

# Contents

Introduction 6
Acknowledgements 15
Notes on Calendar & Transcriptions 15
Chronology 15

Letters & Documents 16–135

1. Elizabeth to Katherine Parr, 31 July 1544
2. Elizabeth to Henry VIII, 30 December 1545
3. Elizabeth to Protector Somerset, 21 February 1549
4. Elizabeth to Edward VI, ?4 February 1553
5. Elizabeth to Mary, 17 March 1554
6. Cardinal Pole to Elizabeth, 14 November 1558
7. Philip Melanchthon to Elizabeth, March 1559
8. Philip II to Elizabeth, 24 April 1559
9. Thomas Gresham to Elizabeth, 25 February 1560
10. William Cecil to Elizabeth, 21 June 1560
11. John Knox to Elizabeth, 6 August 1561
12. De la Valette to Elizabeth, 21 September 1561
13. Elizabeth to the Senate of Hamburg, 18 March 1563
14. Elizabeth's speech to Parliament, 10 April 1563
15. Anthony Jenkinson to Elizabeth, 31 May 1565
16. John Hawkins to Elizabeth, 20 September 1565
17. Mary Queen of Scots to Elizabeth, 15 March 1566
18. Mary Queen of Scots to Elizabeth, 17 May 1568
19. Elizabeth to Mary Queen of Scots, 21 December 1568
20. Ivan the Terrible to Elizabeth, 20 June 1569
21. Ivan the Terrible to Elizabeth, 28 October 1570
22. Elizabeth's patent for Burghley, 25 February 1571
23. Elizabeth to Thomas Smith, 15 September 1571
24. Norfolk to Elizabeth, 21 January 1572
25. Elizabeth to Burghley, 11 April 1572
26. Catherine de' Medici to Elizabeth, 5 June 1572
27. Rudolph II to Elizabeth, 12 April 1577
28. Bess of Hardwick to Elizabeth, 17 March 1578
29. Elizabeth to Anjou, after 16 June 1579
30. Thomas Cely to Elizabeth, 12 December 1579
31. Edmund Spenser to Elizabeth, 22 December 1580
32. William the Silent to Elizabeth, 16 February 1581
33. Mary Queen of Scots to Elizabeth, 8 November 1582
34. Giordano Bruno (?) to Elizabeth, 26 March 1584
35. Elizabeth's warrant for Ralegh, 2 February 1585
36. Philip Sidney to Elizabeth, 10 November 1585
37. Elizabeth's speech to Parliament, 12 November 1586
38. Elizabeth's death warrant for Mary Queen of Scots, 10 December 1586
39. James VI to Elizabeth, March 1587
40. Edward Stafford to Elizabeth, 25 February 1588
41. Drake to Elizabeth, 8 August 1588
42. Elizabeth's speech at Tilbury, 9 August 1588
43. Leicester to Elizabeth, 29 August 1588
44. John Dee to Elizabeth, 10 November 1588
45. Robert Dickons to Elizabeth, 2 February 1589
46. Henri IV to Elizabeth, 15 August 1591
47. Essex to Elizabeth, 18 October 1591
48. Ralegh to Elizabeth, 23 February 1593
49. Elizabeth's translation of Boethius, October to November 1593
50. Richard Young to Elizabeth, 30 November 1594
51. Francis Bacon's play before Queen Elizabeth, 17 November 1595
52. Elizabeth's exemplification for Shakespeare, 4 May 1597
53. Elizabeth to Essex, 17 September 1599
54. Lord Mountjoy to Elizabeth, 2 April 1600
55. Elizabeth's death warrant for Essex, 20 February 1601
56. Anon to Elizabeth, 20 February 1601
57. Elizabeth to James VI of Scotland, 6 January 1603
58. Arabella Stuart to Elizabeth, early January 1603
59. Boris Godunov to Elizabeth, February 1603
60. Postscript: 'The Ocean to Scinthia'

Further Reading 136
Abbreviations 136
Notes 137
Manuscript & Picture Credits 142
Index 143

# Introduction

An encounter by John Simpson of the BBC in the bazaar at Peshawar in the Hindu Kush to my mind best sums up what this book is about: 'Once... I came across a dish of old silver coins and found, among the chunky *dirhams* of Haroun al-Rashid's Baghdad and the bright, wafer-thin coins of Sassanian Persia, a shilling of Queen Elizabeth I. I bought it so I could brandish it on camera, to show how much of a crossroads the bazaar in Peshawar had always been: and ever since I have carried the Elizabethan shilling in my wallet as a kind of token of mysterious journeying. How and when could it have possibly have reached the distant mountains of the Hindu Kush?'

This book is not a biography of Elizabeth, nor a study of her reign; although it might shed light on both. Nor does it propound a thesis. It is, rather, an exercise in kleptomania. Think of it as a treasure-cabinet; or as a market stall upon which you have stumbled during your wanderings through the Hindu Kush. You are invited to rummage and fish out astonishing objects, only in this case they are manuscripts not coins. Manuscripts are quite like coins, in that they often have a strong personal association and – in this case – have links with the Queen; but otherwise they are quite unlike. For a coin is a product of printing. It is hammered from a die; whereas a manuscript is the product of what Keats called 'this warm scribe my hand'. This letter, one could say, flowed from the hand of the living Elizabeth. The historian Diarmid MacCulloch has observed that 'most people from the past before film and sound recording are now no more than bundles of words: we read what is written about them, or fragments of what they wrote or said themselves. If we are lucky, we also have some idea of how they looked'. But an original letter written by Queen Elizabeth is more than a mere bundle of words. It has a physical dimension. So this book is as much about the act of looking as it is about reading. A new type of history perhaps. Many of the sixty documents laid out on this stall will, one hopes, produce a feeling of incredulity; a wonder that such a thing can still exist.

If there is something astonishing about these survivals from the past, there is also something astonishing about Elizabeth. She was a woman who exercised supreme authority in a man's world, while remaining intensely feminine. She assumed the role of Gloriana, the Virgin Queen, to some eyes even usurping the role of the Virgin Mary; but at the same time is held up as a role model for twenty-first century company executives. She is a near-legendary figure from a remote past who remains intriguingly modern. So she is perhaps a natural subject for such an exercise. Had it been a coin of her successor, James I, that John Simpson found in the Hindu Kush, it would not have been quite the same. It has to be Elizabeth.

But we have manuscripts rather than coins on offer. The word manuscript derives from the Latin: 'manu' (by hand) and 'scriptus' (written). Most of the manuscripts here can be described as autograph. This comes from the Greek: 'auto' (self) and 'graph' (write). When we say that a manuscript is autograph, we mean that it has been written by the writer in person, as opposed to a secretary or anybody else. Cognoscenti restrict its use to that of an adjective or adjectival noun, and ignore the perfectly valid secondary meaning (as we shall too) of 'signature'. Two of the components making up these words – 'hand' and 'write' – are straightforward; but the third – 'self' – is more problematic. But it is the self that gives autograph manuscripts their power, an iconic status not unlike that of a religious relic.

One of the distinguishing features of the self is impermanence. It is transitory. We have the letter, but what of the Elizabeth-self that wrote it? In his more than usually gloomy poem 'Aubade', Philip Larkin describes how he lies awake at night thinking about death and the extinction of the self. In the morning, the workaday world reasserts itself:

> ...all the uncaring
> Intricate rented world begins to rouse.
> The sky is white as clay, with no sun.
> Work has to be done.
> Postmen like doctors go from house to house.

Letters, those emissaries of the self that will eventually be snuffed out, are the paper-and-ink embodiments of this everyday world. This is the miracle of the letter written by the long-vanished selfhood of Elizabeth, or – viewed from a Larkinesque angle – its horrible poignancy.

The concept of the autograph – 'self-writing' – lies at the heart of this book. It is not just a collection of texts. Self-writing appears to have come into its own in the mid-fifteenth century, a hundred or so years before Elizabeth was born: it is perhaps no coincidence that the development of handwriting coincided with the invention of that exactly opposite method of writing, the printing press. Perhaps the distinction between that which was autograph, written in a cursive hand, and that which was produced by an anonymous scribe, written in a book hand, was needed to provide the conceptual leap that could lead to the mechanisation of writing. This period also saw the development of the Renaissance portrait, the first time since classical antiquity that recognisable individuals were being depicted from the life, possibly, as David Hockney suggests, employing visual devices that foreshadow photography. A piece of autograph writing is akin to a portrait, and has just a hint of photographic magic about it. There is something strange about these pieces of self-writing, as there is about an old photograph. It is almost as if we have here, displayed on our market stall, a set of vanished selves.

The terms of entry for this book are that the manuscript has either to be written by Elizabeth, or written to her. All of course depends on what one means by 'written', and, indeed, by 'to' and 'by'. Even a collection comprising just letters or manuscripts by Elizabeth faces problems, because she was of course a queen; and a monarch has at least two selves, the public self and the private. So, in the recently published *Elizabeth I: Collected Works*, there is printed the text of the torture warrant signed by Elizabeth, which also appears in this book. But the handwriting of the document is Burghley's, and it's a fair assumption that he wrote it out and handed it to the Queen to sign. Is it really one of her 'works'? A great many of her letters were written for her. One can, however, be fairly sure that she read what she signed; if nothing else, her fantastically elaborate signature would have given her pause for thought. Not for her the complaint of her favourite the Earl of Essex that 'amongst the infinite letters which are offered to us to sign, I must sign some such ere I knew what it was'. At the furthest reach of queenly non-participation is the document issued in Elizabeth's name, recording Shakespeare's purchase of his house in Stratford on Avon. It is 'by' Elizabeth in that it was issued in her name; but she is far removed from any direct personal involvement. It deserves its place on the market stall, though, because it is arguably the most typical thing on display; the type of royal document that was produced in greatest abundance.

The letters 'to' Elizabeth are just as, if not more, problematic. Many of course she would not have seen, for she had secretaries to open her letters for her; and they had their secretaries. It seems unlikely, for example, that she saw the letter to her by Sir Walter Ralegh. So is this letter 'to' her? Or take the letter by Edmund Spenser. Here Spenser is copying, in his capacity as a secretary, a letter that his boss has written the Queen; the copy being intended for the Queen's secretary, Sir Francis Walsingham. So we have a letter in Spenser's handwriting which is not by Spenser, written to the Queen but delivered to someone else. To whom, by whom, is this letter?

And how do you define a letter? A manuscript with a destination might do. Most manuscripts are written with a reader in mind. This is not the case with books. True, they have a target readership. But the book you buy in the bookshop has not been printed with you specifically in mind. Many books go unread. Letters are alive, in a way that the unspent coin or unread book is not. The recipient as well as the sender is important. It is a two-way transaction. The basic principle is simple: if A writes to B, B will end up with the original. If we look in B's in-tray, we will find the original; all A's out-tray will hold, if anything, is a retained copy or draft. The example of Edmund Spenser playing secretary adds a variation to the pattern – for we now have A sending a letter to B with a copy to C – but it does not alter it. There are, for example, three major repositories of Elizabethan state papers in England: the Public Record Office, the British Library, and Hatfield House. Between them they represent Queen Elizabeth's in-tray and her out-tray. They will, therefore, by-and-large hold drafts or copies of her outgoing correspondence, and originals of incoming (plus of course complicating factors such as inter-office copying).

The Public Record Office (PRO) is what it says it is. Papers have long been held by various branches of government, and archives kept since the late thirteenth century. A State Paper Office was established in 1578, when Dr Thomas Wilson – one of the men to whom our torture warrant is addressed – was made Keeper of the Office of Her Majesty's Papers and Records for Business of State and Council. They were at first kept in chests, and then organised into a library under James I. In 1610 James decreed that the papers of Lords Burghley, Salisbury and their predecessors as secretaries of state should go 'into a set form or library, in some convenient place within our palace of Whitehall'. Public records were energetically hunted down by a later Keeper, Sir Thomas Wilson (Dr Wilson's nephew and namesake).

This brings us to Sir William Cecil, Lord Burghley, and his younger son Sir Robert Cecil, Lord Salisbury, both of whom served as Elizabeth's chief minister. Burghley's elder son, Sir Thomas, enjoyed a less distinguished career: from him are descended the elder branch of the family, the Marquesses of Exeter of Burghley House, where family, rather than state, papers are held (this is where the illuminated grant of the barony of Burghley recently came to light). The younger son, Lord Salisbury, thus accumulated both his father's state papers and his own, as well as the confiscated papers of the Earl of Essex and Sir Walter Ralegh, and some of those of the Duke of Norfolk. Papers often stay with the person who generates them: the boundary between what is public and what is private being not always clear (as the controversy over the Churchill papers recently demonstrated). There is, again, a blurring of identities. Some of the state papers in Salisbury's keeping were claimed on his death in 1612 by the energetic Sir Thomas Wilson (quite possibly by prior agreement), and 89 volumes were secured for the State Paper Office.

A further 123 volumes were claimed by the heirs of Sir Michael Hickes, who had served firstly as secretary to Lord Burghley and afterwards as steward to Lord Salisbury. These were sold to the historian John Strype in the 1680s, and were acquired at Strype's death by the Marquess of Lansdowne, now forming part of the Lansdowne manuscripts (MSS) in the British Library. The British Library holds yet another group of Elizabethan state papers. These come from the collection of the great Elizabethan antiquary Sir Robert Bruce Cotton. He, with James I's indulgence – and much to the fury of Sir Thomas Wilson – removed a large quantity of papers for William Camden to use while preparing his famous *Annals* of Elizabeth's reign. Cotton collected papers from many other sources, including material relating to James's mother Mary Queen of Scots, who naturally received sympathetic treatment at Camden's hands; among this material is the letter sent by Eizabeth to Mary about the Casket Letters. Cotton of course accumulated a vast collection of non-Elizabethan material, including the manuscript of *Beowulf*, and his MSS constitute one of the foundation collections of what was to become the British Library. The Cottonian Library was arranged by shelves decorated with busts of the twelve Caesars: Julius, Augustus, Tiberius, Caligula, Claudius, Nero, Galba, Otho, Vitellius, Vespasianus, Titus, and Domitianus; plus Cleopatra and Faustina. The manuscripts, even in the modern setting of the new British Library, are still listed accordingly: the letter by Elizabeth to Mary, for example, is to be found in the volume shelved as MS Cotton Caligula C.I.

Nor is that the whole story. Other bunches of

state papers wandered to different homes, as always reflecting their public-cum-private nature. One batch was inherited by the diarist John Evelyn, whose wife was descended from a steward of the household to the Earl of Leicester: other Leicester papers ended up with Cotton or at Longleat House. The letter on display here from Sir John Hawkins once belonged to Evelyn, and has been docketed in his distinctive hand: 'Sir John Hawkens the greate Sea-man. his Letter to Qu: Eliz'. On 24 November 1665 Evelyn was visited by his friend Samuel Pepys, who recorded in his diary that his host 'showed us several letters of the old Lord of Leicester of Queen Elizabeth and Queen Mary Queen of Scotts and others, very venerable names. But Lord, how poorly methinks they wrote in those days, and on what plain uncut paper'. One hopes Pepys would have made an exception for Hawkins, his fellow naval administrator, who writes in an uncommonly elegant and legible hand; one in fact not unlike that of Pepys himself, and very different from the near-illegible scrawl of Sir Francis Drake (which may say something about their respective characters and habits of command). In 1681 Evelyn lent these papers to his friend and never asked for them back. They are now in the Pepys Library at Magdalene College, Cambridge.

The state papers at Hatfield House are generally the best preserved. Others have faced destruction by fire, damp and vermin. The great Cotton library suffered a disastrous fire in 1731. This explains the scorching round the edges of the first letter in this book. The papers at the State Paper Office only narrowly avoided destruction in the great Whitehall fire of 1619, suffered losses during the Civil War, and in 1750 were found 'to have greatly suffered from vermin and damp'. It is damp that explains the appropriately piratical appearance of the letter by Sir Francis Drake; the 'olde worlde' look that forgers and prop-makers alike strive for. Manuscripts can of course also suffer from well-meaning attempts at restoration. For example, Elizabeth's letter to her sister Mary and the letter by the Duke of Norfolk have both been 'silked'; an attempt to preserve the paper by pasting fabric over it, giving the writing a fuzzy appearance. Quite a few letters in the Cotton library have had their seals, originally on the outside, pasted alongside the signature; an example of this being the letter by Elizabeth to Mary Queen of Scots (our friend MS Cotton Caligula C.I, fol. 94v).

A few of the manuscripts in this book have been written on parchment or vellum. English parchment was usually made from sheep, and vellum from calves ('vellis' being the Old French for calf). It is extremely difficult to tell the difference between the two, although vellum is generally perceived as being of higher quality. We have followed convention and used the term vellum throughout. The great majority of our manuscripts are on paper, which originated in China and was first manufactured in Europe in about 1150. Paper was not made in England until the 1490s, and was largely imported until the eighteenth century. John Spilman, a German goldsmith by appointment to Queen Elizabeth, established a paper mill in 1588 at Dartford in Kent, and was granted a monopoly on paper-making. He produced paper especially for the Queen, distinguished by two types of watermark, one bearing her crowned ER cipher, the other her arms surrounded by the Garter. From a cursory sampling of the Cotton manuscripts this personalised stationery seems to have been used in the early 1590s, although more by her courtiers than Elizabeth herself. All such paper was made from rags and is extremely durable. Modern paper, by contrast, is made from acidic wood pulp, which turns yellow and then brown as it disintegrates, a process memorably described by Robert Frost in his poem 'The Wood-Pile' as 'the slow smokeless burning of decay'. In 1988 Sir Philip Sidney's letter to the Queen was included in *The Faber Book of Letters*. The paper of the printed version has turned brown already; while the original at Hatfield, four hundred years its senior, is doing fine.

All the manuscripts in this book have been written in ink (graphite pencil was not to be introduced until the following century). In Italy they used ink from squids; but in England this was not available, so they used galls, the round nut-like objects produced by the gall-fly on branches of oak trees, instead. The palaeographer Anthony Petti describes the process: 'The usual English recipe was to take three ounces of dry and quite firm gall nuts, break them up and soak them in a quart of wine or rainwater and leave them out in the sun for a couple of days, then stir in two ounces of iron sulphate and leave in the sun for another day. Finally an ounce of gum Arabic was added, the resultant mixture also being left in the sun for a day. Strained and placed in a well-stoppered lead container, the liquid would be serviceable for a considerable time. For extra lustre it was recommended that a slice of pomegranate be added and the mixture simmered on a slow fire'. Writing itself was done with a quill, usually plucked from a goose, which was cut to shape and kept in trim with a penknife. Costume dramas notwithstanding, most of the feathery part was trimmed. The pen was held, as now, with the finger and thumb, with the third finger acting as a rest. Surplus ink was absorbed by dusting the paper with pounce, a fine powder made of pulverized sandarac or cuttle-shell, traces of which can sometimes still be seen adhering to the ink. Once a letter was done and dusted, it would then be folded and sealed, with the address written on the outside. Sometimes slits would be cut in them and they would be closed with silk ties; although this was an extravagance that not everybody could afford. Quite a few of the letters in this collection have been cut, tied and sealed in this way, including the effusion the Earl of Essex sent the Queen, one of 'those elegant, impassioned, noble letters, which still exist, with their stiff, quick characters and their silken ties that were once loosened by the long fingers of Elizabeth' that so impressed Lytton Strachey.

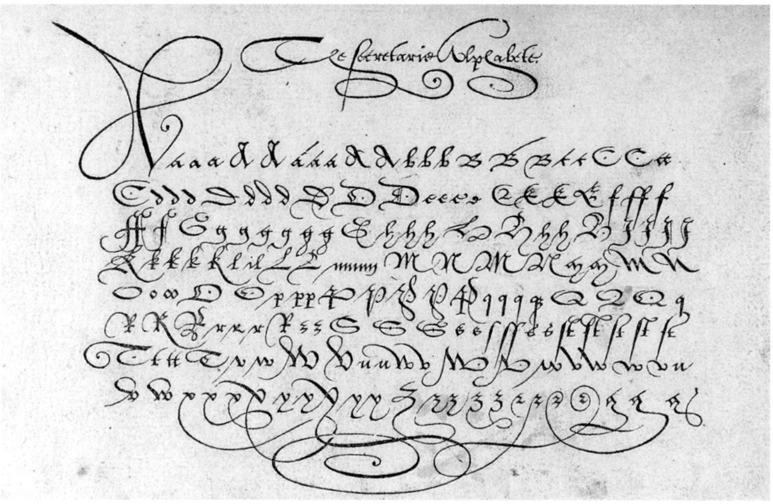

The Secretary alphabet, from John de Beau Chesne and John Baildon, *A Booke Containing Divers Sortes of Hands* (1571)

Which brings us, at last, to the subject of writing itself. The commonest script in use during this period is the Secretary Hand, a native form that evolved from the court hands of the Middle Ages. Roughly speaking, the Secretary Hand could be said to have evolved in the mid-fifteenth century, although some authorities, using stricter criteria, date its first use to the 1520s. By early in the seventeenth century it was already being diluted by the incoming Italic, which forms the basis of our modern hands; and by the eighteenth century only a few traces remained. The most misleading features of Secretary script are the lower-case letters: the 'c' which looks like a 't', the 'e' which can (but does not always) look like a 't' (or a squashed version of the running 'd'), the 'h' which swoops below the line, and the 's' which looks like an 'f' but is made of two pen-strokes.

The Secretary was generally used for business, and by hacks like Shakespeare. Grander people, while capable of writing it, affected the new, imported, elegant, easy-to-read, aesthetically pleasing Italic, also known as the Roman or Italian Hand. Italic was particularly favoured by women. Martin Billingsley in his writing manual *The Pen's Excellencie* (1618) says this is because 'it is conceived to be the easiest hand that is written with Pen, and to be taught in the shortest time: Therefore it is usually taught to women, for as much as they (having not the patience to take any great paines, besides phantasticall and humorsome) must be taught that which they may instantly learne'. The new Italic was also in general use among the nobility and among the rising generation of humanist-educated statesmen like Sir William Cecil. Their handwriting generally uses modern letterforms and should present little difficulty to the modern reader.

As for Elizabeth, early in life she wrote in an Italic hand. The identity of her first teacher is unknown, but from 1545 she appears to have received instruction from her brother's tutor Jean Belmain, and then from Roger Ascham's protégé

William Grindal; a subject to which we shall return in discussing the manuscripts themselves. As an idle rifle through this book will show all too clearly, her handwriting went downhill thereafter. Her later scrawl is matched in its illegibility only by that other grande dame, Queen Victoria. The 1802 catalogue of the Cotton MSS, in describing MS Vespasian F.III, art.29, puts it succinctly: 'Q. Eliz. a memorandum containing some advice, the purport of which is unintelligible'. During the last couple of years of her life, Elizabeth seems to have suffered from gout and rheumatism, and her writing flattened, as in her 'skrating' letter to James VI of 1603. That same year a contemporary noted: 'I have heard it creditably reported that, not long before her death, she was divers times troubled with gout in her fingers whereof she would never complain, as seeming better pleased to be thought insensible of the pain than to acknowledge the disease'.

Her late hand remained predominantly Italic, but has several – general 'skrating' apart – toe-stubbing features, derived from the Secretary script: her lower-case 's' often looks like a lower case 'b' (this derives from the Secretary's terminal 's'); she writes 'e' in two strokes like the modern 'i'; sometimes 'h' is reduced to a downward slash; and her final 's' is sometimes written as 'z' (possibly intended for an 'es'). She also used capital letters – heaven knows why – in mid word. Her spelling, too, can be hard going: a favourite trick is to write 'the' instead of 'they'. Her spelling does, though, provide some tantalising indications of what Elizabeth might have sounded like: for 'sister' she writes 'sistar', for 'Gods' she writes 'Godz', instead of 'things' she writes 'thinkes' (suggesting, as her most recent editors put it, that 'the consonantal values of *g*, *ng*, and *gt* may have been close to that of hard *k* in Elizabeth's speech'). She seems also to have favoured the cockney 'h', giving us 'hit' for 'it' and 'Habilite' for 'ability' (a feature also found in Leicester and Burghley's writing).

While most of the manuscripts in this book are distinguished by an autographic element, if even just a signature, there are some exceptions. One is the illuminated grant of the barony of Burghley. Here the Great Seal serves in the place of a signature (which is why, having smashed the thing, the newly ennobled Burghley has carefully stitched it into a canvas bag). Similarly, the two letters by Ivan the Terrible and that by Boris Godunov rely for their authority on seals rather than signatures. Neither is in the Tsar's handwriting, but all three carried seals and are the actual letters that were sent to the English court. They are – like the grant of Burghley's barony – throwbacks to the pre-autographic tradition.

As its name implies, the Great Seal was the most important of the English royal seals, and was held in the keeping of the Chancery, established in the middle ages as a permanent centre of administration to serve a court that was almost permanently on the move. Presiding over it was the Lord Chancellor, or, if no Chancellor had been appointed, the Lord Keeper of the Great Seal (the office held in Elizabeth's reign by Sir Nicholas Bacon and Sir Thomas Egerton). Those documents that Elizabeth did sign were usually issued under either the Privy Seal or her Signet. Both denote particular branches of the administration (the signet being also the Queen's personal seal); in the words of Dianne Tillotson: 'Most of the documents which were sent out from the chancery into the great wide world were authenticated with the great seal. The privy seal and the signet were mainly used for documents passed between the secretariats and so are less likely to be found among the papers of the recipients of grants, now scattered around regional archives and private libraries'. The Great Seal is most commonly found on Letters Patent, an open document conferring or confirming a right, settling a dispute, or whatever; whereas the two lesser seals are usually found on warrants issued by one branch of the administration to another (thus Essex's death warrant is issued under the Privy Seal and addressed to the Lord Keeper, who in turn made out another warrant so that

Obverse of the second Great Seal, designed by Nicholas Hilliard

the deed could be done). The two lesser seals are single-sided and were attached directly to the document, with a diamond square of paper placed over the wax, impressed with Elizabeth's arms. The Great Seal by contrast is double-sided and suspended by either a vellum tag, or silk ties.

Elizabeth employed two Great Seals during her reign, each of which – following the mediaeval pattern – shows her enthroned in majesty on the obverse, and mounted on horseback on the reverse. It has been suggested that the artist responsible for designing the first of the Elizabethan Great Seals was the court miniaturist Levina Teerlinc. But if, as we argue, she was responsible for executing the portrait on the newly discovered Burghley grant, such a supposition would seem unlikely, since the drawing is supposed to be a copy of the seal's obverse; something it doesn't do very well (whatever its other merits). But there is no dispute about the artist responsible for the second seal. On 8 July 1584 the new seal-matrix was commissioned from Nicholas Hilliard (a goldsmith as well as miniaturist) and Derek Anthony, Graver of the Mint, 'as our Great Seal by much use waxes unserviceable'. Hilliard's seal, in use from 1586, gives us one of the most familiar images of the reign.

Elizabeth's signature – properly called her Sign Manual – has been described as 'her queenly trademark', and is even more famous than the seal Hilliard designed for her. At the very outset of her reign, her signature did not differ greatly from that she used as a princess, her name being followed by a paraph similar to the quatrefoil flourish used by her father. But from about the time of her coronation on 15 January 1559 (and possibly marking the event), she began signing herself 'Elizabeth R'. This is a linguistic mish-mash, of English (Elizabeth) and Latin (Regina). Her grandmother, Elizabeth of York, favoured this hybrid, but otherwise Tudor queens had been linguistically more consistent and stuck to plain English: Elizabeth's mother, Anne Boleyn, signed herself 'Anne the Quene', Lady Jane Grey as 'Jane the Quene', and Elizabeth's half-sister as 'Marye the Quene'. Elizabeth retained her 'Elizabeth R' trademark, with the same calligraphic flourishes and number of twirls, until the end of her life. Although as the years passed – whether through dimming eyesight or weakening wrist or some psychological cause – her signature grew larger and LARGER and LARGER.

1559

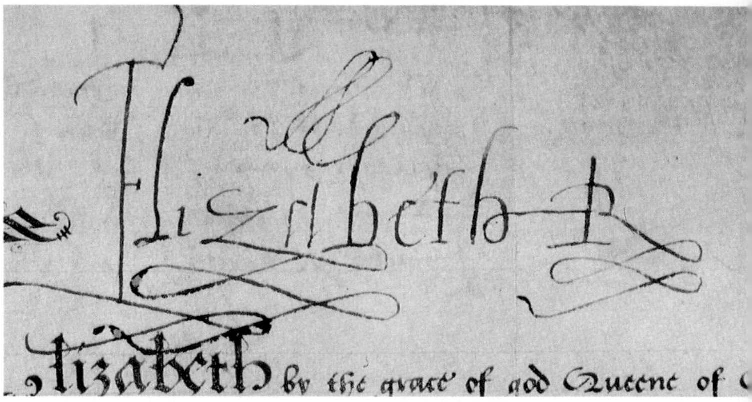


1568

1570

Documents signed by Elizabeth in 1559, 1568, 1570 (with the stamp), 1580, 1588 and 1602, showing actual size the gradual enlargement of her signature.

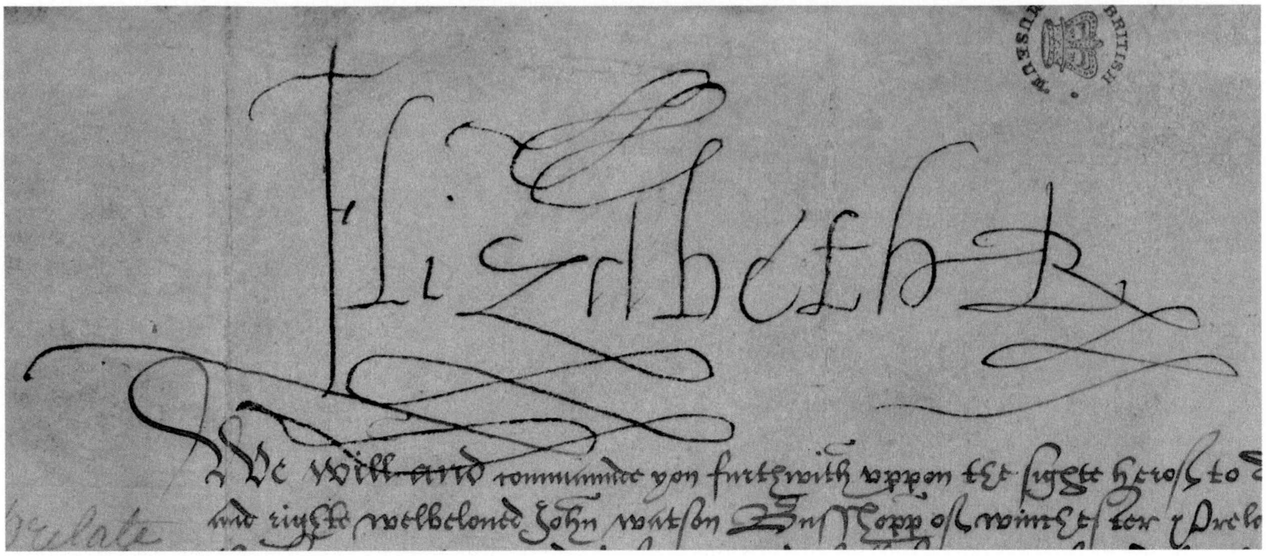
1580

1588

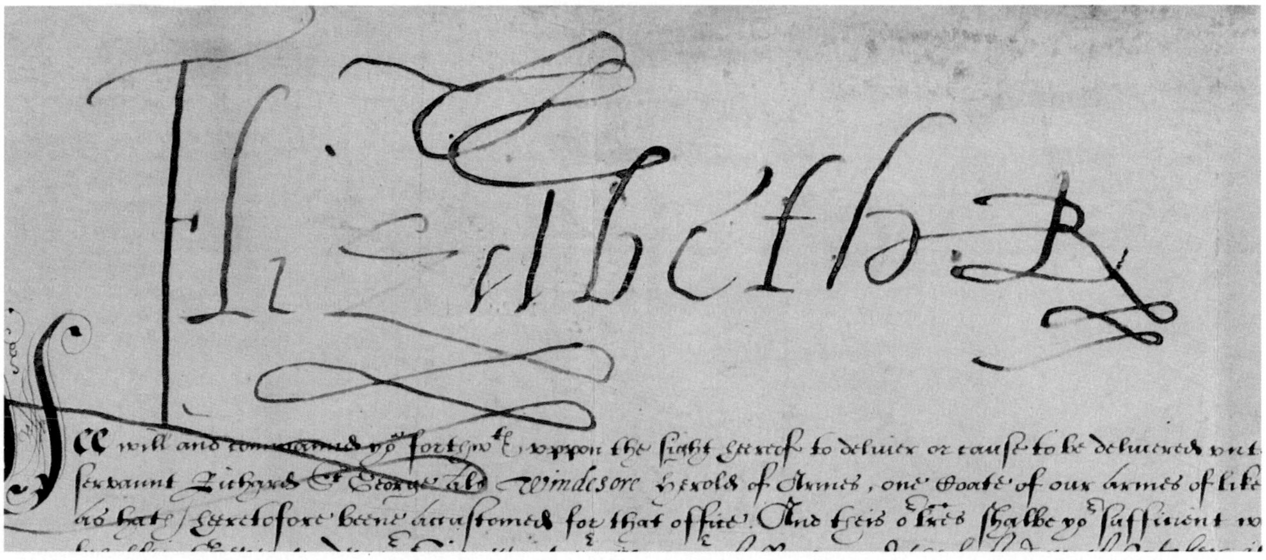
1602

It is not just that Elizabeth's signature is remarkable for its elaboration. It is remarkable that she didn't use something simpler. For she insisted on signing things herself. So under the circumstances one might have expected her to settle for something a little less fantastical. Powerful bosses are famous for hurried, scrawled signatures. Not so Elizabeth. The remarkable thing about all this is that her predecessors, Henry VIII, Edward VI and Mary, often had recourse, when authorising routine documents, to woodcut stamped signatures. With a boy-king like Edward this is not surprising; but with Henry and Mary it perhaps does say something about their style of monarchy. With Henry, one has the impression that he just couldn't be bothered. But at least a woodcut signature can be clearly identified as such. In 1545 Henry VIII, who already had his routine documents signed for him by the crude woodcut stamp, brought into use a 'dry stamp'. This was an uninked blind-stamp which was impressed into the paper, leaving a light but accurate impression of the King's Sign Manual. A specialist calligrapher – Henry's was called William Clerk – would then ink over the outline, thus producing a near perfect facsimile of the royal signature. Henry at first kept the use of this device under his close personal supervision, but it was then handed over in its 'little coffer of black leather' to one of his Gentlemen of the Privy Chamber, John Gates. As David Starkey puts it, Henry 'had alienated his signature as completely as earlier Kings had alienated their seals to their Chancellors'. All sorts of things could now easily be done in the King's name. There is good reason to believe that Henry's will was 'signed' only after he had died. It seems that the dry stamp was also used in Edward's reign and under Mary.

None of this applies to Elizabeth. Although there may be one exception. On 10 March 1570 she issued a warrant authorizing Sir William Cecil to affix her signature by stamp to a series of letters sent into the shires to raise levies against the Rebellion of the Northern Earls (finding that 'we can not in due time with our hand writing signe them all according to our desire'). An example of one of these letters, bearing her stamped signature, is with the warrant at the Public Record Office. Both have been nibbled by mice in a similar fashion and clearly belong together. The warrant is a draft only, and the accompanying document obviously a retained sample. I do not know whether any letters with her stamped signature were, in the event, ever sent out. Certainly it did not set a precedent.

Elizabeth was, as everybody knows, given to vacillation; and there is at least one example in this book of her countermanding an order, in the case of the execution of the Duke of Norfolk. When it came to the execution of her cousin Mary Queen of Scots, the delay was near endless. At long last she was persuaded to sign the warrant. When news of the execution was brought to her, she tried to avoid responsibility by blaming her Council and Secretaries of State. They had, she furiously protested, despatched the warrant without her permission. But the validity of her signature was never in question. The warrant itself has vanished, but there remains a copy among the papers of Robert Beale, the trusted Clerk to the Council and the man they chose to send galloping up to Fotheringhay, taking with him with the original document bearing the Queen's signature. Beale has written on his copy, now in the British Library: 'Her Majestys hand was also in the Coppie' (i.e. the original warrant). It says a good deal about Elizabeth that she did not, like her father, her brother or sister, take the easy option and delegate her sovereignty and moral agency to a stamp.

# Acknowledgements

My first thanks are due to Simon Adams who has not only corrected numerous errors of fact and interpretation, but has been generous in sharing his profound knowledge of the period and its sources. I think I should add that he read the penultimate draft only, which has allowed me plenty of scope to introduce fresh errors or misinterpret his suggestions. I am also grateful to Henry Woudhuysen, who early on sent me his unpublished paper 'The Queen's Own Hand', which has proved an invaluable guidebook on my journey (a far longer one than I ever anticipated). Susan Wharton did a great deal of work on the translations (hers being those without the howlers). Another colleague from Sotheby's days, Peter Beal, offered guidance and encouragement throughout. I am likewise grateful to Thomas G. Barnes for general as well as specific advice and encouragement. I should also like to thank Jon Culverhouse and Victoria Leatham (not least for Hamlet's Ferrari), Julia Hamilton, Sally Plum, Belinda Ross, Mark Dunton, Karen Hearn, Simon and Judy Rodway, the late Tim Clark (for teaching me about unicorns), Roy Davids (for teaching me about manuscripts), Joan Winterkorn (ditto), John Wilson (ditto), Stephen Roe, Gavin Littaur, Philippa Windsor, Susan Frye and Georgianna Ziegler. A year ago I was fortunate to meet Richard Lourie, who suggested I look into the correspondence between Elizabeth and Ivan the Terrible, thus jolting me from a set of biographical tramlines: for some reason, while biographers of Ivan write at length about Elizabeth, hers hardly ever mention him (Peter Beal reminds me that she even features in Eisenstein's *Ivan the Terrible*). I am grateful to Susan Doran, for allowing me to gatecrash the 'Elizabeth I: Monarchy and Myth' conference at St Mary's College, Strawberry Hill, in June 2002 (an instructive if humbling experience). This book has been prepared from original manuscripts, and many more have been examined and photographed than made it into the final selection, but never once have I received anything but helpfulness and patience from their custodians, from Robin Harcourt Williams at Hatfield, my first port of call, to Richard Luckett at the Pepys Library, my last: my gratitude and thanks, then, to all those at the British Library, the Public Record Office, Hatfield House, the Lambeth Palace Library, the Bodleian Library, the Pepys Library, the Shakespeare Birthplace Trust, and Burghley House (where first I stumbled across Levina's Elizabeth rolled up in the corner of a cupboard ten years ago). As always, the London Library has proved itself invaluable (although there does seem to have been rather a run on books about Elizabeth of late). *Elizabeth I: Her Life in Letters* would have been hard to write – indeed would not have been thought of – without Marcus, Mueller and Rose's *Elizabeth I: Collected Works*. I have likewise drawn on the pioneering work of G. B. Harrison and Maria Perry. Samantha Bodey, Simon Roberts and the Book Department of Phillips (now Bonhams) have been selfless in allowing me to work on this book undistracted. My thanks, finally, to those who produced the book: Lara Speicher, Kathleen Houghton, Belinda Wilkinson, Peter and Alison Guy, and Catherine Britton. The whole project was the brainchild of David Way – I was several thousand miles away, somewhere to the northeast of Peshawar, when he came up with the idea – so he must bear the blame for its inception, if not its taphonomy.

TFMP

March 2003

# Calendar

From 1582-83 there were two calendars in use in Europe. Catholic countries adopted the reformed Gregorian calendar (New Style) while England retained the Julian calendar (Old Style). Under the old calendar the year started on 25 March (Lady Day), under the new it began on 1 January. The new also ran ten days in advance of the old. In dating manuscripts we have followed the usual practice of giving the year according to the New Style, while conforming to whatever day and month is given in the manuscript (mostly Old Style).

# Transcription

No printed version can hope to reproduce the nuances of a hand-written text. Indeed, that is the whole point of this book. In quoting from the documents on display, I have adopted the pattern set out by Samuel Schoenbaum in his *William Shakespeare: A Documentary Life* (1975): 'In a book such as this, in which facsimile reproductions are married to the text, I have thought it advisable to preserve the idiosyncracies of old spelling in quotations from manuscript and early printed sources. I have, however, normalized long *s* and final *j*, and the *i-j*, and the *u-v* equations (e.g. I give *upon* for *vpon*, *have* for *haue*, and *joyed* for *ioyed*). I have also extended abbreviations, except for certain common and untroublesome forms (e.g. $y^e$, &, $W^m$, $M^r$). Expansions are introduced silently' (p.xvi). I have parted from Schoenbaum in expanding '$y^e$' to 'the'; the 'y' here being a relic the Old English and Icelandic runic letter 'thorn' which represents the 'th' sound.

# Chronology

1533 (7 September) Elizabeth born
1547 Henry VIII dies, Edward VI succeeds
1553 Edward VI dies, Mary succeeds
1558 (17 November) Mary dies, Elizabeth succeeds
1568 Mary Queen of Scots comes to England
1585 First colony in Virginia
1587 Mary Queen of Scots executed
1588 Defeat of the Spanish Armada
1601 Essex's rebellion and execution
1603 (24 March) Elizabeth dies

L. Eliz. Hen 8 daughter to the Q her mother in law



L'inimica fortuna inuidiosa d'ogni bene, et voluitrice de cose humane
priuo per un'anno intero della Ill.ma presentia vostra, et non ess
anchora contenta di questo, vn'altra uolta me spoglio del mede
bene: la qual cosa a me saria intollerabile, s'io non pensassi be
di goderla. Et in questo mio exilio certamente conosco la clem
sua altezza hauer hauuto cura, et sollicitudine, della sanità m
quanto fatto haurebbe la maiestà del Re. Per la qual cosa n
sono tenuta de seruirla, ma etiandio da figlial amore reuer
intendendo vostra Ill.ma Altezza non me hauer domentica
volta che alla maiestà del Re ha scritto: il che a me ap
quella prieghare. Pero insino a qua non hebbi ardire a
per il che al presente uostra Eccell.ma altezza humilmēte
che scriuendo a sua maistà si degni de raccomend
gando sempre sua dolce benedettione, similmēte pr
l signore Iddio gli mandi successo boniss.mo acquis
soui inimici, acciochè piu presto possia uostra a
me con lei rallegrarsi del suo felice retorno. N
dio che conserui sua Ill.ma altezza alla cui gr
asciando le mani m'offero et raccomn
cobo alli 31 di Iulio

*'I am bound not only to serve you but to revere you with a daughter's love'*

# I The first letter

31 July 1544

Autograph letter by Princess Elizabeth, to her stepmother Queen Katherine (Parr), in Italian, written while her father Henry VIII was away campaigning in France; subscribing herself 'Your most obedient daughter and most faithful servant, Elizabeth', 'From St James's this thirty-first of July'

This charred remnant is all that remains of Elizabeth's earliest known letter, written when she was ten years old: it was caught in the same fire that nearly destroyed the manuscript of *Beowulf* and the rest of the Cotton Library in 1731 (see Introduction, p. 9). Elizabeth was, famously, a precocious child. A few years later, her tutor Roger Ascham was to boast that 'She talks French and Italian as well as she does English, and has often talked to me readily and well in Latin, moderately in Greek'. In February 1603, a month before she died and by then a near-legendary figure, she remarked to the awe-struck Venetian Ambassador – after dressing him down him in fluent Italian – 'I do not know if I have spoken Italian well; I think so, for I learned it as a child and believe I have not forgotten it.' This letter bears out that claim. Who first taught her Italian is unknown, but she was later to receive lessons from a native, Giovanni Battista Castiglione, possibly a cousin of his namesake Baldassare, author of the classic manual of Renaissance manners, *Il Cortegiano* (translated into English in 1561 as *The Courtyer*), wherein aspiring courtiers are advised 'to be seen in tunges, and specially in Italian, French, and Spanish'.

Princess Elizabeth *c.*1546/47 by an unknown artist

Etiquette dictated that Elizabeth should not write directly to her father, the King. So here she writes to her stepmother Katherine Parr instead. In Katherine, her father's sixth and last wife, Elizabeth appears to have found something of a second mother. The rhetorical flourish referring to her 'exile' has sometimes been read literally and taken as an indication that Elizabeth had fallen from favour. But in fact the reverse was the case, for she had been restored to her place in the succession, from which she had been excluded on the execution of her mother, only the month before. Henry had then gone off to the wars. While he was away in France Katherine ruled as Queen Regent. Elizabeth was to join her that August. It was her first prolonged stay at court since infancy, and it is perhaps fitting that her first experience of court life should have been during a woman's rule.

[from line 5] *. . . And in this my exile, I know well that in your kindness, your Highness has had as much care and solicitude for my health as the King's Majesty. So I am bound not only to serve you but to revere you with a daughter's love, since I understand that your most Illustrious Highness has not forgotten me every time you write to the King's Majesty, which would have been for me to do. However, heretofore I have not had the temerity to write to him, so I now humbly entreat your most Excellent Highness that, in writing to his Majesty, you will deign to recommend me to him, praying ever for his sweet blessing and likewise entreating our Lord God to send him best success in gaining victory over his enemies, in order that your Highness and I may rejoice the sooner at his happy return . . .*

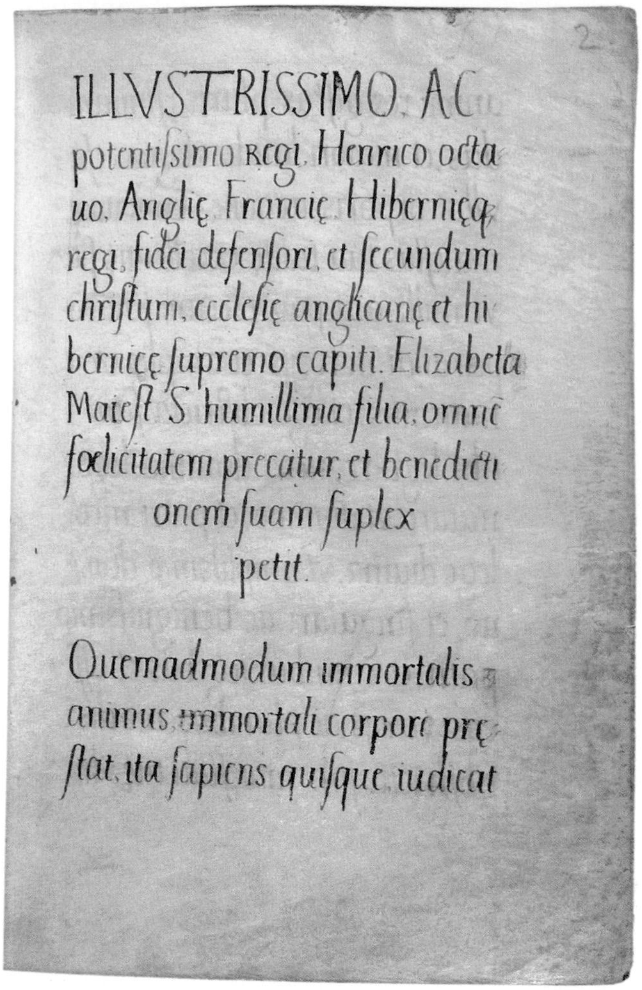

2

ILLVSTRISSIMO. AC
potentissimo regi. Henrico octa
uo. Angliȩ. Franciȩ. Hiberniȩq;
regi, fidei defensori, et secundum
christum, ecclesiȩ anglicanȩ et hi
berniȩ supremo capiti. Elizabeta
Maiest S humillima filia, omnē
foelicitatem precatur, et benedicti
onem suam suplex
petit.

Quemadmodum immortalis
animus immortali corpore prȩ
stat, ita sapiens quisque iudicat

*'a king whom philosophers regard as a god on earth'*

# 2 Her father's daughter

30 December 1545

Autograph epistle in Latin by Princess Elizabeth, addressed to her father Henry VIII, prefacing her trilingual translation of her stepmother Katherine Parr's *Prayers and Meditations*, rendered from the English into Latin, French and Italian, for presentation to the King as a New Year's gift; subscribed 'From Hertford, the 30 day of December 1545'

This is Elizabeth's only surviving letter to her father, Henry VIII. To her contemporaries she was very much her father's daughter, in a way that her half-sister Mary – born of a Spanish mother – never was; and it was of course her father's determination to marry her English mother, Anne Boleyn, that gave rise to the breach with Rome: the only flaw in his calculations being the fact that Elizabeth was born a girl. She owed everything to him. During her sister Mary's reign a contemporary reported that 'she prides herself on her father and glories in him'. But quite what, in her inner recesses, she thought of the man who had her mother executed for reasons of political expediency is less clear. It has been argued that, as her mother's daughter, Elizabeth knowingly let Henry's dynasty die out. It has also been argued that she hero-worshipped him and would have remembered her mother's death primarily as a temporary impediment to her acquisition of new clothes.

Henry VIII 1540 by Hans Holbein the Younger

Katherine Parr's *Prayers and Meditations* was written under the influence of Elizabeth's godfather Thomas Cranmer and espouses the moderate form of Protestantism which Elizabeth was to favour all her life. Her trilingual translation is the twelve-year-old Elizabeth's New Year present to her father. The binding she has embroidered herself. It incorporates Henry and Katherine's initials interwoven into one monogram, with at the corners the white Tudor rose; later to be inextricably associated with the cult of Gloriana. Elizabeth has written on vellum – by no means an easy thing to do – in a formal hand clearly modelled on that of her brother Edward's tutor, the aptly named Jean Bellemain. Roger Ascham's star pupil William Grindal had been appointed Elizabeth's tutor in 1544, and within a few years she was to abandon Bellemain's French Italic in favour of the Cambridge Italic as taught by Ascham (*3 & 13*). The Latin dedication, composed by Elizabeth to go with her translation, has been described as her earliest expression of political philosophy. She tells her father that 'Nothing ought to be more acceptable to a king, whom philosophers regard as a god on earth, than this labour of the soul, which raises us up to heaven and on earth makes us heavenly and divine in the flesh'; adding that she sees herself 'not as an imitator of your virtues but indeed as an inheritor of them'.

[translation] *To the most illustrious and most mighty King Henry the Eighth, King of England, France, and Ireland, Defender of the Faith, and second to Christ, Supreme Head of the English and Irish Church, Elizabeth, his Majesty's most humble daughter, wishes all happiness, and begs his blessing…*

My Lorde hauinge receiued your Lordeships letters I perceiue in them your goodwil towarde
me bicause you declare to me plainlie your mynde in this thinge and againe for that you
wolde not wische that I shulde do any thinge that shulde not seme good unto the counsel
for the wiche thinge I giue you most hartie thankes. And wheras I do understande
that you do take in euel parte the letters that I did write unto your Lordeshipe I am
verye sorie that you shulde take them so for my mynde was to declare unto you plain=
lie as I thogth in that thinge wiche I did also the more willingelye bicause (as I write
to you) you desired me to be plaine with you in al thinges. And as concerninge
that pointe that you write that I seme to stande in my none witte in beinge so wel
assured of my none selfe, I did assure me of my selfe nomore than I trust the trueth
shal trie, And to say that wiche I knewe of my selfe I did not thinke shulde haue
displeased the counsel or your grace. And surelye the cause whie that I was sorye
that ther shulde be anye suche aboute me was bicause that I thogth the people wil say
that I deserued throwgth my lewde demenure to haue suche a one, and not that I mislike
anye thinge that your Lordeshipe, or the counsel shal thinke good for I knowe that you
and the counsel ar charged with me, or that I tak apon me to rule my selfe for I kno=
we the ar most deceued that trusteth most in them selues, wherfore I trust you shal
neuer finde that faute in me, to the wiche thinge I do not se that your grace has
made anye directe answere at this time, and seinge the make so euel reportes al=
readie shalbe but a increasinge of ther euel tonges, howbeit you did write that if I
wolde bringe forthe anye that had reported it you and the counsel wolde se it redreste
wiche thinge thogth I can easelye do it, I wolde be lothe to do it for bicause it is my
none cause, and againe that shulde be but a bridinge of a euel name of me that I
am glade to punesse them, and so get the euel wil of the people, wiche thinge I
wolde be lothe to haue. But if it mougth so seme good unto your Lordeshipe
and the reste of the counsel to sende forthe a proclamation in to the countries
that the refraine ther tonges declaringe how the tales be but lies it shulde
make bothe the people thinke that you and the counsel haue greate regarde
that no suche rumors shulde be spreade of anye of the kinges Maiesties
Sisters as I am thougth unwordie, and also I shulde thinke my selfe to receue
suche frendeshipe at your handes as you haue promised me, althogth your Lorde=
ship hathe shewed me greate alreadie. Howbeit I am aschamed to aske it
anye more bicause I se you ar not so wel minded therunto. And as concerninge

Your assured frende to my litel
power

Elizabeth

*'my lewde demenure'*

# 3 A teenager in love

21 February 1549

Autograph letter by the Princess Elizabeth, to Edward Seymour, Duke of Somerset, Lord Protector, objecting to being put under the custody of a new governess (Lady Tyrwhitt), lest this give rise to rumours of her 'lewde demenure'; and insisting that the Council put out a proclamation on her behalf ensuring that 'no suche rumors shulde be spreade of anye of the Kinges Majesties Sisters as I am thougth unwordie', 'Writen in hast From Hatfield this 21 of Februarye'

To her exasperated admirer Ivan the Terrible, Queen Elizabeth was a complacent old maid; to her admiring courtiers at the end of her reign she was the glorious Virgin Queen. But she was young once, if not quite foolish; virginity was, to reverse the normal order of things, more the province of her later years. She was fifteen when she wrote this letter. Her father Henry VIII had died two years before and had been succeeded by her half-brother, the nine-year-old Edward VI. Edward's maternal uncle Edward Seymour – to whom this letter is written – had assumed the title of Duke of Somerset and the office of Lord Protector. Meanwhile his dashing younger brother Thomas Seymour, the Lord Admiral, married Henry's widow, Katherine Parr. Elizabeth was a member of the couple's household and soon became the object of Seymour's attentions. Katherine it seems did little to curb him. Elizabeth's governess, Kat Ashley, was to recount how on one occasion Katherine held Elizabeth while 'My Lord Admiral did cut her gown in a hundred pieces', and how in the mornings he would creep into her bed-chamber and tickle her. Matters grew more serious after Katherine died in childbirth in September 1548. An affair of the heart had become an affair of state. Seymour pressed his suit with some success. It was said that Elizabeth blushed whenever she heard his name mentioned, and liked hearing him praised. By now Kat Ashley, who had previously been censorious, gave the courtship her enthusiastic backing. The overly ambitious Seymour was arrested on 17 January 1549.

Kat Ashley was sent to the Tower, and Elizabeth threatened with having Lady Tyrwhitt – who had a reputation for being a religious firebrand – as governess. Sir Robert Tyrwhitt, her husband, meanwhile attempted to extract incriminating information from the girl. But he did not get very far, eventually reporting back to the Protector that 'She hath a very good wit and nothing is got out of her but by great policy'. No action was taken against Elizabeth, and that summer Kat Ashley was back in service. But her suitor, Seymour, fared less well. He was executed for high treason on 20 March. On hearing the news Elizabeth is supposed to have remarked that 'this day died a man of much wit and very little judgement'. Not long afterwards Somerset himself fell from power. One historian has described this episode as being 'the fiery crucible in which all that remained of irresponsible childhood was remorselessly burnt to dross and ashes: out of it came a woman with a purpose, schooled to self-repression, prudence, and mistrust'.

[from line 12] *...And surelye the cause whie that I was sorye that ther shulde be anye suche aboute me was bicause that I thogth the people wil say that I deserved throwgth my lewde demenure to have suche a one, and not that I mislike anye thinge that your Lordeshipe, or the counsel shal thinke good for I knowe that you and the counsel ar charged with me, or that I tak apon me to rule my selfe for I knowe the ar most disceved that trusteth most in them selves, wherfore I trust you shal never finde that faute in me...*

16

Like as a shipman in stormy wether plukes downe the sailes taryinge
for bettar winde, so did I, most noble Kinge, in my vnfortuna
chanche a thurday pluk downe the hie sailes of my ioy and cōfor
and do trust one day that as troblesome waues haue repulse
me bakwarde, so a gentil winde wil bringe me forwarde to
my hauen. Two chief occasions moued me muche and
grieued me gretly, the one for that I douted your Maiestie
helthe, the other bicause for al my longe taryinge I wente
without that I came for, of the first I am ~~wil~~ releued in
a parte, bothe that I vnderstode of your helthe and also
that your Maiesties loginge is far frō my Lorde Marque
chamber, Of my other grief I am not eased, but the best
is that whatsoeuer other folkes wil suspect, I intende not
to feare your graces goodwil, wiche as I knowe that
I neuer disarued to faint, so I trust wil stil stike by me
For if your graces aduis that I shulde retourne (whos
wil is a cōmandemente) had not bine, I wold not haue
made the halfe of my way, the ende of my iourney.
And thus as one desirous to hire of your Maiesties helt
thogth vnfortunat to se it I shal pray God for euer to
preserue you. From Hatfilde this present saterday.

Your Maiesties hūble siste
to cōmandemente. Elizabeth

*'Like as a shipman in stormy wether plukes downe the sailes'*

# 4 Before the storm

?4 February 1553

Autograph letter by Princess Elizabeth, to her half-brother King Edward VI, regretting that she has received an order to turn back while on her way to visit him, the blow being twofold in that she not only failed to see him but was given cause to doubt his health, 'From Hatfild this present saterday'

The opening of this letter – 'Like as a shipman in stormy weather plucks down the sails, tarrying for better wind' – employs a favourite rhetorical device; another of Elizabeth's letters to Edward begins 'Like as a richman...' Nevertheless, the image of her in a storm-tossed world plucking down her sails does stick in the memory. This may in part be because it invokes that favourite allegorical figure of the Renaissance, Dame Fortune, who is often shown clutching a billowing sail. Although undated, it seems pretty certain that this letter was written in 1553, during the last months of Edward VI's life. John Dudley, Duke of Northumberland, had seized power from Protector Somerset in 1549. He planned to divert the succession away from Mary and Elizabeth to his own family. To this end he married his son Guildford Dudley to Lady Jane Grey, descendant of Henry VII's younger sister. This would have the added advantage of securing a Protestant succession, something on which the dying King was adamant. That June Edward drew up his 'Device for the Succession' which overthrew the terms of his father's will and, in its final form, left the crown to Lady Jane and her heirs male. This was put into effect by Letters Patent issued on 21 June, in which the exclusion of Mary and Elizabeth was justified on the grounds that they were bastards, of the half-blood.

Edward VI c.1546/47 by an unknown artist

Nevertheless, Edward had been very close to Elizabeth. As if suspecting some attempt at alienation, she protests in this letter: 'whatsoever other folks will suspect, I intend not to fear Your Grace's goodwill, which as I know that I never deserved to faint, so I trust will still stick by me'. It was clearly in Northumberland's interests that the two should not meet, which would explain why the meeting was cancelled and why – presumably – this letter was never delivered to Edward. Elizabeth is known to have made plans for visiting him on Thursday 2 February (Candlemas), which may mean that this letter, dated 'this present saterday', was written on the 4th. Or it might have been written later that spring when it had become clear that Edward was suffering from his final illness, coughing up livid, black sputum which observers said 'smelled beyond measure'. As the King's life ebbed to a close, it was indeed a time for taking in sails; in Joel Hurstfield's words, 'England was tossed about amid the squalid manoeuvres of a divided government without a mature king to guide it'. The fifteen-year-old King was to die at six in the evening on 6 July. That afternoon a fearful storm blew up, turning the summer's day as black as night.

*Like as a shipman in stormy wether plukes downe the sailes tariinge for bettar winde, so did I, most noble Kinge, in my unfortuna[te] chanche a thurday pluk downe the hie sailes of my joy and comfor[t] and do trust one day that as troblesome waves have repulse[d] me bakwarde, so a gentil winde wil bringe me forwarde to my haven...*

If any euer did try this olde sayinge that a kinges worde was more than a nother mans othe I most humbly beseche your M. to verefie it in me and to remember your last promis and my last demaunde that I be not condemned without answer and due profe wiche it semes that now I am for that without cause provid I am by your counsel frome you commanded to go unto the tower a place more wonted for a false traitor than a tru subiect wiche thogth I knowe I deserue it not yet in the face of al this realme apperes that it is provid wiche I pray god I may dy the shamefullist dethe that euer any died afore I may mene any suche thinge and to this present houre I protest afor God (who shal iuge my trueth) whatsoeuer malice shal deuis) that I neuer practiced conciled nor consentid to any thinge that migth be preiudicial to your parson any way or daungerous to the state by any mene. and therfor I humbly beseche your maiestie to let me answer afore your selfe and not suffer me to trust your counselors yea and that afore I go to the tower (if it be possible) if not afor I be further condemned. howbeit I trust assuredly your highnes wyl giue me leue to do it afor I be thus shamfully cried out on as now I shal be yea and without cause. let consciens move your hithnes to take some bettar way with me than to make me be condemned in al mens sigth afor my desert knowen. Also I most humbly beseche your highnes to pardon this my boldnes wiche innocency procures me to do togither with hope of your natural kindnis wiche I trust wyl not se me cast away without desert wiche what it is I wold desier no more of God but that you truly knewe. wiche thinge I thinke and beleue you shal neuer by report knowe unles by your selfe you hire. I haue harde in my time of many cast away for want of comminge to the presence of ther prince and in late days I harde my lorde of Somerset say that if his brother had bine sufferd to speke with him he had neuer sufferd but the persuasions wer made to him so grete that he was brogth in belefe that he coulde not liue safely if the admiral liued and that made him giue his consent to his dethe. thogth thes parsons ar not to be compared to your maiestie yet I pray god as euil persuations persuade not one sistar again the other and al for that the haue harde false report and not harkene to the trueth knowen

therfor ons again kneling with humblenes of my hart bicause I am not sufferd to bow the knees of my body I humbly crave to speke with your highnis wiche I wolde not be so bold to desier if I knewe not my selfe most clere as I knowe my selfe most tru. and as for the traitor Wiat he migth peraduenture writ me a lettar but on my faithe I neuer receued any from him and as for the copie of my lettar sent to the frenche kinge I pray God confound me eternally if euer I sent him word, message, token or lettar by any menes, and to this my truth I wil stande in to my dethe.



I humbly craue but only one worde of answer from your selfe

Your highnes most faithful subiect that hathe bine from the beginninge and wylbe to my ende

Elizabeth

*'I am by your counsel frome you commanded to go unto the tower'*

# 5 Waiting for the tide

Noon 17 March 1554

Autograph letter by Princess Elizabeth, to her half-sister Queen Mary, written in a desperate attempt to secure an audience after receiving news that she is to be sent to the Tower, protesting at any involvement in Sir Thomas Wyatt's rebellion or disloyalty to her, and concluding: 'I humbly crave but only one worde of answer from your selfe/Your highnes most faithful subject that hathe bine from the beginninge, and wylbe to my ende./Elizabeth', undated

This – probably the most famous of Elizabeth's letters – is all about timing; or rather prevarication and mistiming, arts for which the mature Queen was to become notorious. Northumberland's attempt to secure the succession for his son and Lady Jane Grey had failed (*4*), and Elizabeth's Roman Catholic half-sister Mary had come to the throne. As next in line and a Protestant, Elizabeth was in great danger, especially during the earlier part of the reign. The most dangerous moment came with Wyatt's rebellion, made in protest at Mary's marriage to Philip II. After the rebellion had been crushed, Mary's Chancellor Bishop Gardiner gave a Lentern sermon in which he promised to be 'merciful to the body of the commonwealth', adding that this could not be 'unless the rotten and hurtful members thereof were cut off and consumed'. On 12 February Lady Jane was beheaded at Tower Green. On 16 March Gardiner and the Council waited on Elizabeth and told her that she was to be removed from Whitehall to the Tower.

Queen Mary 1554 by Hans Eworth

When the following day two counsellors arrived to take her there by river Elizabeth persuaded one of them to allow her to write this letter to Mary, requesting a personal interview. She then wrote her letter very very slowly, so that, by the time she had finished – taking care to enter in slashes in the space above her signature to prevent anyone tampering with the text – the daylight low-tide that enabled boats to pass safely under the narrow arches of London Bridge had turned, sparing her for another day. Recent analysis of tidal predictions has established that the last daylight opportunity would have occurred shortly after 1300 hrs, which would place the writing of the letter at midday. (It is a curious fact that, in the face of such pinpoint accuracy, Elizabeth's twentieth-century editors follow one another in dating this famous letter to 16 March, even though it is beyond dispute that it was written on the Saturday before Palm Sunday, which that year fell on the 18th). The next day, Palm Sunday, Elizabeth finally entered the Tower. This was the place where her mother Anne Boleyn had been executed. She was, she later claimed, in such despair that at one point she thought of sending to her sister to ask that she might be beheaded with a sword, as her mother had been, instead of the axe.

*If any ever did try this olde sayinge that a kinges worde was more than a nother mans othe I most humbly beseche your Majestie to verefie it in me and to remember your last promis and my last demaunde that I be not condemned without answer and due profe wiche it semes that now I am for that without cause provid I am by your counsel frome you commanded to go unto the tower a place more wonted for a false traitor, than a tru subject. . .*

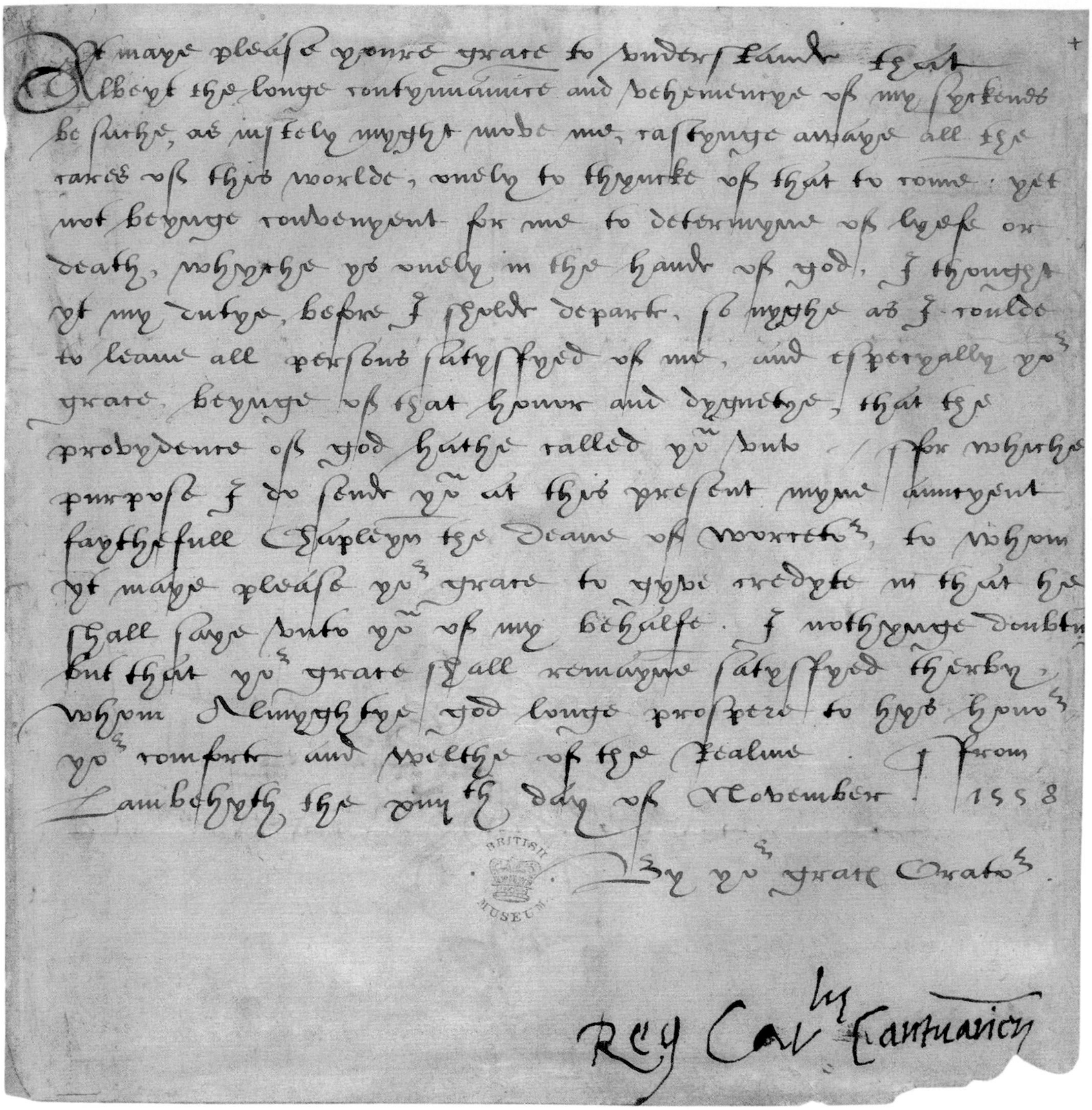
It maye please youre grace to understande that
Albeyt the longe contynuance and vehemencye of my syckenes
be suche, as justely myght move me, castynge awaye all the
cares of this worlde, onely to thynke of that to come: yet
not beynge convenyent for me to determyne of lyfe or
death, whyche ys onely in the hande of God, I thought
yt my dutye, before I shulde departe, so myche as I coulde
to leave all persons satysfyed of me, and especyally yor
grace, beynge of that honor and dygnytye, that the
provydence of God hathe called you unto / For whyche
purpose I do sende you at this present myne auncyent
faythefull chapleyn the deane of Worceter, to whom
yt maye please yor grace to gyve credyte in that he
shall saye unto you of my behalfe. I nothynge doubtyng
but that yor grace shall remayne satysfyed therby,
whom Almyghtye God longe prospere to hys honor
yor comforte and welthe of the realme. From
Lambehythe the xiiij th daye of November 1558

By yor grace Orator

Reg. Car. lis Cantuarien.

*'before I sholde departe, so nyghe as I coulde to leave all persons satysfyed of me'*

# 6 The death of the old order

14 November 1558

Letter dictated and signed by Reginald, Cardinal Pole, Archbishop of Canterbury, to Princess Elizabeth, written in expectation of imminent death ('...the longe contynuaunnce and vehemencye of my syckenes be suche, as justely myght move me, castynge awaye all the cares of this worlde, onely to thyncke of that to come...'), sending his chaplain (Seth Holland) with a private message, and putting his trust in God for the good care of the realm, 'From Lambehyth the xiiii$^{th}$ day of November. 1558', signed as 'Reginald Cardinalis Cantuarensis'

Reginald Cardinal Pole was a great-nephew of Edward IV and cousin of Queen Mary, whom his mother Margaret, Countess of Salisbury, had helped bring up. As a young man he had been much favoured by Henry VIII, but earned the King's bitter hostility by outspoken criticism of his divorce and schism from the papacy, as a result spending twenty years in exile in Rome. After attaining the purple, he was one of three legates appointed to preside over the opening of the Council of Trent, and at the conclave of 1549-50 came within one vote of being elected pope. In Rome he associated with Catholic evangelical circles practising a Bible-based Christianity and tending towards belief in justification by faith, thus having much in common with Martin Luther. Among the group were Michelangelo and his muse Vittoria Colonna, to whom Pole acted as spiritual mentor.

On Mary's accession in 1553 Pole returned to England as the Pope's Legate. On 30 November 1554 he formally absolved Parliament and received the country back into the fold. He was consecrated Archbishop of Canterbury on 22 March 1556, the day after his predecessor Thomas Cranmer was burnt at Oxford. But his ministry was frustrated by hostility between his erstwhile friend, Pope Paul IV, who was violently anti-Spanish, and Queen Mary's consort, Philip II of Spain. The Pope first revoked Pole's legatine authority and then summoned him to Rome to answer charges of heresy. Pole stayed put.

This letter was written at the very end of Mary's reign, long after Elizabeth had been released from the Tower (4). After several false pregnancies, Mary's health had been steadily deteriorating and on 6 November 1558 she was at last prevailed upon to nominate her half-sister Elizabeth as her heir. Meanwhile her cousin the Cardinal was also ailing. He sent Elizabeth this letter on 14 November. In the private message that accompanied it he told her that there was no hope of the Queen's life, and prayed that her successor would maintain the true faith. Elizabeth is said to have sent him a reassuring reply. Towards midnight of 16 November Mary received last rites. At between five and six the following morning she died. The Cardinal's attendants tried to keep her death from him, but one of his chaplains let slip the news. Pole it is said 'remained silent for about a quarter of an hour, but though his spirit was great, the blow nevertheless, having entered into his flesh, brought on the paroxysm earlier'. That afternoon he heard vespers and compline, and in the evening of the same day – twelve hours after his cousin – he died.

[from line 5]*...not beynge convenyent for me to determyne of lyefe or death, whyche ys onely in the hand of god, I thought yt my dutye, before I sholde depart, so nyghe as I coulde to leave all persons satysfyed of me, and especyally your grace, beynge of that honor and dygnetye, that the provydence of god hathe called you unto./For whiche purpose I do sende you at this present myne auncyent faythefull Chapleynn the Deane of Worcetor, to whom yt maye please your grace to gyve credyte in that he shall saye unto you of my behalfe...*

Calend. Martij 1559.
Melanthon to: Reginae.

Inclytae &
Serenissimae
Reginae Angliae
& Franciae,
Dominae
Elisabethae
vera pietate
& om. virtu
tibus ornatae

domini nostri Ihesum christum
ut R. Celsi. v. servet incolumem,
in gubernet ac protegat eã
Datae Cal. Martij. 1559
Regiae M. V.
studiosus
Philippus Melanthon

*'the Church like the wounded traveller'*

# 7 Protestantism returns to England

March 1559

Autograph letter by Philip Melanchthon, to Queen Elizabeth, in Latin, advising her on the settlement of the Church at her accession to the throne; the letter carried home by a returning Marian exile, the Rev. William Barlow; signed 'Philippus Melancthon'; docketed by Sir William Cecil

Queen Elizabeth ascended the throne on the death of her Catholic half-sister Mary on 17 November 1558. Later in her reign, her accession day was to be added to the calendar of official festivals of the Church of England. In the next century, whenever English Protestants felt under threat, the 17th of November would be ostentatiously celebrated. In some ways, though, Elizabeth makes for an unlikely Protestant icon. She was no zealot. She did not want, as Francis Bacon famously said, to 'make windows into men's hearts and secret thoughts'. The more earnest Protestant brethren were to regard her with growing suspicion, and she caused something of a scandal by maintaining a crucifix and candles in her private chapel. She held the Calvinist firebrand John Knox in particular detestation (*11*). Philip Melanchthon was more her style. He had been Martin Luther's chief ally and took over as leader of the German reform movement on his death in 1546. By 1559 he was widely vilified for his moderate views: facing his own death a year later, he said it was not to be feared, for it freed one from the fury of theologians. Henry VIII and Edward VI had both invited him to England, but he remained at Wittenberg, where he taught divinity and classics. As a child Elizabeth had studied his *Loci communes*, the first systematic presentation of the principles of the Reformation.

Elizabeth in her coronation robes by an unknown artist (a copy painted in *c.*1600)

In March 1559, four months into Elizabeth's reign, the Protestant settlement of England was by no means a foregone conclusion. Two bills for an Act of Uniformity (introducing a Protestant form of service) and an Act of Supremacy (legitimising royal ecclesiastical power) were before Parliament. The government was defeated first time round but managed to pass both acts that April, although with Elizabeth's title downgraded from 'Supreme Head' of the Church to 'Supreme Governor'. She was, after all, a woman. The Supremacy Act became law on 28 April, and those bishops who refused to comply could at last be ejected and replaced. Returned exiles accounted for seventeen of the first generation of Anglican bishops. Among them was William Barlow, bearer of this letter, whom Elizabeth made Bishop of Chichester.

[Summary of the letter] *The government should be chiefly directed to advance the proper worship of God, and prosperity of the Church. He wishes her a long and happy marriage. He also exhorts her to assist the Church, which is like the wounded traveller, and advises her at once to establish its doctrines and rites in a definite form, lest afterwards dissensions should arise: this will be easier for her to do in England, where the government is monarchical, than elsewhere; and her example may even avail with other nations. It is desirable that this form of doctrine should be expressed without ambiguity in those points which are chiefly in dispute, and that they should be supported by clear testimonies, for which purpose he wishes that there might be a synod for the settling of all doubtful questions. The Rev William Barlow will be the bearer of this letter, whom he commends as being a learned man, one who right worships God, and loves ecclesiastical concord.*

+

Señora

no escrivo mas vezes a V. al. por saver que el
conde de feria le da siempre quenta de todo
lo que ofrece y agora lo hago solamente movido
del gran deseo y cuydado que tengo de ver tan bien
puestos y establecidos los cosas de V. al. como las
mias propias, pues en efeto las tengo por
tales, para que con ser esta el conde a V. al. le diga
lo que cerca dellos me ocurre y parece que deve
de proveer con tiempo, ruego mucho a V. al. le
crea como a my mismo y haga mirar en
ello como negocio en que no le va menos que
la conservacion y seguridad de su reyno, y sea
cierta V. al. que en esto y en qualquiera otra
cosa que le tocare me hallara siempre tan verda-
dero y buen herm.no como lo he sido por lo pasado
y se lo dira el conde a quien me remito en
lo demas por no cansar a V. al. con larga carta
cuya ser.ma persona y real estado nuestro señor
guarde y prospere como deseo, de bruselas
a 24 de abril 1559

buen herm.no de V. al.

Yo el Rey

*'this business affects nothing less than the safety of your kingdom'*

# 8 Little sighs that border on laughter

24 April 1559

Autograph letter by Philip II of Spain, to Queen Elizabeth, in Spanish, explaining that he is taking the unusual step of writing to her in person because her kingdom is endangered by a grave threat, upon which the bearer of the letter, Count Feria, will enlarge; signed 'I the King'

It was with some reluctance that the former King of England, Philip II of Spain, left a widower by the death of Queen Mary, agreed to marry his sister-in-law Elizabeth. He had protected her during her sister's reign and had persuaded the reluctant Mary to recognise her as heir, knowing full well that the crown might otherwise pass to the half-French Mary Queen of Scots, a disaster for Habsburg interests. Everybody knew that Elizabeth must marry, if only (as Philip put it) to 'relieve her of those labours which are only fit for men'. Thus it was that in January 1559, with a heavy sense of duty, Philip authorised his ambassador Feria to propose. Amazingly, Elizabeth did not accept at once. She stalled. After a while Philip – the greatest match in Christendom – grew tired of waiting; and decided to marry the King of France's daughter instead.

Feria reported Elizabeth's reaction on 11 April: 'she had heard your Majesty was married, smiling, saying your name was a fortunate one, and now and then giving little sighs that bordered upon laughter'. She told him Philip could not have been all that much in love with her, as he 'had not the patience to wait four months'. Nevertheless, Feria added excitedly, Philip's French marriage had thrown Protestant heretics into 'a state of great alarm at the thought that everybody is arming against them'. This suggested a new ploy. On 24 April Philip wrote this letter for Feria to deliver to Elizabeth: 'I have thought well to send you enclosed the letter for her written with my own hand, the tenor of which you will see by the copy'. Feria was instructed 'to confirm the Queen and her friends in the fear you say they feel of the peril and danger in which they stand, so that they may understand thoroughly that they are ruined unless I succour and defend them... when you have frightened the Queen about this... you will assure her from me that I will never fail to help her in all I can to preserve her realm and settle her own affairs exactly the same as if they were my own'. To receive this great blessing Elizabeth should above all 'forbid any innovations in religion'. Feria presented the letter to Elizabeth on the 28th. The next day he reported back: 'After giving your Majesty's letter to the Queen I spoke to her in conformity with what had been written to me. She heard me as she had heard me many times before, only that on this occasion I spoke in your Majesty's name... I tried to frighten her all I could... She answered amiably that she thanked your Majesty for your message'. She then brazenly told him she was planning a Protestant settlement after all. There was little Feria could do: 'It is very troublesome to negotiate with this woman, as she is naturally changeable, and those who surround her are so blind and bestial that they do not at all understand the state of affairs'. Upon which Feria was recalled to Spain, and the comedy ended.

[from line 11] *...this business affects nothing less than the safety of your kingdom, and you may be assured that in this as in any other matter which affects you I shall be as attentive as I have been in the past, but now I let the Count speak for me, so as not to burden your Highness with a long letter...*

1560

Feb. 25

(345)

78

It maye please yo[u]r most Excellent Ma[jes]tie to understand, that for the better proffe to yo[u]r highnes for the conveyance of soche bullion and golde as I shall provyde for yo[u], I have sent yo[u] this letter enclossed in the stonne worke, being no smale comforte unto me that I have obteyned to the knowledge theroff for the better conveyance of yo[u]r treasure, which thing must be kept as secretlie as yo[u]r Ma[jes]tie can devize, for yf yt shulde be knowen or persevid in Flanders it were as moche as my liffe and goods were worth, besides the losse that yo[u]r highnes shulde susteyne therbie, which I shall not let to put in effecte. Havinge no dowght but that yo[u]r Ma[jes]tie will have a consideration of my service as ther shall appertayne. Lykewyse according to my most bounden dewtie here I have sent you a perfect note of soche mony as I have taken up at Andwarpe at this present.

| | |
|---|---|
| Of Lazerus tucker | xxviij m li. vj c lxvj li. xiij s. iiij d. |
| Of Anthony ffucker | xx m li. |
| Of Paullus van Dalle | xviij m li. iij c xxxiij li. vj s. viij d. |
| Of Balthezer and Conrat Schetz | xvij m li. vj c lxvj li. xiij s. iiij d. |
| Of Jeronymus Selinger | v m li. |
| Of Sebastian Sterhamor | v m li. |
| Of Clayse Johnson | iiij m li. iij c xxxiij li. vj s. viij d. |
| Of Allexsander Bonvisi | iiij m li. |
| Of Cosmus Stotle | iiij m li. iij c xxxiij li. vj s. viij d. |
| Of Claudo Fourche | iiij m li. iij c xxxiij li. vj s. viij d. |
| Of Lewras Reymes | iij m li. iij c xxxiij li. vj s. viij d. |
| Of Andreas van Berme | iij m li. iij c xxxiij li. vj s. viij d. |
| Of Hans ffucker | xx m li. vj c lxvj li. xiij s. iiij d. |
| Of Frederigus Rolthope | iij m li. v c xxxiij li. vj s. viij d. |
| Of Paulus Rolthope | iij m li. j c lx li. iij s. iiij d. |
| Some totall | cxxxv m li. iij c lx li. iij s. iiij d. |

Other I have not to molest yo[u]r Ma[jes]tie withall but I shall most humblie beseche yo[u]r highnes to be a comforte unto my poore wiff in this my absens in the service of yo[u]r Ma[jes]tie. As knoweth the Lorde whome preserve yo[u]r noble Ma[jes]tie in helth, and long liffe and long reigne over us with increas of honor. ffrome my house in London the xxv^th of ffebruarie an[n]o 1559.

By yo[u]r Ma[jes]ties most humble and faithfull obedyent subiect

137a Thomas Gressham

*'the conveyans of soche bullion, and golde as I shall provyde for you'*

# 9 At the sign of the grasshopper

25 February 1560

Autograph letter by Sir Thomas Gresham to Queen Elizabeth, informing her that this letter is 'inclossed in the stonne worke' used for the safe carriage of bullion from Flanders to England, itemising the loans secured on the Antwerp Exchange from fifteen bankers, totalling £128,449-3*s*-4*d*, and finally begging her (before setting off to serve as Ambassador to the Duchess of Parma, Regent of the Netherlands) 'to be acomforte unto my pore wife in this my absens in the serviz of your Majestie'; 'Frome my house in London the xxv$^{th}$ of Februarie anno 1559'

Sir Thomas Gresham – 'the Wealthiest Citizen in *England* of his age, and the founder of *two* stately Fabricks, the *Old Exchange*, a kind of Colledge for merchants, and *Gresham Colledge*, a kind of Exchange for Scholars' – is here raising money to finance the first war of Elizabeth's reign, her eventually successful attempt to eject the French from Scotland (*10*). The Crown's entire income for a year normally came to about £250,000, so the loan secured by Gresham of nearly £130,000 represented a considerable sum. The Crown was responsible for all government spending, whether on the upkeep of the Queen and her places and court, military and naval expenditure, ruinously expensive wars, or funds paid out in her capacity as paymaster for Protestant Europe. Most of the Queen's income – amounting to some £200,000 – comprised 'ordinary' revenue, which was derived from sources such as Crown lands and customs. With this she had to fund the entire machinery of government. A smaller portion – about £50,000 – comprised 'extraordinary' revenue. This was raised by Parliament through taxation and, never popular, had to be kept to a minimum. Furthermore it could only be used for military and naval expenditure. Any other moneys needed had to be raised through loans, for which Gresham, as Crown Agent at the Antwerp Exchange, was responsible; the total loan secured by him coming to £247,000, more than a year's ordinary revenue.

As the export of bullion from the Low Countries was prohibited, Gresham had recourse to various subterfuges such as, in this instance, 'the stonne worke'. He was a dab hand at the game, on one occasion smuggling home an arms shipment invoiced as velvets and crimson satins. He was later to recommend that in raising such loans 'the Queen's Majesty in this time should not use any strangers, but her subjects'. Among the alien merchants on the present list is 'Hans Fucker', down for £9,666-13*s*-4*d*, who can probably be identified with Hans Jacob Fugger of the Augsburg family of banker-princes, a great art-collector, bibliophile, and patron of the composer Lassus. Gresham weaned the Crown from dependency on such sources by establishing a bourse in London, its premises adorned with his famous grasshopper crest. Here the Queen came in 1571, causing 'the same burse by an herald and a trompet to be proclaimed the Royal Exchange'. It could be said that this was the moment when England financially came of age.

*Yt maye please your most Excellent Majestie to understand, that for the better profe to your hightnes: for the conveyans of soche bullion and golde as I shall provyde for you, I have sent you this letter inclossed in the stonne worke being no smale comforte unto me: that I have obteyned to the knowledge therof for the better conveyans of your treasure, which thing must be kept as secretlie as your Majestie can devize, for yf yt shulde be knowen or perseved in fla[n]ders it were as moche as my liffe and goods were worth, besides the lose that your hightnes shuld susteyne therbie, whiche I shall not let to put in perse havinge no dowght but that your Majestie will have a consideracion of my Service as ther unto aperteyneth...*

long in plantyng, as I thynk it wilbe to morrow in ye mornyng
before the battry will shote of. The frenche seke all ye
wayes they can to putt a feloshipp in ye cotts of vs. so as we
see what they shote at. Wherin if there wer not more
trust that ye matters wold kepe them a sonder and vs to
githar, than in any certenty of ye natio of Scotland, I wold
feare more than I doo. But suerly the hatred to ye french
is such, and ye causees so many, the benevolence at this
tyme towards england is so grete, and ye wt such desert, as
I see not that in long tyme ye french shall recover the mynde
of scottish men ageynst vs as in tymes past hath bene.

Sence ye Quenes deth, here be none in scotland that dare
openly shew favor to ye french. the Bishopps yt be most
offended, dare not shew any contenãce to theis men, nor dare
come out of ye castle for hatred of ye comon people. We did
offer to ye archb: of Sandrews a gard to come to ye embassadors
but he durst not, and so ye fr: embassad: went into ye
castell to hym and others. I will no more molest yor
Maty, but vse my contynuall prayor, that God wold direct yor
hart to procure a father for your children, and so shall ye children
of all your realme bless your sede. nether peace nor warr
wt out this will proffitt vs long. Which in ye name of God
(I am now a precher) I humbly beseche yor Maty to consider ernestly
for otherwise suerly God will requyre a sharpe accompt at yor
hand, for your tyme lost, and ye danger of bloodshed of your
miserable people. I trust of your Mats pardon. fro edenburgh
the 21. of June at iij of clock in ye afternoone. 1560



Your Mats most humble and vnworthy
Serv. W. Cecill

*'that God wold direct your hart to procure a father for your children'*

# 10 Some mistimed advice

21 June 1560

Autograph letter by Sir William Cecil, to Queen Elizabeth, written after he had successfully negotiated the Treaty of Edinburgh, the first part of the letter containing an account of how the French party were being harassed in Edinburgh, the end given over to a plea that Elizabeth marry, 'from edenburgh the 21. of June at iiii of clock in the afternoone. 1560'

To anyone familiar with Elizabethan state papers, the angular Italic handwriting of Elizabeth's chief minister, Sir William Cecil, first Baron Burghley, will be instantly recognisable. He seems to have read everything and written to everybody and his hand crops up everywhere; not least among the vast quantity of state papers preserved at the Public Record Office, at Hatfield House, and at the British Library. And yet few letters by him to the Queen have survived. This may be because they were, like a married couple, seldom apart. This archival intimacy is illustrated by the filing-note made on this letter. Cecil has docketed it, in that distinctive Italic, as having been sent from himself: '21 Junii 1560/W. Cecill to the Q. Majesty'.

Lord Burghley (detail) after *c.*1585 by an unknown artist

Their temporary separation had come about through Cecil's mission to Scotland that summer. French influence there had for some years been dangerously strong: not only was Mary Queen of Scots married to the King of France, but her French mother, Marie of Guise, ruled as Regent in Scotland. Added to which Mary was descended from Henry VIII's sister Margaret, and reports reached England that, when Mary's husband Francis II was crowned in September 1559, the arms of England were put on display. This was an insult Mary was never allowed to forget. The Protestant Lords of the Congregation appealed to their English co-religionists for support. Money was raised by Gresham, and a force dispatched (9). It met with qualified success. A reluctant Cecil was sent up to Scotland to settle things. A combination of circumstances, including the death of Marie the Regent that June and the beginnings of civil war in France, induced the French to make concessions. The resulting Treaty of Edinburgh recognised Elizabeth's right to the throne, and bound Mary and her husband to abstain from using her arms and title, while the government of Scotland was to be transferred to a Protestant council of Scottish nobles. But Cecil's temporary absence had, as he feared, generated its own problems. When he got home, he discovered a certain coolness on the Queen's part, a reaction, it may be, to losing the policy initiative to her minister. She had also fallen head over heels in love with Lord Robert Dudley, the future Earl of Leicester (13). That September Lord Robert's wife died in what many thought were highly suspicious circumstances. This was not the marriage Cecil had been advocating. He even complained to the Spanish Ambassador that the Queen would send him to the Tower rather than let him resign.

[from line 18] *. . . I will no more molest your Majesty, but use my contynuall prayor, that God wold direct your hart to procure a father for your children, and so shall the children of all your realme bless your sede: nether peace nor warr without this will proffitt us long, which in the name of God (I am now a preacher) I humbly besech your Majesty to consider ernestly for otherwise suerly God will requyre a sharpe accompt at your hand, for your tyme lost, and the daunger of bloodshed of your miserable people. I trust of your Majestes pardon . . .*

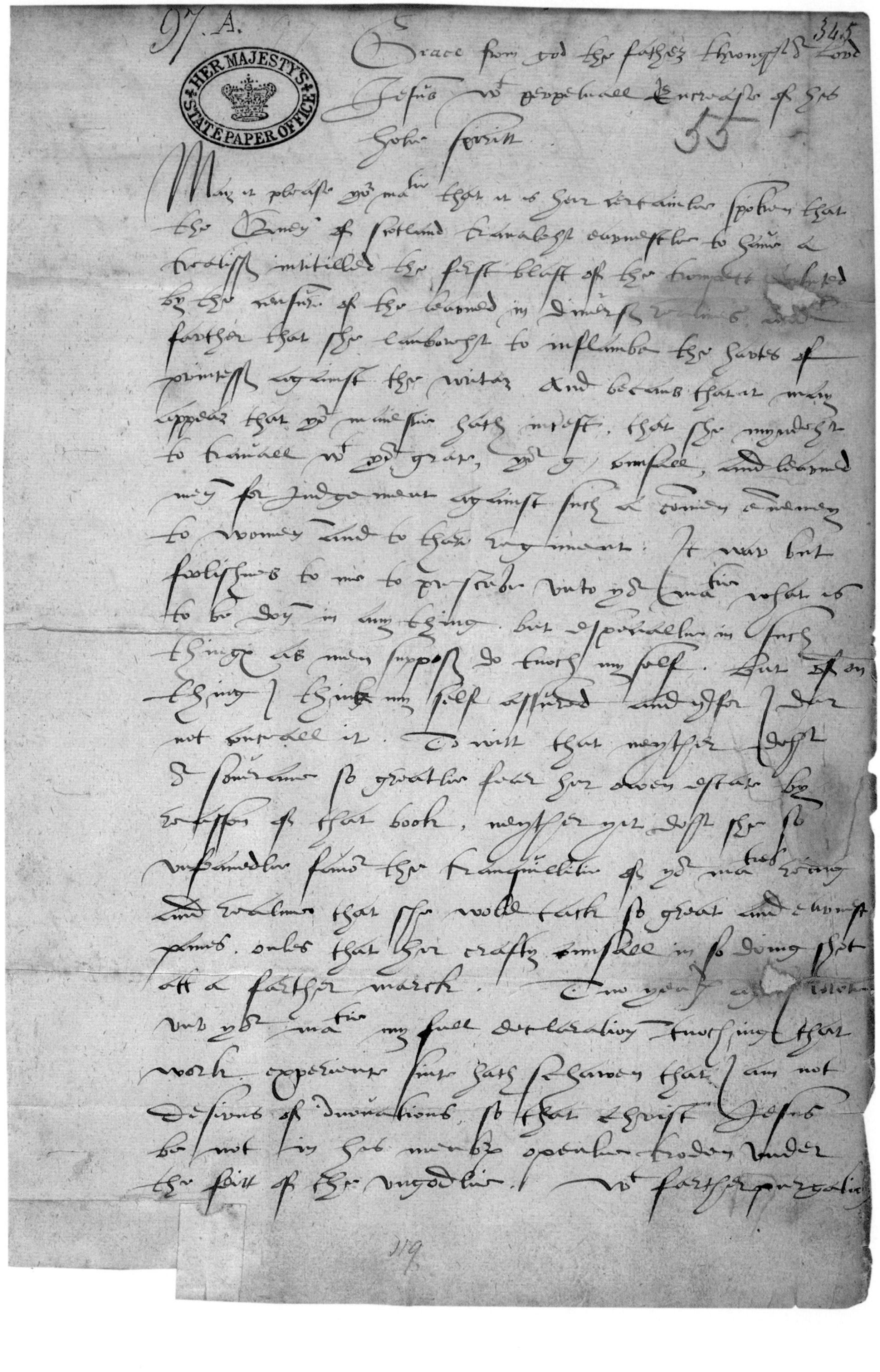

97. A. 345

HER MAJESTY'S STATE PAPER OFFICE

Grace from god the father throught our Lord
Jesus wt perpetuall encrease of his
holie spirit. 55

May it please your maiestie that it is here certanlie spoken that
the Quene of Scotland travaleth earnestlie to have a
treatise intitled the first blast of the trumpett confuted
by the censure of the learned in diverse realmes, and
farther that she laboureth to inflambe the hartes of
princes against the writer. And becaus that it may
appear that your maiestie hath interest, that she myndeth
to travell wt your grace, your graces counsell, and learned
men for judgement against such as ar named enemyes
to women and to thare regiment. It war but
folishnes to me to prescribe unto your maiestie what is
to be done in any thing, but especiallie in such
thinges as men suppose do tuche my self. But of on
thing I think my self assured and therfor I dare
not conceall it. To witt that nether doth
our soverane so greatlie fear her awn estate by
reasson of that book, nether yet doth she so
unfeanedlie favour the tranquillitie of your maiesties reing
and realme that she wold tak so great and earnest
paines, onles that her craftie counsell in so doing shot
att a farther mark. Two yeares ago I wrote
unto your maiestie my full declaration tuching that
work, experience since hath schawen that I am not
desirous of innovations, so that Christ Jesus
be not in his membres openlie troden under
the feit of the ungodlie. With farther purgation

119

*'such a common enemey to womenn and to thare regiment'*

# 11 The monstrous regiment

6 August 1561

Autograph letter by John Knox to Queen Elizabeth, written days before the return to Scotland of Mary Queen of Scots, whom he accuses of wishing to suppress his book *The First Blast*, and warning Elizabeth that Mary does not 'unfeanedlie favor the tranquillitie of your Majesties reing and realme that she wold tack so great and earnest panes, onles hir crafty counsall in so doing shot att a farther marck', while assuring her that, for himself, 'I am not desirus of Innovations, so that Christ Jesus be not in his membris openlie troden under the feitt of the ungodlie'; docketed by Sir William Cecil, subscribed 'from Edinburgh the 6 of August 1561/your majesties servand to command in godliness John Knox'

In the words of Robert Louis Stevenson, John Knox was 'not abashed by the tinsel divinity that hedged kings and queens from his contemporaries'. Queen Elizabeth loathed him. His famous tract *The First Blast of the Trumpet against the Monstrous Regiment of Women* (where 'regiment' means rule or regime) was published – with mistiming of near genius – in May 1558, six months before Elizabeth came to the throne. Page one is headed 'The First Blast to Awake Women degenerate' and opens: 'To promote a woman to bear rule, superioritie, dominion or empire above any realme, nation, or citie, is repugnant to nature' and a 'contumelie to God'. Its principal targets were Mary of Guise, Regent of Scotland, 'an unruly cow', and Mary Tudor, 'unworthy by reason of her bloody tyranny [even] of the name of woman'. Knox returned to Scotland following the Protestant uprising of the Lords of the Covenant in 1559 (*10*). After the Treaty of Edinburgh he was responsible for the ecclesiastical settlement of August 1560 which abolished the authority of the Pope, idolatry, and the mass (with death the penalty for a third offence).

This letter, with one written to Elizabeth two years before, was published in Knox's own *History of the Reformation*, a work 'unsurpassed for its vigorous representation of the principal acts and actors of the historic drama in which he himself plays the leading part'. It was written a fortnight before Mary's arrival in Scotland from France on 19 August. That Sunday she ordered mass to be said in her private chapel. The following Sunday Knox preached that 'one mass was more fearful to him than 10,000 armed enemies'. Mary summoned him and accused him of inciting her subjects to rebellion and of writing *The First Blast* (which had been published anonymously). After their interview he wrote to Cecil that 'in communication with her I espied such craft as I have not found in such age', a sentiment echoed in this letter to Elizabeth, in which he warns her of the meeting that, outside Schiller's play and Donizetti's opera, was doomed never to happen: 'she myndeht to travall with your grace'. Perhaps, for all her loathing, she did take some notice.

*Grace from god the father throught our Lord Jesus with perpetuall Encrease of his holie spiritt./May it please your majestie that it is heir certainlie spoken that the Quen of scotland travaleht earnestlie to have a treatiss intitilled the ferst blast of the trompett [con]futed by the censure of the learned in divers realmes, and farther that she lauboreht to inflambe the hartes of princess against the writar And becaus that it may appear that your majestie hath interest, that she myndeht to travall with your grace, your graces counsall, and learned menn for Judgement against such a common enemey to womenn and to thare regiment. It were but foolishnes to me to prescribe unto your majestie what is to be donn in any thing, but especiallie in such thinges as men suppos do tuoch my self…*

123

75

523. 359 (410.)

Madame, d'autant que ce gentilhomme present porteur qui est de voz subiectz, m'a faict grand instance et prière d'avoir son congé pour s'aller ung peu repatrier,
ce que je luy ay accordé en fin pour estre fort raisonnable, ayant esgard
a la longueur du temps quil a demeuré en ceste paouvre Isle faisant la
guerre ordinaire au Turc nre (notre) commun ennemy, ou il a tousiours faict
d'homme de bien et vray gentilhomme, Je n'ay voulu permectre quil
partist pour sans estre acompaigné de cestes lres (lettres) pour tesmoigner Madame
ayant sceu de luy le vouloir quil a de se prosterner a voz piedz en signe de sa
bonne obeissance quil est personnaige digne des faveurs et recueil que vre (votre)
Maiesté est accoustumée de faire a ses vassaulx et bons subiectz, Et d'autant
quil m'a promis vous discourir les affres (affaires) de nre (notre) estat et en quoy nous avons
a employé noz temps en ces guerres de ces cartiers, surquoy me reposant
s'il plaist a vre (votre) maiesté luy faire cest honneur que de l'ouyr, je fairay ceste
cy plus ~~longue~~ briefve En suppliant le createur quil vous doint Madame
en parfaicte santé longue et tresheureuse vie, De Malte ce [illegible]
iour de Septembre 1561

1561
Sept. 21

4

Vre (votre) treshumble, et tresobeissant serviteur
Le Me (Maistre) de l'hospital de Jherusalem

Jehan de Valette





97

*'this poor island waging war against the Turks our universal enemy'*

# 12 Christendom at peril

21 September 1561

Letter signed by Jean Parisot de la Valette, Grand Master of the Order of the Knights of St John of Jerusalem, to Queen Elizabeth, in French, commending the bearer, an Englishman who has long and faithfully served in Malta against the Turk, and who will inform her of the state of the Order; the body of the letter in a French hand; docketed by Sir William Cecil with the date and by a clerk: 'master of the hospital of Jerusalem to the Queen's majestie'

The Knights of St John owe their origin to a hospital for pilgrims established at Jerusalem in the eleventh century. After the Crusaders were driven out of Palestine the Knights emigrated first to Cyprus and then to Rhodes, from where they were expelled by Suleiman the Magnificent in 1522. They established a new base at Malta in 1530. By this time they had become primarily a fighting order in defence of Christianity, drawn from all over Europe. Jean de la Valette, greatest of all their Grand Masters, was elected in 1557. His younger contemporary, the French historian Brantôme describes him 'a very handsome man, tall, calm and unemotional, speaking several languages fluently – Italian, Spanish, Greek, Arabic and Turkish'. By 1561, the date of this letter, he was busy overhauling the island's defences: for Malta was, as it was to be in the Second World War, the key to the Mediterranean, from which Suleiman could attack – in Churchill's phrase – the underbelly of Europe. The expected attack came three-and-a-half years later on 18 May 1565. The siege was not lifted until 8 September.

The Great Siege of Malta (detail) by Matteo Perez d'Aleccio

The importance of the siege was recognised in far-away Protestant England. Elizabeth herself wrote that 'if the Turks should prevail against the Isle of Malta, it is uncertain what further peril might follow to the rest of Christendom'. A German visitor at the end of her reign noted that she kept a picture of the siege in her apartments at Whitehall: this would have been one of a set painted by Matteo Perez d'Aleccio, a pupil of Michelangelo and Official Painter of the Great Siege (illustrated above). When the siege was lifted, the Archbishop of Canterbury appointed a Form of Thanksgiving to be used in all churches over the next six weeks. Unfortunately the English branch of the order had been disbanded by Henry VIII, and only three Englishmen are known to have taken part. One was probably Sir Edward Stanley, a recusant supporter of Mary Queen of Scots and uncle to Lord Derby for whose company, Lord Strange's Men, Marlowe wrote *The Jew of Malta*. Another was Sir Oliver Starkey, the only English knight of the order, and Latin Secretary to La Valette, by whose side he is buried in the great crypt in Valetta's cathedral. It was Starkey who wrote the epitaph on La Valette's tomb, describing him as 'the shield of Europe, whence he expelled the barbarians by his holy arms' and 'the first to be buried in this beloved city, whose founder he was'.

[summary of the letter] *This gentleman, bearer of the present letter, who is one of your subjects begs me to grant him leave to return to his home country, which request I have found very reasonable, having regard to the length of time he has spent in this poor island waging war against the Turks our universal enemy, where he has always proved himself to be a true gentleman*

197 / 184

179

Magci Dni, Amici clarissmi Qui has nras perfert, Gulielmus Herle, fidelis nr et dilectus Famulus, negotia certa habet hoc tempore necessario obeunda in Germania. Cupimus igitur, ut, nro nomine, vobis sit quam commendatus: vtque illi, in rebus suis expediendis, siue in vra Ciuitate, siue in vra ditione, vra beneuolentia et gratus fauor ostendatur. Et parem humanitatem nos similiter erga vros soies, quandocunque par vsus feret, libenter declarabimus. Bene valete, Ex Regia nra westmonasterij, XVIIIo Martij. Ano Dni, Mo Do LXIIo. Regni vero nri Vo.

Elizabeth R

R. Aschamus

*'R. Aschamus'*

# 13 The uses of scholarship

18 March 1563

Letter signed by Queen Elizabeth, in Latin, the text in the Italic script of her Latin Secretary Roger Ascham, addressed to the Council, Proconsul and Senate of the City of Hamburg, recommending to their care her agent William Herle, then undertaking certain negotiations for her in Germany; Westminster, 18 March 1563

This routine letter of introduction was written and composed by Roger Ascham in his capacity as Elizabeth's Latin Secretary, his signature appearing at the foot of the letter. Ascham is famous for teaching the young Elizabeth her beautiful Italic handwriting. But in fact, while greatly admiring her calligraphy, he never claimed to have instructed her in the art. The man who tutored her between the ages of eleven and fifteen was Ascham's protégé William Grindal. Ascham himself took over the job only after Grindal's death of the plague in 1548, and stayed with her for not much more than a year; a period which sees no marked change in her writing. During Grindal's tutelage Elizabeth's hand does indeed change from the French Italic, as taught by Jean Belmain (*2*), to the Cambridge Italic (*3*), as exemplified by Ascham. The direct influence was presumably Grindal's, but as nothing in his hand is known to survive this cannot be verified. To throw further confusion on the matter, Ascham wrote in several distinct styles. In the letter illustrated he has used something close to his everyday handwriting; for calligraphic fireworks, of which he was more than capable, one has to look elsewhere. Compared to other routine diplomatic letters written for other monarchs – for example those penned by Charles I's Latin Secretary, the German poet Georg Rudolph Weckherlin – this letter by Ascham is a lacklustre affair. It is perhaps telling that, even though Elizabeth employed one of the greatest writing masters of the day, the focus is on her handwriting rather than his. In public she was to hog the calligraphic limelight until the end of her life, while in private her 'skrating hand' disintegrated into an illegible scrawl (*57*).

In addition to his secretarial duties, Ascham once more served as the Queen's classical tutor; in 1562, he told a friend, he was reading Greek and Latin with her every day. It was a culture of scholarship in which the whole court shared, indeed it was a lunchtime conversation with Sir William Cecil and others later in 1563 that inspired Ascham to write his masterpiece, *The Schoolmaster*. He was perennially hard up, but at least service with Elizabeth provided some sort of security: nor was he the plotting type. One thinks, by contrast, of another scholarly secretary, William Barker, racked by a fellow humanist in the Tower (*23*); or of Henry Cuffe, Professor of Greek at Oxford, hung, drawn and quartered after serving as secretary – cum evil genius – to the Earl of Essex (*55*). The beneficiary of this letter, William Herle, was a creature of this demi-monde. He, too, was an exceptional linguist and always short of cash. He was an expert in Dutch and Baltic trade and acted as agent for both Leicester and Sir William Cecil. He also worked under cover at home, acting as Walsingham's contact with 'Henry Fagot' (*51*). One of his tasks in Germany was to gloss over Elizabeth's gun-running to Ivan the Terrible, which she had denied to the Hamburg Senate 'on her royal word' (*20*). Hamburg nevertheless offered opportunities for legitimate business. It had a bourse, established in 1558, and was a leading city of the Hanseatic League, controlling trade between Germany and England's east coast.

No. 15.

30

~~his unmeke~~

~~muche ... dear~~

Sins ther can be no ~~never~~

~~[illegible]~~ dewar det than princes word ~~ought no man~~ ~~neede for to~~ to kipe that unspotted for my part I was one that wold be lothe that ~~that which~~ the selfe thinge that kipes the marchants credit from crase shulde be the cause that princes ~~sayings~~ speche shulde merite blame and so ther honor quaile ~~and sinc~~ a answer therfor I wil make ~~[illegible]~~ and this it is ~~The grete~~ The two peticions that ~~bothe ha~~ you presented me expresse in many wordes as of your cares the gretest conteined thes two thinges in somme, my mariage and my successor of wiche two the last I thinke is best be touched and of the other a silent thoght may serue for I had thoght it had bine so desired as none other trees blossomes shulde haue ~~[illegible]~~ bine minded or ~~[illegible]~~ had bine denied you but to the last thinke not that you had nede this desire if I had seen a time so fit and it so ripe to be denounced The gretenes of the cause therfor and nede of your retournes dothe make me say that wiche I think the wise may easely gesse that as a short tyme for so longe a continuance ought not passe by rote as many telleth tales even so as cause by conference with the lerned shal shewe ane matter worthy utterance for your behalfes so shal I more gladly pursue your good after my dayes than with my prayers be a meane to linger my living threde. And this muche more than I had thoght wil I add for your comfort I haue good record in this place that other menes than you haue mencioned haue bine thoght of ~~[illegible]~~ perchanche for your good as muche as for my surty no les wiche if presently coulde conveniently haue bine executed ~~finished~~ had not bine differed but I hope I shal die in quiet with nunc dimittes wiche can not be without I se some glimse of your folowing surty after my grave bones

And by the way if any here doute that I am as it wer by vowe or determination bent never to trade that way of life put out that heresie your belefe is awry for as I think it best for a private woman so do I strive with my selfe to think it not mete for a prince and if I can bend my liking to your nede I wil not resist suche a mynde

*'my marriage and my successar'*

# 14 The oracle speaks

10 April 1563

Autograph draft of Queen Elizabeth's reply to the petitions presented by the House of Commons and the House of Lords, on the subject of 'my marriage and my successar'

In an interview with William Maitland, the Scottish secretary, Elizabeth made her views on the question of the succession plain. If she had no children of her own she knew that some third party would succeed her, but for her to nominate a successor would be 'to require me in my own life to set my winding-sheet before my eye'. 'Think you', she asked, 'that I could love my winding-sheet? Princes cannot like their own children, those that should succeed them... so long as I live, I shall be Queen of England; when I am dead, they shall succeed me that has most right'. To which she added: 'I know the inconstancy of the people of England, how they ever mislike the present government and has their eyes fixed upon that person that is next to succeed... I have good experience of myself in my sister's time how desirous men were that I should be in place, and earnest to set me up'.

Elizabeth I 1572 by Nicholas Hilliard

In January 1562, *Gorboduc*, the first English tragedy and the first play to be written in blank verse, was performed before the Queen. It described the terrible things that happen when a king dies with the question of the succession left unsettled. Matters were brought into sharp focus when Elizabeth suffered an attack of smallpox late in 1562. It looked for a while as if she might die, and Cecil was forced to draw up emergency plans proposing that a 'Council of Estate' govern the realm in the event of an interregnum. She of course survived. That January the Commons petitioned her to marry and name a successor, pending birth of an heir. The House of Lords followed suit. Elizabeth replied to both petitions, promising an answer in due course. This is that answer, delivered on her behalf and in her presence by the Lord Keeper, Sir Nicholas Bacon, to both Houses at the prorogation of Parliament.

When she was young Elizabeth had, so her tutor Ascham wrote to a friend at the time, a prose style 'that grows out of the subject; chaste because it is suitable, and beautiful because it is clear'. It is not a subject he returned to later, even when praising her other manifold virtues in *The Schoolmaster*. Obviously, what she said to Maitland concerning the succession she could not repeat to Parliament. They got, instead, this speech. She promises that she will think about marrying, despite her private inclinations to the contrary. This part of the speech one can just about follow. But when it comes to the succession she speaks in such opaque terms that, as G.R.Elton puts it, 'her words, sonorous though they were, carried no meaning that anyone could get hold of'. The speech closes with the gnomic utterance: 'I hope I shall die in quiet with *Nunc Dimittis,* which cannot be without I see some chances of your following surety after my graved bones'.

[in margin] *And by the way if any here dowte that I am as it wer by vowe or determination bent never to trade that life put out that heresie your belefe is awry for as I thinke it best for a privat woman so do I strive with my selfe to thinke it not mete for a prinse and if I can bend my wyl to your nide I wyl not resist suche a mynde*

the Orientall Regions. ffor into Consideration that the same wood was
brought thither by the Course of the Sea. And that there muste of
necessytie be a passage out of the sayde Orientall Sea into the
Septentrionall Sea. ffor how ells coulde that wood come to
that flowde of vayatte other reasons are to be alledged for the proffe of
the said passage which for feare to be tedious I omitt. Wherefore
moste gratious princes pondering the aforesaide and Consideringe your
worthye Navye, havinge nowe god be praysed, quietnes with all foreyn
princes. And also men apt, skylfull, reddy to venture theire lyves in worthy
attempts. And also with what smalle charge it wilbe compassed in respecte
of the worthy attempte, nothinge inferyoure to straungers in any respecte
yf it wold please your moste excellent Matie to sett forwarde this famous
discovery of that renowned Cathaye. And to geve order in tyme for
the same for that suche affayres maye not nor cannot be don in haste
I doubte not but in shorte tyme by the trafficque thereof your Matie
shall growe to infynyte ryches. And be accompted therby the ffamous
princesse of the worlde to thencrease of your renowne to the discomayinge
of your Enemyes. And to the greate wealthe of your Realme & subiectes
besyde the great benefyte by the mayntenance of your Navye. And to
the furtheringe hereof & full atchyvinge of this enterpryse, yf yt
wolde please your highnes to imploye me your poore servante in the same
and thinke me worthy to take the said charge, I am and wilbe moste
redye to serve your Matie as dewtye byndeth me. And to venture my lyfe
as fervente zeale moveth me, which yf I maye lyve to accomplishe
I shall attayne the ende of my desyer, which is and alwayes hathe bean
to doe service bothe acceptable to your Matie and also beneficiall to my
natyve countrye, which god graunte, who longe preserve your highnes
in prosperous successe in all your greate attempte.

ultimo Maij 1565

Your Maties moste humble & faithfull servante

Anthony Jenkinson

*'the Hedd and horne of an Unycorne'*

# 15 An Arctic unicorn

31 May 1565

Autograph petition by Anthony Jenkinson to Queen Elizabeth, requesting a patent for the discovery of a north-east passage to Cathay, citing among other evidence of its existence the discovery of a unicorn horn off the coast of Siberia, which was presented to Ivan the Terrible while Jenkinson was at the Tsar's court; docketed by Sir William Cecil 'ult. Maii. Jenkynson for the discovery of the Cathay'

Anthony Jenkinson was one of the most remarkable of Elizabethan travellers and a trusted confidant of Ivan the Terrible, at whose court he spent considerable time and for whom he at one time acted as envoy to Persia. It is probably through him that Ivan made a proposal of marriage to Elizabeth (*20*). In this petition Jenkinson presses upon Elizabeth the realisation that Spain and Portugal had already seized the western routes to China and the Far East (Cathay), the land of spices and unimaginable riches, and that England would be best advised to sail there directly via the North Pole, through which he believes there is a navigable passage. As evidence for such a passage he cites the discovery of a unicorn's head washed up on an island off the coast of Siberia, subsequently presented to Ivan the Terrible. (It would in fact have been the tusk of a narwhal or 'sea unicorn'). Not long after submitting this patent Jenkinson was joined in his enterprise by Sir Walter Ralegh's half-brother Sir Humphrey Gilbert, who eventually secured a petition for a north-west, as opposed to north-east, passage (one through Canada rather than Russia). Sir Martin Frobisher made his three Arctic voyages attempting this passage. Gilbert then turned his attention to North America itself rather than the land that lay beyond: a quest taken up after his death by Ralegh (*35*).

A skirmish between Frobisher's men and the Inuit in 1577, after John White

The unicorn was an animal of potent symbolic power; and a unicorn's horn – possibly even the one described in Jenkinson's petition – played a part in the strange story of Ivan the Terrible's final days. It had been foretold that he was to die on 18 March 1584. On the 15th he summoned some courtiers into his treasure chamber. Among them was the English Ambassador who described the events in his diary. Showing them his richest gemstones, Ivan exclaimed: 'I am poisend with disease: you see they shewe their virtue by the chainge of their pure culler into pall: declares my death. Reach owt my staff roiall; an unicorns horn garnished with verie fare diomondes, rubies, saphiers, emeralls and other precious stones that ar rich in vallew; cost 70 thowsand marckes stirlinge of David Gower, from the fowlkers of Ousborghe. Seeke owt for som spiders'. He then ordered his doctor to scrape a circle on the table with the horn. Any spider placed within the circle died, any placed outside ran away and lived: 'It is too late, it will not preserve me'. On the evening of the appointed day, Ivan tried to set up a chessboard but could not get the king to stay upright. It was then that he suffered a paroxysm and died.

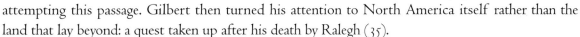

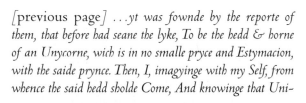

[previous page] *...yt was fownde by the reporte of them, that before had seane the lyke, To be the hedd & horne of an Unycorne, wich is in no smalle pryce and Estymacion, with the saide prynce. Then, I, imagyinge with my Self, from whence the said hedd sholde Come, And knowinge that Unicornes, are Bredde in the Lande of Cathaye, Chynaye and other* [page illustrated] *the Orientall Regions, Fell into Consideration, that the same Hedd w[as] Broughte thyther by the Course of the Sea...*

Pleaseth yt your matie to be informed that the xxth day of September I arryved in a port of cornewall called Paddystow, wth yor maties ship the Jesus in good saftye thanks be to god, our voiage beinge resonably well accomplyshed accordinge to our pretence.

Your maiesties commandment at my departinge from yor grace at Enfeld I have accomplyshed so as I doupt not but yt shalbe found honorable to your highnes, for I have allwayes bene a helpe to all spanyards & portyngalls that have come in my way, wthout any force or preiudice by me offred to any of them although many tymes in this trade they have bene under my power.

I have also discovered the cost of Florida in those parts where ther ys thought to be any great welth, & because I wold not be tedyous unto yor highnes, I have declared the comodyties of yt to Mr wynter who wyll shewe my lord Robert of yt at large. Thus I end my most bounden dewty wth I rest prayinge to almyghty god for the preservacion of your maiesty in most prosperous estate.

From paddystow the xxth day of September 1565

Your maiestyes most humble and obedyent servaunt

John Hawkins

*'I have allso discoveryd the cost of floryda'*

# 16 Potatoes and tobacco

20 September 1565

Autograph letter by Captain John Hawkins, to Queen Elizabeth, announcing his arrival home 'in a port of cornewall called paddystow, with your majesteis ship the Jesus in good savytye Thankes be to god, owr voiage beynge resonably well accomplyshed accordynge to our pretence', having 'discoveryd the cost of floryda', 'from paddystow the xx$^{th}$ day of september 1565'

This letter was written the day Hawkins arrived home after his second slaving voyage to the New World, very probably bringing with him – into England for the first time – the sweet potato and tobacco. The voyage of 'Juan Achines', as the Spanish called him, had taken him to the west coast of Africa and then on to the Spanish Main (the north coast of South America). Skirting Jamaica and Cuba, he then landed at Florida, where the French Huguenot René Laudonnière had established a colony at Fort Caroline on the Rio de Mayo. He was received by his co-religionists as a brother. He gave them much needed supplies, and offered them a passage home; an offer that was refused. On 20 September – the day of our letter – Laudonnière's colony was to be wiped out by the Spanish, who twelve days earlier had established a rival base at St Augustine: this now stands as the oldest continually inhabited European settlement in North America.

The *Jesus of Lubeck*, which Hawkins is careful to state is in 'good safety', was the Queen's contribution to the venture. She was a crumbling 700-ton vessel purchased by Henry VIII in 1545 from the Hanseatic League. Like her contemporary, the *Mary Rose*, she was a top-heavy galleon designed to function as a floating castle. In the 1570s, this type of ship was to be replaced by galleons of a longer, sleeker design, mounting more cannon and sailing nearer the wind. Hawkins has usually been credited with this reform, although recent research has shown that not all the credit is his. The most famous of the new galleons was the *Revenge*, chosen by Sir Francis Drake as his flagship against the Armada (*41*). Drake was Hawkins's cousin and very probably accompanied him on his Florida voyage.

The 'pretence' of the voyage was to break into the closed market of the Spanish Americas. On the way out Hawkins stopped at Sierra Leone, cramming the holds of his ships with slaves. These were then sold on to the labour-hungry Spanish colonists of the New World, usually after Hawkins had put on a show of force for the benefit of the colonists who were breaking the official embargo against unlicensed traders. Hawkins, by all accounts an otherwise humane commander, had no qualms about the business. Of this we have heraldic proof. For, having dispatched this letter, he travelled up to London, where the delighted Queen rewarded him with a grant of arms. He chose as his crest a 'demi-Moor proper bound and captive, with amulets on his arms and ear *or* [gold]', or – in layman's terms – a bound and captive African slave.

[from line 6] *...your majestyes commaundment at my departyng from your grace at Enfyld I have accomplyshed so as I doupt not but yt shalbe found honorable to your highnes, for I, have allwayes byne a hellp to all spanyardes & portyngalls that have come in my way, withowt any force or prejudice by me offred to any of them although many tymes in this tract they have byne under my power. I have allso discoveryd the cost of floryda in those partes wher ther ys thought to be any great wellth...*

that will heir of o[u]r estait, considdering the samin will favo[u]r us sumquhat
as to help & support us (gif neid beis) to defend us & o[u]r realme
against all & quhatsumeuer o[u]r saids rebellis & thame yat traytourslie
will mentein or assist thame contrair us. War it bot onlie for yair
awin example that the lik offence be no[t] comittit against thame be
yair subiectis likewise in yair realmes, Praying yow yairfoir to
remember yo[u]r awin hono[u]r & yow neir of blude we ar to yow
thinking upon the word of God q[uhi]lk commandis that all princes
suld favo[u]r & defend the iust actiounis of uther princes alsweill
as thair awin q[uhi]lk we doubt no[t] bot ye will do unto us knawing
o[u]r caus to be so iust as all the world may testifie. We thoght to
have writtin to yow this lettre w[i]t[h] oure awin hand, yat ye mycht
have better understand all o[u]r meaning & takin mair familiarlie w[i]t[h]
bot of trewth we ar so tirit & evill at eise, quhat throw rydding
of twenty millis in v hours of the nycht as w[i]t[h] the frequent seiknes
& evill dispositioun be the occasioun of o[u]r chyld, yat we could no[t]
at this tyme as we was willing to have done q[uhi]lk we hope ye
will excuse till heireftir. That we may god willing at the first
occasioun q[uhi]lk salbe offerit mair amplie to mak discours unto yow
of the haill discourse of the proceidings / And thus richt excellent
richt michtie princes & o[u]r gude sister we committ yow to the
protectioun of almichty God. Off oure castell of Dunbar the
xiij day of Marche And of o[u]r regne the xxiiij yeir 1565

Zour richt gud sister and
Cusignes Marie R

*'the frequent seikness & ewill dispositioun be th'occasioun of our chyld'*

# 17 Flying murder

15 March 1566

Letter dictated by Mary Queen of Scots, with signature and subscription in her hand ('Your richte gud Sister and Cusignes Marie R'), to Queen Elizabeth, written in broad Scots, describing the murder in her presence at Holyrood House of her favourite and secretary David Riccio, and her subsequent flight in fear of her life, when six months pregnant with the future King James; explaining at the end of the letter that she had intended writing by her own hand but exhaustion has forced her to dictate it, 'Off oure castell of dunbar the xv day of marche And of our Regne the xxiiii yeir, 1565'

The pregnant Mary Queen of Scots was having supper with her secretary David Riccio and a few others in her private apartments at Holyrood on the evening of Saturday 9 March 1565, when she was joined by her husband, Henry Darnley, and soon after by a gathering of Protestant Lords, one in full armour with a night-gown over the top. While Darnley restrained Mary, and another pointed a pistol at her belly, her secretary was dragged out of the room, clutching at her hem and screaming 'Justizia, justizia! Sauvez ma vie, madame, sauvez ma vie!' He was then stabbed to death, receiving in all fifty-six wounds.

Lord Darnley 1560, a courting miniature for Mary Queen of Scots, attributed to Levina Teerlinc

Riccio, a Savoyard, had originally been a bass singer in Mary's chapel quartet. He was, by general account, a small, misshapen man. When Mary's passion for her handsome but dim, and probably syphilitic, husband Darnley waned, she grew close to Riccio. He was promoted to the post of French Secretary, even though 'he was not very skilful in dyting of French letters'. In 1565, Mary's Protestant half-brother, the Earl of Moray, disaffected by her marriage to the Catholic Darnley, had attempted a coup (the Chaseabout Raid). On its failure, Moray fled to England. Mary then had a woodcut stamp made of Darnley's signature as king. This she entrusted to Riccio, who took over the duties of Secretary of State. All of which united both Darnley and the Protestant Lords against the secretary. After the murder, Mary was held prisoner at Holyrood. But she managed to persuade Darnley to abandon his fellow conspirators, and with him escaped at midnight on 11 March. They reached Dunbar at dawn, after five hours of hard riding and one change of horses, from where, a few days later, Mary dictated this letter, breathlessly describing her adventure to her sister queen: 'as first hes takin our houss slane our maist speciall servand in our awin presence & thaireftir haldin our propper personis captif tressonneblie, quhairby we war constranit to escaipe straitlie about midnyght out of our palice of halliruidhouss to the place quhair we ar for the present, in the grittest danger feir of our lywis & ewill estate that evir princes on earth stuid in'.

She had, she tells Elizabeth, wanted to write the letter herself, but was too exhausted. Her words were taken down by an anonymous professional scribe using Scots orthography, rendering for example 'where' as 'quhair'. Mary did not herself attempt to write a letter in the vernacular until 1568, although Sir Nicholas Throckmorton describes her speaking to him 'in Scots' at an audience held in August 1560.

[from line 11] . . . *We thotht to have writtin to you this letter with oure awin hand, that therby ye myght have better onestand all our meaning & takin mair familliarlie therwit Bot of trewt we ar so tyrit & ewill at eass, quhat throw rydding of twenty millis in v horis of the nyght as wit the frequent seikness & ewill dispositioun be th'occasioun of our chyld/that we could not at this tyme as we was willing to have done. . .*

Sil vous plest avoir pitie comme iespere de mon
extresme infortune de la quelle ie laysseray a me
lamanter pour ne vous importuner & pour prier
dieu quil vous doint en sante tres heurheuse
& longue vie & amoy passance & la consolation
que iantands resevoir de vous a quie ie presante
mes humbles recommandations de Wirkinton
ce xvii de mey

Votre tres fidelle & affectionnee bonne
soeur & cousine & eschapee prisonniere
MARIE R

*'I have nothing in the world, but what I had on my person when I made my escape'*

# 18 An unexpected guest

17 May 1568

Autograph letter by Mary Queen of Scots, to Queen Elizabeth, in French, announcing her arrival in England and describing the misfortunes she has suffered from the time of the murder of her secretary, David Riccio (*17*), and expressing confidence that Elizabeth will invite her to court and aid her against her enemies; subscribing herself 'Your most faithful and affectionate good sister & cousin & escaped prisoner/Mary R', from 'Wirkinton ce xvii de mey'

This letter caught Elizabeth and her ministers off guard, and landed them in a dilemma from which they would not be extricated until Mary's execution nearly twenty years later. The last Elizabeth had heard from her cousin was of her escape from Lochlevin, where she had been imprisoned by the Protestant Lords. Elizabeth drafted a congratulatory letter on 17 May on first hearing of Mary's escape, in hopes that she could mediate. But Mary and her army had meanwhile been defeated by the Regent Moray. She fled southwards to Dundrennan Abbey, with her famous long hair cut short and wearing a hood to avoid recognition. But instead of making for France, where she was Queen Dowager, Mary embarked on a small fishing boat and crossed the Solway Firth into England. On the evening of 16 May she landed at the Cumberland port of Workington. Next day, she wrote this letter to Elizabeth, in full expectation that she would be invited to court and that assistance against her enemies in Scotland would be forthcoming. Cecil's immediate reaction is recorded in a memorandum bound with the letter, headed 'Thynges to be Considered uppon the scottish Q. coming into... England', which begins with the stipulation that no 'english scottish or french' be allowed to visit her without permission and that 'good hede be taken' to apprehend any secret letters to her. In the circumstances, Mary's description of herself as an 'escaped prisoner' is somewhat wide of the mark. She also describes herself as having only the clothes she stands up in. This gave rise to a curious piece of gossip (gleefully recorded by the Spanish Ambassador), which shows that the romantic view of the two queens is not the sole preserve of later centuries. According to the Ambassador, Elizabeth responded to Mary's plight by sending her a parcel of linen. When opened this was found to contain two worn-out chemises, a length of black velvet and a pair of shoes. Elizabeth's representative was so embarrassed that he was forced to pretend that some sort of mix-up had occurred, and that the parcel had really been intended for one of Mary's maids.

[translation, from overleaf] ...*God, through his infinite goodness, has preserved me, and I escaped to my Lord Herris's, who, as well as other gentlemen, have come with me into your country, being assured that, hearing the cruelty of my enemies, and how they have treated me, you will, conformably to your kind disposition and the confidence I have in you, not only receive for the safety of my life, but also aid and assist me in my just quarrel, and I shall solicit other princes to do the same. I entreat you to send to fetch me as soon as you possibly can, for I am in a pitiable condition, not only for a queen, but for a gentlewoman; for I have nothing in the world, but what I had on my person when I made my escape, travelling across the country the first day, and not having since ever ventured to proceed, except in the night, as I hope to declare before you,* [illustrated] *if it pleases you to have pity, as I trust you will, upon my extreme misfortune...*

21 December 1568

~~272~~ 274 ~~295~~

~~276~~ (274) 367

Madame, Whiles your cause hath bene here treated upon, we thought it not needfull to write any thing therof unto yow, supposing alwaies that your Commissioners, wolde therof advertise as they sawe cause. And now sithen they have broken this conference, by refusing to make answer as they say by your commandement, and for that purpose they returne to yow; Although we thinke yow shall by them perceive the whole proceadinge: Yet we cannot but let yow understand by these our lres, that as we have bene very sory of long tyme, for your mishappes and greate troubles, So find we our sorrowes now dubled in beholding such thinges as are produced, to prove your self cause of all the same. And our grief herin is also increased, in that we did not thinke at any tyme, to have seen or hard such maters of so greate apparaunce and moment to chardge and condempne yowe. Neverthelees, both in frendship, nature, and Justice, we are moved to cover these maters, and stay our iudgement, and not to gather any sence therof to your prejudice, before we may heare of your direct answer therunto, according as your Commissioners understand our meaning to be, whiche at their request is delivered to them in writing. And as we truste they will advise yow for your honor to agree to make answer, as we have motioned them, So surely we cannot but as one Prince and nere Cousine regarding an other, moost ernestlye as we may in termes of frendship require and chardge yow not to forbeare from answering. And for our parte as we are hartely sory, and dismaide to find suche mater of your chardge, So shall we be as hartely gladde, and well content to heare of sufficient mater for your dischardge. And althoughe we doubt not, but yow are well certified of the diligence and care of your ministers having your Commission; yet can we not beside an allowance generallie of them, specially note to yow, your good choice of this bearer the Bushoppe of Rosse, who hathe not onely faithfullie and wiselie, but also so carefullie and dutyfullie, for your honor and weale behaved himself, and that bothe privatelie and publikelie, as we cannot but in this sorte commende him unto yowe, as we wishe yow had many suche devoted discrete servauntes. For in our iudgement, we thinke, ye have not any that in loyaultie, and faithfullnes can overmatche him: And this we are the bolder to write, considering we take it the beste triall of a good servaunte to be, in adversitie, out of which we wishe yow to be delivered, by the iustification of your Innocency. And so trusting to heare shortlie from yow, we make an ende. Geven at Hampton Courte under our Signet the xxj^th of December, 1568 in the Leaventhe yeare of oure Reigne.

Your good Sistar and Cousin

Elizabeth R

This lre was sent to the Scots Q by the Bishop of Ross

367

*'maters of so greate apparaunce and moment to chardge and condempne yowe'*

# 19 The riddle of the Casket Letters

21 December 1568

Letter signed and subscribed by Elizabeth to Mary Queen of Scots ('Madame'), the text in the hand of a secretary, written after Mary had withdrawn her commissioners from the Conference of Westminster (in protest at not being allowed to plead her case in person) and pressing her to answer the charges laid against her; Elizabeth also commends the bearer, Mary's agent the Bishop of Ross; 'Geven at Hampton Courte under our Signet the xxi^th^ of December, 1568 in the Leaventhe yeare of oure Reigne'

What was in effect Mary's first trial – the second being the one that brought her to the block – was styled a 'conference' held in York and Westminster at the end of 1568. Ostensibly it was called so that Moray and the Scottish lords who had deposed her could answer for their act. But in reality it was Mary who was being charged, accused of complicity in the murder of her husband Darnley by Bothwell, the man she afterward married. On 6 December the notorious 'casket letters' were produced as evidence of her guilt. These purported to be love-letters from Mary to Bothwell, written while Darnley was still alive. Mary was not at the conference and never had the chance to examine them. She declared them forgeries. On 14 and 15 December their handwriting was compared by the commissioners with sample letters by Mary 'of long standing', and declared genuine. Copies were made. The originals then made their way back to Scotland and were soon lost sight of. They have been debated ever since. It may be that they comprised elements of genuine letters but had been tampered with. Or maybe not.

The difficulty of pronouncing on the genuineness of letters without being able to examine the originals is obvious. Take, for example, the letter illustrated opposite. Why, one might ask, has it been written by a secretary, when Elizabeth and Mary usually wrote to each in their own handwriting; why is it in English, when they normally wrote to each other in French; and why has the original survived when most of those addressed by Elizabeth to Mary have not? The letter is indeed a fake, of sorts. For it was drafted not by Elizabeth, but by Sir William Cecil (and he did not write French). And even when, as here, the letter is not in dispute, interpretations can vary wildly. Agnes Strickland wrote in the nineteenth century that 'here Elizabeth, under cover of condolence, viciously alludes to the love letters of the silver gilt casket'; while in the late twentieth Maria Perry sees Elizabeth signing her name with extra flourishes 'almost as though she were trying to convey some mitigating message of hope', with one swirl resembling 'the knot of true love, or true friendship, with which she decorated the embroidered prayer books in her youth' (2).

As for Mary's guilt, that January Elizabeth was to declare the case against both her and Moray unproven. He, the one who had nominally stood accused, was allowed back to Scotland to continue ruling in Mary's stead; while Mary was to begin that long period of imprisonment, culminating in her execution, which was to transmute her into a figure of legend (33).

[from line 6] *...we cannot but let youe understand by these our lettres, that as we have bene very sory of long tyme, for your mishappes and greate troubles, So find we our sorrowes now dubled in beholding such thinges as are produced, to prove your self cause of all the same. And our grief herin is also increased, in that we did not thinke at any tyme, to have seen or hard such maters of so greate apparaunce and moment to chardge and condempne yowe ...*

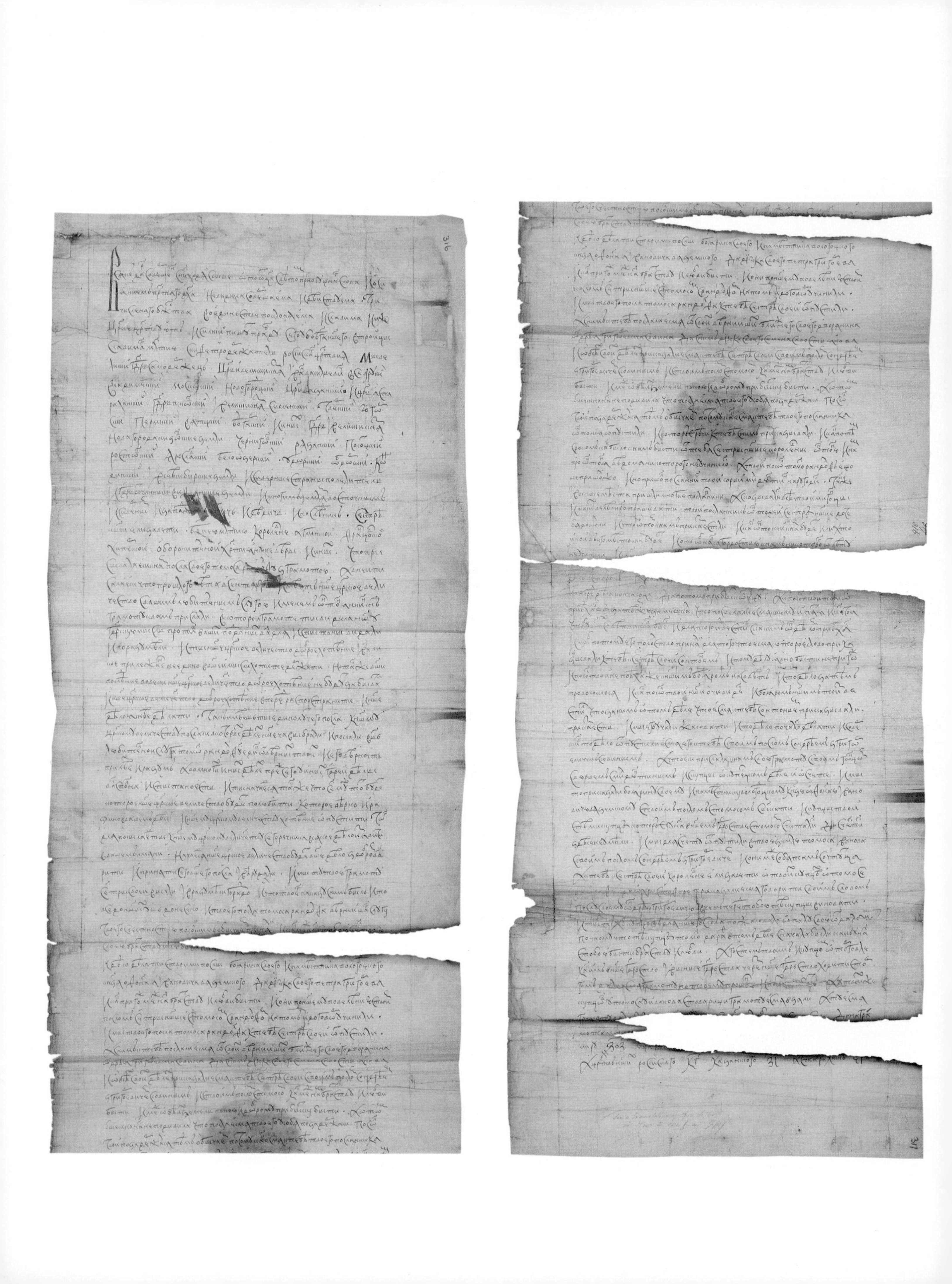

316

317

*'Our letter, written in the Empire of Muscovia, at our auncient towne of Vologdaye, from the beginning of the world seven thousand seaventie and seaven'*

# 20 Dreaming of England

20 June 1569

Letter by Tsar Ivan IV, 'the Terrible', to Queen Elizabeth, in Russian, upbraiding her for the manner in which she appears to be putting England's commercial interests above 'our highnes affaires' and asking why the message sent via her ambassador Anthony Jenkinson has not yet been answered, written in the 'fuortieth [year] of our age, the xxxth yere of our Lordshippe, and the 23 yere of our Empire, since the wynning of *Casane* xvii yere, and of *Astrecane* xv yere' [shown here in two sections]

Ivan 'the Terrible' was the first Duke of Moscow to proclaim himself Tsar of Russia. 'Terrible' is in fact a mistranslation of the Russian *Grozny*, which properly means 'awesome', but it is one that is to be found in every language and, in Benson Bobrick's words, 'what began as a mistranslation can be called a verdict of history'. Ivan was also sometimes called 'the English Tsar', being on especially close, if sometimes tetchy, terms with the English and their Muscovy Company. He held their agent Anthony Jenkinson in particularly high esteem (*15*). But he was above all fascinated by Elizabeth. In November 1567 he had sent a secret message to her by Jenkinson. In this he proposed that they should offer each other political asylum should the need arise. Ivan had already vacated his throne once and was to make a show of abdicating again a few years later. He was paranoid of plots against him and no doubt assumed, having himself dealt with two of her predecessors in quick succession (and as many changes in religion), that Elizabeth was in much the same position. It is widely believed – although concrete evidence is lacking – that it was on this occasion that he also sent her, via Jenkinson, a proposal of marriage. Such a proposal would not have been out of character. His letters are peppered with references to her 'maidenly state' and his bitter rival, Eric of Sweden, was one of her most persistent suitors. Ivan was, admittedly, already on his second wife. But, like Elizabeth's father, he was not one to let such considerations stand in his way. In 1582 he sent an embassy to court the Queen's young cousin, Lady Mary Hastings. He was then on wife number seven. Lady Mary, being a sensible girl, refused him; and was known thereafter as 'the Emporis of Muscovia'. Boris Godunov was to maintain this tradition (*59*).

Ivan the Terrible by an unknown artist

In this letter, Ivan refers back to the message entrusted to Jenkinson in 1567. Our quotation is taken from a contemporary translation held among the state papers, and is the version that Elizabeth would have read.

*. . . your messenger,* George Middleton, *was come to the* Marve *[Narva], and with him manie other[s], naminge themselues to be your messingers, and wee willed to enquire of them whether your, our sisters, messenger* Anthonie *were come to youre presense, and whether they had anie thinge to saie to us of the messaidge, or whether* Anthonie *should come, or anie other in his stead; and they beinge embrased with pride, would make us no aunswere, that they would not come to our neare and privie counsaile, and would make them privie of none of theire affaires; all that they saide was of marchunt affaires, and settinge our highnes affares aside, as it is the use of all countries that princes affaires should be first ended. . .*

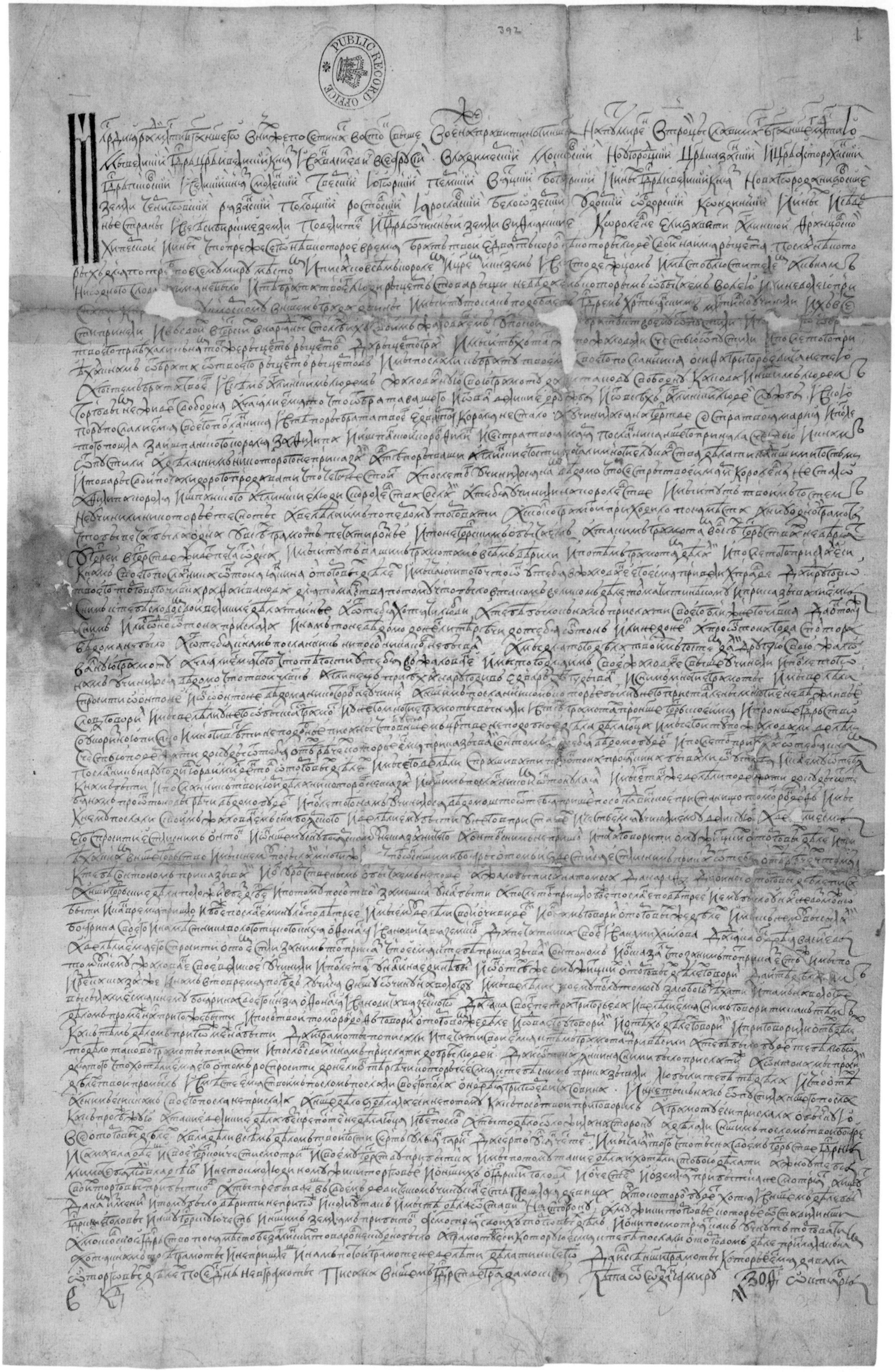
392
PUBLIC RECORD OFFICE

*'And you flower in your maydenlie estate like a maide'*

# 21 Insults for an old maid

28 October 1570

Letter by Tsar Ivan IV, 'the Terrible', to Queen Elizabeth, in Russian, giving an indignant account of his dealings with England from the time of her brother Edward and sister Mary up to the present, and complaining bitterly that she sends a ragbag of mere merchants to treat with him and that every letter she sends 'hath had a contrarie seale, wich is no princelie fashion', and that the English are interested in nothing but trading and she herself is no better than an old maid, ending the letter by stating that he is withdrawing all privileges from them; cut with slits where originally tied and folded, papered seal on the reverse showing the Imperial two-headed eagle, 'Written at our honor of *Musko*, since the foundation of the world 7069 yeres, the xxviii daie of October'

This has fair claim to be the rudest letter Elizabeth ever received. It was prompted by two letters she had sent Ivan, both dated 18 May 1570, one public, the other under her privy seal. The latter contained her long-delayed reply to his request for a treaty of mutual asylum (20). She managed to avoid mentioning the possibility of her own flight, while offering Ivan refuge in England; so long as, that is, he paid for his own upkeep. Such masterly condescension clearly proved too much for him. Nor, from her 'maydenlie estate', did she make any mention of marriage.

While such an exchange might be seen as belonging to the realms of comedy rather than tragedy, our letter dates from truly terrible times. For earlier that year Ivan had massacred very nearly the entire population of Russia's second city, Novgorod; and in July initiated a series of equally hideous executions in Red Square, beginning with the dismemberment of his elderly Chancellor and the skinning alive of his State Treasurer. Indeed, Benson Bobrick believes that 'such a letter could probably not have gotten past Ivan's Foreign Ministry had he not recently liquidated its most outstanding personnel'. Elizabeth responded by sending out the intrepid Anthony Jenkinson, who secured an audience with Ivan in March 1572. He managed to patch things up and English privileges were restored (protestations to the contrary notwithstanding, Ivan was quite as keen a tradesman as Elizabeth). As with the previous letter from Ivan (20), our quotation is taken from a contemporary translation and is the version that Elizabeth would have read.

*...wee had thought that you had beene ruler over your lande, and had sought honor to your self and proffitt to your Countrie, and therefore wee did pretend those w[e]ightie affaires between you and us. But now wee perceive that there be other men that doe rule, and not men, but bowers [i.e. boors] and marchaunts, the wich seeke not the wealth and honnor of our majesties, but they seke there owne proffitt of marchandize. And you* flowe *[i.e. flower or flourish]* in your maydenlie estate like a maide; *and whosoever was trusted in our affaires and did deceave us, it were not meete that you should creditt them. And now seeinge it is so, wee doe sett aside those affaires; and those bowrish Marchaunts that have beene the occasion that the pretended welthes and honors of our Majesties hath not come to passe, but doe seeke their owne wealthes, they shall see what traffique they shall have here; for our cittie of* Musko, *before their traffique to it, hath not greatly wanted Englyshe commodities. And the priviledge that wee gave to your Marchaunts, and sent to you, that you would send it us againe, and whither it be sent or no, wee will give commaundement that nothing shalbe donne by it. And all those priviledges wich wee have given aforetime be from this daie of none effect...*

Elizabeth Dei gracia Anglie Francie
et Hibernie Regina fidei defensor &c. Archiepiscopis
Regalis
Idcirco
habendum
et tenendum
Volentes
Et
In cuius rei testimonium
Dat per manum nostram apud Palatium nostrum Westm' vicesimo quinto die Februarii Anno regni nostri tricesimo
Powle

*'Baron of Burghley in the County of Northampton'*

# 22 The greatest in the realm

25 February 1571

Letters Patent issued under the Great Seal of England by Queen Elizabeth, in Latin, creating Sir William Cecil, Councillor and Principal Secretary, Baron of Burghley, listing as witnesses over thirty peers, bishops and officers of state, 'given under our hand at our Palace of Westminster on the twenty-fifth day of February in the thirteenth year of our reign'

Elizabeth, in Fuller's phrase, 'honoured her honours by bestowing of them sparingly', so much so that Cecil was the only one of her ministers to receive a peerage. This deed granting him his title is unusual in several respects. As a class of document, bearing a portrait of the Queen, it is not untypical: it was, it seems, up to the recipient to commission any embellishment, and this was usually carried out by a scribe along recognized lines. For humbler royal documents the initial 'E' was usually left blank, an example of this being the exemplification granted to Shakespeare (52). The swirling pattern of the ermine trim on the coronation robe follows the standard pattern for such initial letter portraits and is based upon the design of Elizabeth's first Great Seal. The seal itself, made of friable beeswax, has been smashed and the crumbled remains stitched into a cloth bag inscribed in Burghley's distinctive hand: '25 febr.13.EI/barony of Burghley'. (Nowadays the Great Seal is made of cellulose acetate plastic to obviate this problem.)

Coloured initial letter portraits are rare, but normally adhere to the set formula. This example, however, is uncharacteristic in ways that may shed light on a minor art-historical riddle. While the general outline of the portrait follows convention, it is both more assured in its handling and yet at the same time far more distorted than usual: to the modern eye it has something of the sculptural quality of a Henry Moore figure. Despite its oddity it cannot – as can so many initial letter portraits – be described exactly as naïve. Furthermore the three historiated initial letters in the top line (of the words 'Dei', 'Anglie' and 'Francie') are illuminated in a style more befitting a Book of Hours than a deed, and are clearly the work of an artist rather than a notary-cum-scribe. The portrait itself is obviously not by Nicholas Hilliard, who in 1571 was on the threshold of his career. Prior to his ascendancy the most prominent miniaturist at Elizabeth's court was Levina Teerlinc. She was the daughter of the great Bruges illuminator Simon Bening and had come to England in about 1545; like Burghley, she had been in royal service through several reigns and would, one imagines, have been well acquainted with him. She was one of the Queen's gentlewomen and as the royal 'pictrix' received the considerable sum of £40 a year. But despite such pre-eminence, no signed or documented work by her is known. Nevertheless a small group of miniatures has been assigned to her; and our portrait is clearly by the same hand. For example, a miniature of Lady Katherine Grey shows the same modelling and angle of the head and unmistakable Cupid's-bow mouth set above a rounded chin. Another miniature of the Maundy Ceremony shows similarly elongated figures with heads turned at the same angle: this is telling because usually in initial letter portraits the Queen is shown full-face. A miniature of Lord Darnley (17) displays similar characteristics. But despite all these foibles, this deed is a striking work of art; and, if by Teerlinc, is an important addition to her canon, and might help explain something of her contemporary reputation.

Elizabeth R

By ye Quene.





Right trusty and welbeloved we grete you well, and fyndyng the
traytorouss attempte lately discovered, yt nether Barker nor Banis[ter]
ye D. of Norfolk men have uttred ther knolledg in ye under practis[es]
of ther Mr, and of them selves, nether will discover ye same wt[out]
torture. forasmuch as ye knolledg herof concerneth our suerty and
estate, and that they have untruly allredy answerd, we
will and by warrant herof authoriss you to procede to
ye furder examynation of them uppon all poynts that you ca[n]
thynk by your discretions mete for knolledg of ye truth. and [if]
they shall not seme to you to confess playnly ther knolledg, then [we]
warrant you to cause them both or ether of them, to be br[ought]
to ye rack, and first to move them wt feare therof to
deale playnly in ther answers, and if that shall not move the[m]
then you shall cause them to be putt to ye rack, and to [fynd]
the tast therof untill they shall deale more playnly, or untill
you shall thynk mete. and so we remitt the whole proced[yng]
to your furder discretion requiryng you to use spede herin, and to requ[ire]
ye assistance of our lieutenant of ye towre. Gyven under our signet
ye xvth of Septemb. 1571

*'you shall cause them to be putt to the rack, and to feel the tast thereof'*

# 23 Scholars at play

15 September 1571

Warrant written by Lord Burghley and signed by Queen Elizabeth, directed to Sir Thomas Smith and Dr Thomas Wilson, charged with investigating the Ridolfi Plot, authorizing the use of torture on Barker and Bannister 'the D. of Norfolkes men', held in the Tower of London, who have not 'uttred ther knolledg', 'Gyven under our signet the $xv^{th}$ of Septemb. 1571'; docketed: 'Receaved at the Tower the xvi daie of $7^{ber}$ at eleven of the clocke in the forenowne. 1571'

Most unusually this torture warrant for two of Norfolk's servants suspected of complicity in the Ridolfi Plot (24) has been written out by Burghley in person, rather than being entrusted to a clerk. Since the warrant did not reach the Tower until eleven the following morning, it cannot have been a case of pressing urgency. Perhaps Burghley handled it himself for reasons of confidentiality; for Elizabeth was not keen to acquire a reputation as a torturer. It was not until the following decade that torture became at all routine; and this appears to be the first time Elizabeth allowed it to be used. It was not part of the criminal process under common law and required exercise of the royal prerogative (usually by the Council); in all fifty-three warrants are recorded as having been issued during the reign. The standard Tudor authority on the constitution, *De Republica Anglorum*, states that England, as a free nation, scorns 'contumely, beatings, servitude and servile torment', and that sufficient evidence could be gathered 'without racking'. Sir Thomas Smith – author of these words – happens also to be one of the people to whom this warrant is addressed: in this instance he and Thomas Wilson (author of *The Art of Rhetoric* and translator of Demosthenes) consented to torture only 'because it is so earnestly commanded to us'. Father Gerard (50) was later to describe how, when he was in the Tower, 'they produced a warrant for putting me to torture. They had it ready by them and handed it to me to read. (In this prison a special warrant is required for torture.) I saw that the warrant was properly made out and signed.'

The two servants named in this warrant, William Barker and Lawrence Bannister, were Members of Parliament in the Duke's interest. Barker, one of Norfolk's under-secretaries, was a distinguished translator of Xenophon; while Bannister was the Duke's 'Officer in the North'. Barker was examined on no fewer than twenty-one occasions, Bannister on ten. It seems that the threat of torture was enough to make both speak. Barker was especially voluble and was a key witness against the Duke. Norfolk for his part maintained at his trial that it was Barker and the Bishop of Ross (agent to Mary Queen of Scots) who had done the plotting, exclaiming 'I would sooner have trusted one Bannister than fifteen Barkers', and later writing to his children that 'the Bishop of Ross, and especially Barker, did falsely accuse me, and laid their own treasons upon my back.'

[from line 6] *. . . we will and by warrant herof authoriss you to procede to the furder examynation of them uppon all poyntes that you ca*[n] *thynk by your discretions mete for knolledg of the truth. and* [if] *they shall not seme to you to confess playnly ther knolledg, then w*[e] *warrant you to cause them both or ether of them, to be broug*[ht] *to the rack, and first to move them with feare therof to deale playnly in ther answers, and if that shall not move them then you shall cause them to be putt to the rack, and to fe*[el] *the tast therof untill they shall deale more playnly, or until you shall thynk mete. . .*

to extend hys charytable and fryndlye favor nowe in fartherynge them whoe are otherwyse
destytute, and I wold hope that they schald be as obedyent to hyme as ever they weare to
me, and then that they schald be browght upe in gods true feare, wherby they schall the
better learne to knowe ther obedyent dutye to your majestye and ther cuntrye. And
thus hopynge more in your majestyes most mercyfull goodnesse that ytt wyll please the
same to extende your gracyousnes then in enye suti or labor that I cane make, beynge most
unworthye to presume thus muche as to wryte, yff ytt weare not by your hyghenesse
most gracyouse leave I doe most humblye apon my knees take my leave most lowlyye
besechynge your excellent majestye to excuse the yll and scrybblynge wrytynge hereoff, wyche
God knowes proceades off my unablenes for beynge overwhelmyd wt sorowe and care. God
longe preserve your majestye and blysse thys your realme wt your longe contynuance to the
glorye off God, to the increace off true gospellers, and comfort off all good subjects
Amen Amen. The 21 off Januarye 1571

Wrytten by the wofull hand off a dead man
your majestyes most unworthye subject, and yeat ny yours
in my humble prayer untyll the last brethe,

Tho. Howard.

*'Wrytten by the wofull hand off a dead mane'*

# 24 A dead man speaking

21 January 1572

Autograph letter by Thomas Howard, fourth Duke of Norfolk, to Queen Elizabeth, written from the Tower of London after having been sentenced to death for high treason, praying her forgiveness for his manifold offences and that he may leave this vale of misery with a lighter heart and quieter conscience; and requesting that Lord Burghley should act as guardian to his 'poor orphans'; docketed by Burghley as having been received from Norfolk's gaoler, Sir Henry Skipworth, on 22 January

The Duke of Norfolk was the first noble casualty of Elizabeth's reign: he was England's only duke and thus her most senior peer, second in precedence only to the Queen herself. He was also England's richest man, with his own mini-kingdom at Kenninghall in Norfolk. But by the time he came to write this letter, all that was past. He had been found guilty of high treason and sentenced to death. As a traitor he suffered attainder, which stripped him of all rights, including all titles and his ability to pass on those titles. There were to be no further Dukes of Norfolk until 1660. He had been found guilty of being party to two interlinked plots, both aimed at marrying him to Mary Queen of Scots and placing her on the English throne. The first had coincided with the Rebellion of the Northern Earls, from which the Duke – not an incisive character – had withdrawn at the last moment. The second was a madcap scheme proposed by the London-based Florentine banker Roberto Ridolfi, by which Mary's claim was to be supported by a Spanish invasion of England. With the help of William Herle (*13*) and a good deal of torture, or its threat (*23*), the scheme had been unravelled and the Duke's rather half-hearted participation laid bare. He had been tried and found guilty by his peers on 16 January 1572, with execution of the sentence fixed for 21 January, the day on which he wrote the present letter. A principal target of both plots had been Lord Burghley (formerly Sir William Cecil), representative of the new non-aristocratic order, who had been made a baron (the lowest title in the peerage) the year before (*22*). Much has been made of Norfolk's pathetic request that Burghley look after his motherless children, 'to extend hys charytable and fryndlye favor nowe in fartheryng them whoe are otherwyse destytute' (as this letter puts it). But the request probably reflects the fact that Burghley, as Master of the Court of Wards, had many such noble orphans in his keeping, including, a few years later, the young Earl of Essex.

Apart from his high rank, the other attribute that made Norfolk suitable for Mary was the Roman Catholic sympathies of his family. But by a strange quirk of fate Norfolk's boyhood tutor had been the Protestant martyrologist John Foxe, to whom he was devoted. Foxe had dedicated to him the first, Latin, version of what in expanded form was to become the famous *Book of Martyrs*; and was to attend him on the scaffold.

[from line 8]*... I doe most humblye apon my knees take my leave, most lowlylye besechyng your excellent majestye to excuse the yll and scryblyng wrytyng hereoff, wyche god knowes proccedes off my unablenes beyng overwhelmyd with sorows and care. God long preserve your majestye and blysse thys your realme with your longe contynuance to the glorye off god, to the increace off true gospellers, and comfor off all good subjects Amen Amen. The 21 off Januarye 1571/Wrytten by the wofull hand off a dead mane your majestyes most unworthye subject, and yeat your majestyes in my humble prayer untyll the last brethe,/Tho. Howard*

E (7) 13

My lord me thinkes that I am more beholdinge to the hindar
part of my hed than wel dare trust the forwards side
of the same and therfor sent to the Leveftenant
and the S: as you knowe best the ordar to
defar this execution til the here furdar
and that this may be done I doute nothinge
without curiositie of my further warrant
for that their rasche determination upon
a very unfit day was countermanded by
your considerat admonition the causes that
move me to this ar not now to be expressed
lest an irrevocable dede be in meane while
committed. If they wyl nides a warrant
let this suffice all writen with my owne
hand. Your most lovinge soveraine

Elizabeth R

Printed in Ellis 2. 263.

*'me thinkes that I am more beholdinge to the hindar part of my hed'*

# 25 At two in the morning

11 April 1572

Autograph letter by Queen Elizabeth, to Lord Burghley, deferring execution of the Duke of Norfolk; docketed by Burghley: 'The Q Majesty with hir own hand. for staying of the Execution of the D O [N] R[eceived] at 2. in the morning'

By 1572, after fourteen years of disuse, the scaffold on Tower Hill was falling to pieces. A new one had to be erected. Only members of the nobility were executed by beheading on Tower Hill, and none had been condemned so far in Elizabeth's reign. Unlike her father, she did not use execution as an instrument of policy; the worst fate that befell any of her servants being the suspension from office of her secretary William Davison, scapegoat for the execution of Mary Queen of Scots. Norfolk had been found guilty of plotting treason not once, but twice. In all, five warrants were signed by Elizabeth for his execution, and all but the last retracted. After the first postponement in January 1572, Burghley complained: 'The Queen's Majesty hath been always a merciful lady, and by mercy she hath taken more harm than by justice, and yet she thinks that she is more beloved in doing herself harm. God save her to his honour long among us.' On signing the second warrant that February, Elizabeth suffered a species of nervous collapse, so serious that rumours circulated that she had been poisoned. Leicester and Burghley, their rivalry forgotten, sat up all night by her bedside. The third warrant was issued and retracted at the end of the month. Then one was signed on 9 April. This was followed by the letter illustrated here: in referring to the 'hindar part' of her head, Elizabeth is invoking that part of the brain traditionally held to govern the affections. Norfolk was, after all, not only England's only duke, but also her cousin on her mother's side; a mother who had also been executed. It took a meeting of Parliament that May to persuade the Queen to finally sign the warrant and let the act go ahead. Norfolk was executed on 2 June.

Norfolk suffered greatly from Elizabeth's squeamishness and the deferred sentence, both mentally and physically. It may be, as Elizabeth Jenkins has written, that 'Hysterical subjects, it is said, suffer particularly from their memories, and are to an unusual degree dominated by their past; to be obliged to set in motion the machinery of axe and block, which had an awful significance for herself, produced a nervous resistance that was going to need very careful handling.' Elizabeth, too, could be ruthless, as the bloody reprisals exacted after the Northern Rebellion show (24). But whatever her motives, she somehow managed to retain her humanity, the use of the 'hindar part of my hed'. For those who do not share what Brecht called 'the usual disastrous respect which we feel for murderers' this maddening, indecisive, worrying letter may be judged one of the noblest written by anyone who has exercised near absolute power.

*My lord me thinkes that I am more beholdinge to the hindar part of my hed than wel dare trust the forwards side of the same and therfor sent to the Leuetenant and the S: as you knowe best the ordar to defar this execution till the here furdar and that this may be done I doute nothinge without – curiocitie of my further warrant for that ther rasche determination upon a very unfit day was countermaunded by your considerat admonition the causes that move me to this ar not now to be expressed lest an irrevocable dede be in mene while committed. If the wyl nides a Warrant let this suffice all writen with my none hand. Your most lovinge soveraine/Elizabeth R*

5 Jun 72. England: Eliza: R: 1572 France 82

86

Madame en voyent le Roy mon filz mon
cousin le duc de Mommoransi et le sieur
de Foys innocasion ne volu parla presante
autre cet que leurs ay prie vous dire de
mapart (lui declarer) de layse et plesir que je resans e
ay de voyr conservase et renouvellayse une
si bonne et ferme amytie entre vous et le
Roy mon filz le quel lembrase de tele afecsion
quil desire partous moyens la fayre ymmortele
come ausi tele desire de mon coste qui me fayst
desirer que ynsin que ne avons yespargner rien
pour cet afayre que je voldroys que dieu
ma[?] fayte si heureuse que chause comme
du Roy monsigneur et de moy vous feust ausi
si agreable come de bon cuour avons donne charge
au dict nos cousins de le vous aufrir pour vous
envoier le mari a de filz ynsi quil vous plera
ese avons quelque autre chause plus cher
que celuy si qui est mon filz le duc daussi bon
cuour et volante nous le vous aufrions car je
vous cour desire pouvoyr avoyr cet heur e honneur
quinsin que je vous ayme come mere sa fille que
par une si bonne et heureuse aucasion je my puise
nomer tele et remetant au dict quil vous en
diron de nos[tre] part je fayre fin priant dieu
me fayre la grase que puisse conoystre par ef
fayst lamitie et afection que vous porte

Vostre bonne seur et cousine
Caterine

From the Quene mother

A Madame ma bonne Seur
La Royne Dangleterre

*'I already love you as a mother does her daughter'*

# 26 Before the massacre

5 June 1572

Autograph letter by Catherine de' Medici, Queen Mother of France, to Queen Elizabeth, sending two ambassadors, Francis Duke of Montmorency and Paul de Foix, to England, to open formal marriage negotiations on behalf of her son the Duke of Alençon, and hoping thereby that she can, at last, take Elizabeth as her daughter

Hated by the English as instigator of the Massacre of St Bartholomew's Day, Catherine de' Medici has not been loved in France either. The great nineteenth-century historian Jules Michelet called her that 'maggot which came out of Italy's tomb'. Her Italian origins were part of the problem. While on her mother's side she was a Bourbon, on her father's she was a Medici, a minor member of a banking family. By Salic law she was, as a woman, debarred from the throne of France. And yet for some forty years she ruled, or helped to rule, a country to which she did not fully belong, as queen consort, regent and queen mother, as wife to one king, the ever-unfaithful Henri II, and mother to three, Francis II, Charles IX and Henri III. Hers was in many ways an heroic achievement. But Catherine had no desire, like Elizabeth, to marry her country. She saw herself rather as the mother of a dynasty, and wanted to catch Elizabeth in her net.

Catherine de' Medici *c.*1555 by François Clouet

Catherine offered Elizabeth two of her sons. The first was the Duke of Anjou, later Henri III, who although heterosexual was notorious for his fondness for women's clothes and male favourites. He refused to compromise his religion for Elizabeth's sake; besides, he was scandalised by her carryings-on with Leicester. The next son to enter the lists was François Duke of Alençon (29). This is the letter sent by Catherine with her ambassadors formally charged with opening the negotiations. When the ambassadors arrived, they found Elizabeth still touchy about the rebuff she had received from the elder brother. During their first interview, she mocked them by saying that Catherine seemed to be offering 'all her children, one after another'. She also thought it ridiculous that she should be asked to marry a man twenty-two years her junior. Elizabeth formally declined their marriage terms on 24 July. But then, four days later, said that Alençon could visit her if no preconditions were set. And so the marriage charade – which suited France as much as England – got under way. But, within a month, a calamity befell which made it well nigh impossible for Elizabeth's subjects to accept such a woman as her mother-in-law. On 24 August, the feast of St Bartholomew, and succeeding days, thousands of Protestants in Paris and the provinces were slaughtered. Catherine's exact role in the massacre is uncertain, but she probably had a hand in giving the orders. She was to give various explanations to various people at various times, while enjoying the adulation of a grateful Pope and the Catholic world; and, whatever her responsibility, her name has become inextricably linked with the crime.

[from line 11] *...we shall spare no effort in this matter and I pray God that the offer from my lord the King and myself may be agreeable to you, either as a husband or as a son, as you please...if we had anything dearer to us than my son the Duke, we would offer it to you with the same good heart and goodwill; for I have always longed to have the happiness and honour (since I already love you as a mother does her daughter) to call myself such...*

66

Nos mutuae amicitiae, quae eidem cum M^te sua intercessit, colendae
augendaeque nusquam facile defuturos esse, quinimo nostrum erga
Ser^tem V. fraternae beneuolentiae studium quauis occasione promptis-
sime comprobaturos. Quam nostram integerrimam voluntatem
cum Ser^tis V. p^tus Sidneius vberius declaraturus sit, ad illum nos
remittentes, quod reliquum est, Ser^tem V. diu incolumem vi-
uere ac omni foelicitate frui ex animo optamus. Dat[um] in Arce
nostra Regia Pragae, die decima quarta mensis Aprilis. Anno Domini Millesimo, Quingentesimo, Septuagesimo Septimo. Regnorum no-
strorum Romani secundo, Hungarici quinto, Bohemici itidem secundo.

Ser^tis V.

Bonus frater et
Consanguineus

Rudolphus



V^t Jo: Bap: Webe[illegible]

Obernburger

# 27 Rapt in secret studies

12 April 1577

Letter signed, in Latin, by the Holy Roman Emperor Rudolf II, to Queen Elizabeth, thanking her for her letter of condolence on the death of his father the Emperor Maximilian, received from her emissary Philip Sidney, 'twenty-fourth day of the month of April, Anno Domini 1577, in the second year of Our reign as Roman Emperor, the fifth as King of Hungary and the second as King of Bohemia'

Rudolf II of Habsburg, Holy Roman Emperor, King of Bohemia and Hungary, was, in the words of his biographer R.J.W. Evans, 'without doubt one of the most extraordinary of European rulers. His personality, attractive and repulsive by turns, has exercised down succeeding centuries a fascination not restricted to his chosen residence of Prague'; and there were parallels with Elizabeth: 'Both the unmarried Emperor and the Virgin Queen were widely regarded as figures prophetic of significant change in their own day, as symbolic of lost equilibrium when they were dead'. Rudolf was probably the greatest collector and patron of the late Mannerist period, gorging a *fin-de-siècle* fascination for alchemy, astrology and other arcane sciences, and attracting to his court such luminaries as Tycho Brahe, Johannes Kepler, Giordano Bruno and John Dee. He grew increasingly reclusive as the years passed, until he was forced to cede power to his brother Matthias; sharing the fate of Shakespeare's Prospero: 'The government I cast upon my brother,/And to my state grew stranger, being transported/And rapt in secret studies'.

Rudolf II as Vertumnus (god of the seasons) 1590/91 by Giuseppe Arcimboldo

When Rudolf inherited his throne he was twenty-four. Queen Elizabeth sent an embassy under Philip Sidney, himself only twenty-two and 'fêted abroad as the most notable Englishman of his age, the Byron of late Renaissance Humanism'. Rudolf's father, Maximilian, had been notably tolerant of his Protestant subjects, and it was feared that Rudolf, who had been brought up at the court of his uncle Philip II, might not be so accommodating. Sidney would have been ideal for the job, for King Philip, whose name he bore, was his godfather. Sidney was at the same time entrusted with a covert mission, which was to sound out on his journey to and from Prague the possibility of forming a defensive Protestant league against Habsburg and Papal encroachments. Although young, Sidney was already well travelled. He also had links with some of the arcane figures from the Rudolfine circle. Before setting out he called on John Dee (*44*), and was later to befriend Giordano Bruno (*34*), receiving the dedication of two of his books.

Sidney was granted an audience with the Emperor on Easter Monday, 8 April, after which he received this formal letter of thanks to take back with him to the Queen. Sidney reported home: 'He answered me in Latin with very few words... the Emperor is wholly by his inclination given to the wars, few of words, sullen of disposition, very secret and resolute, nothing the manner his father had in winning men in his behaviour, but yet constant in keeping them. And such a one as though he promise not much outwardly, hath as the Latins say *Aliquis in Recessu* [something in reserve]'.

may yt plese your moust exelente magystye I am outterly
onhable to expresse the monyfolde causes I haue
to yelde your magystye my moust humbyll
thankes and presently yn that I understand
by my vary good lorde of lesester that yt hath
plesed your magystye of your moust especyall
and gracyous goodnes to grante vnto my
poure docter lenex the costody of hur chylde
nott wthstandynge that ther were dyvers
meanes youssed to your heghnes for the
conterary whereby the more am I bounden to
rest your fatheffoull and thankefoull
sarvante for the same, and I do beseche
your magystye that I may commette
wolly vnto your moust gracyous consyderation
my sayde poure docteres case of whoes only
goodnes I repose my wolle trust, beseching
your magystye also to haue yn remembrance
the forder sutte of my lord and me ore
theyes two oure chyldernes behalfe and so
as we are moust bownden we wyll never seasse to pray
to the almyghte god longe to prosper your
magystye yn all Joy perfytt healthe and felycyte
yt longe and happy reyne over vs at shefelde
the xvij of marche

your magystyes moust
bounden subgett and sarvant



E Shrowesbury

*'to grante unto my poure dawter lenex the costody of har chylde'*

# 28 The woman who built houses

17 March 1578

Autograph letter by Elizabeth, Countess of Shrewsbury (Bess of Hardwick), to Queen Elizabeth, expressing her gratitude after hearing from the Earl of Leicester that her daughter Lady Lennox has been granted custody of her child, Lady Arabella Stuart (following the death of Arabella's grandmother), 'at shefelde the xvii of marche'

Unlike her father, Queen Elizabeth neither married nor procreated, or built a single palace. What she did build was designed to last no longer than that summer's progress, or the succeeding Accession Day's tournament. Not for nothing was hers the age of the theatre. The fabulous palace of Nonsuch, built by her father, seems – having vanished – to be her most fitting abode; a palace where she stayed a good deal, but did not even own (for Mary her sister, not liking the place, had sold it). Bess of Hardwick was in a different mould. She sought to perpetuate herself through her children and her building. The pursuit of both was made possible by her four marriages, which left her, after the Queen, the richest woman in England. Her second marriage, to Sir William Cavendish of Chatsworth, provided her with six marriageable children from whom she could forge her dynasty. This letter was written when on her last marriage, to the enormously rich Earl of Shrewsbury. She and Shrewsbury were to have a spectacular falling-out a few years later; and it was to be after his death, when left with his fortune, that she was to begin building her most famous house, Hardwick Hall, that palace of glass that survives to this day, its turrets crowned by the initials 'E S'.

Arabella Stuart 1577 by an unknown artist

This letter is not concerned with her architectural ambitions but rather her dynastic plans. These were, if anything, even more grandiose: to place a grandchild on the throne of England. The Earl of Shrewsbury had in his keeping Mary Queen of Scots. Mary's mother-in-law Lady Lennox (Darnley's mother) visited the Shrewsburys in 1574. The two mothers contrived to introduce Bess's last unmarried daughter, Elizabeth Cavendish, to Lady Lennox's remaining son, Charles Stuart, Lord Lennox (Darnley's younger brother). Elizabeth and Lennox fell in love and married. The Queen took a dim view of the matter, and old Lady Lennox was sent to the Tower. The couple had a child, Lady Arabella (or Arbella) Stuart, born in early November 1575 (58). The child's father died of consumption soon afterwards. His title should have gone to Arabella, but James VI refused to recognise her. After Lennox's death the child's wardship appears to have gone to her Lennox grandmother. She died on 9 March 1578. A few days later Bess wrote the Queen this letter expressing her relief that the wardship had been passed to her 'poure dawter lenex', the child's mother. 'My vary good lorde of lescester', bearer of the good news, was a frequent guest at the Shrewsbury houses and entertained Bess when she came to court later that year.

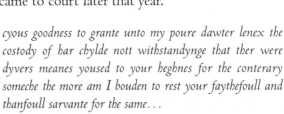

*may yt plese your moust exelente magystye I am utterly onhabyll to expresse the monyfolde causus I hav to yelde your magystye my moust humbyll thankes and presently yu that I onderstand by my vary good lorde of lescester that yt hath plesed your magystye of your moust especyall and gracyous goodness to grante unto my poure dawter lenex the costody of har chylde nott withstandynge that ther were dyvers meanes yoused to your heghnes for the conterary someche the more am I bouden to rest your faythefoull and thanfoull sarvante for the same...*

O Monsieur L'ennuy qui tient ma fantasie envelouppé en
tant de paine me pousse a vous suplier de bien poiser quelle
la fin & sequele de cest voyage nous peult effectuer di je
entierement ou plus tost de Creve Coeur Si l'affaire
ne s'achevera par mariage Combien je me suis
mauldicte depuis la concession du passeport en pensant
qui jamais vous procurast ou quelque desastre ou
deshonneur Vous ne pouvés imaginer la moindre
part de mes doleurs Je ne fais aultre chose que resver
desirant plus que de vivre de m'asseurer tousjours qu'il
ny aura diminution de vos bonnes graces ny de vostre
singuliere affection en mon endroict quelle fin que ceste
cause aura Et me seroit le plus grand desplaisir que mon coeur
receust onques de me mettre en doubte en quoi me pourrez
fort consoler pour recevoir cest honneur d'en estre asseurée de vostre main qui jamais
n'escripvit chose qu'il me piquast Je me imagine
mon treschier a vous dire franchement qu'il y a de vos
fideles ministres qui vous hastent la demeure craignant
que la rupture de ce negoce ne leur soit imputé a
faulte de ne s'y estre sagement employé ou a magnanimité
d'en avoir esté assés circumspect Et pourtant j'ay pris
la hardiesse un aultre coup comme celle qui vous souhaite tout
l'heur & riens moins du monde de vous importuner
de ceste ou qui je me persuade de ne avoir rien obmis
que je vous dois administrer Mercedant toute devotion
a vous complaire en ce qui sera convenable pour nous
deux n'ayant la pire aymant mieulx ainsi vous
ayant en plus d'esgard comme Dieu scait
& me en portera tesmoignage A qui je prie de
me conserver en vostre bonne grace & vous conceder cent ans de vie

Vostre tresassurée Comme estant
tant obligée

Elizabeth R

*'You cannot imagine the half of my suffering. I do nothing but daydream'*

# 29 A frog goes a-wooing

After 16 June 1579

Autograph letter by Queen Elizabeth, to François, Duke of Anjou (formerly Alençon), in French, written in a state of considerable anxiety after having granted him a passport: she is terrified lest she lose his affection, and while admitting that it is rash of her to write, and that her letter may be importunate, she hopes that she is still in his good graces

Elizabeth, who was fond of nicknames, called the Duke of Anjou the Frog. By all accounts ugly, heavily pockmarked, twenty-two years younger than Elizabeth, and quite possibly homosexual, he was perhaps not the ideal catch. Marriage negotiations had dragged on since 1572 (26). Hers was, one contemporary complained, 'the weaving of Penelope, undoing every night what was done the day before and then reweaving it anew the next, advancing in these negotiations neither more nor less than has been done and undone countless times without reaching a conclusion one way or the other'. Mary Queen of Scots attributed Elizabeth's new interest in the Frog to her learning of Leicester's remarriage the previous September. This, said Mary, 'hath so offended this Queen, that it is thought she hath been led, upon such miscontentment, to agree unto the sight of the Duke d'Alençon [Anjou], notwithstanding she had deferred three whole days, with an extreme regret, and many tears, before she would subscribe the passport'. So Elizabeth invited the Frog to England; an invitation which may – or may not – have given rise to the nursery rhyme 'A frog he would a-wooing go'. He had been preceded by his Master of the Wardrobe, Jean de Simier – 'the Ape' – who prepared the ground by doing a bit of wooing for him (and, ever helpful, telling the Queen about Leicester's marriage). Simier was, according to Camden, 'a choice Courtier, a man thoroughly versed in Love-fancies, pleasant Conceits and Cort-dalliance'. He thoroughly charmed Elizabeth.

Anjou's elder brother, by now King of France, had his misgivings about the match, as indeed he did about his brother. Nevertheless, armed with his passport, Anjou slipped away from his brother's court and sailed for England, arriving at Greenwich on 17 August. He travelled incognito, as the seigneur du Pont-de-Sé. The thirteen-day visit was a great success and Elizabeth seemed to have been genuinely smitten with her Frog. He clearly found the Queen more agreeable than expected. When the visit ended the parting was, according to the Spanish Ambassador, 'very tender on both sides'. Simier escorted Anjou to Dover and reported back to the Queen that his last night in England was restless, and that he frequently extolled her 'divine beauties, and his extreme regret at being separated from your Majesty, the gaoler of his heart and mistress of his liberty'. From Boulogne Anjou sent her 'a little flower of gold, with a frog thereon, and therein Monsieur his physiognomy, and a little pearl pendant'. Meanwhile all hell broke out in England. Not only was Anjou a Frenchman, but he was the son of that 'Jezebel of the Age', Catherine de' Medici (26). But, in truth, with Anjou's departure any realistic possibility of Elizabeth marrying and having children was closed forever.

*. . . how I have cursed myself since the granting of the passport, thinking that my own hand might have procured for you dishonour or disaster. You cannot imagine the half of my suffering. I do nothing but daydream, wanting less to live than to be assured that I have not gone down in your estimation, and that your affection for me has not diminished for whatever reason. It would be the greatest reward that my heart ever received to be reassured of this, and you would console me greatly by a letter in your own hand, which never wrote anything insincere. . .*

my delute remembryd yor power obediant servant Thomas Cely of
Brystowe wysshythe yor majeste helthe & yspryte to godes good wyll &
plesuer amen &c for that my bryngyng up hathe not byn syche to wryte
dewtyfully unto yor majeste I crave pardon yf my pen run a stray for that I
am wher I can not atayn to counsell. nether wyll I that any man
shall understand that I wryte for that I am sworn by the Inquizision
of spayne nether to speke nether yet to wryte nothynge tochyn the
secretes of the ynquizision or ther howes wher I was thri yeer in clos
pryzon for gods cawes & yours & all my goodes taken frome me most unjustly for
god I take to wytnes I never did any thynge contrary to spayn in all
the dayes of my lyffe not withstandyng thes grete ynjuryes they have
condemnyd me to the galys for fower yeers threy of them with in ij
monethes be past my frendes hathe procuryd yor majestes favorable
leteres for me but they do not avayell but I pray god I may be thankfull
for yor hyghnes good wyll toardes me: ther ys in the galy wher I am a
woman which woman ys a cortezan & ys dayly in the copeny with the captayne
wher she dothe here myche she ys of alexandrea & ys amyga to won of
the captayns of the ynfantarya thys woman dothe tawlke with me very
often & I make her wether wyth her & for syche tawlke as pasythe
with the captayne I am abel to understand I am yn won of the chambers
yn the galy wher I do her plezuer to suffer her frendes to tawlke
with her & she dothe what she can for me: I thowghte yt good to
move yor majeste for that ther comunycasi hathe byn siche that
afore I most ynder venter my lyffe to wryte for that they
toche yor majeste & yor contre very myche I do thynke yt good to
trobble my lord tresurer with thes affares: for that I wyll not
troble yor hyghnes with a longe leter: my lorde tresurer ys wyse &
polytyke he wyll with forty wordes put in to yor hyghnes more yn a quarter
of a hower then I shall with writynge of 4 shetes of paper I have
writen unto yor majeste ij leteres tochynge other affares but I
wrote in the last leter which I sent by won peres of lemothe
that I wold be worthe a hundred thowzan powndes a yeer to yor
subjectes & forty thowzan pownde a yeer to yor cofferes I fyer
nothynge from you I seke you dowet I wayte for my lyberte:
trewly lyberte I dezier & won yeer I have to acomply & ij monethes
& have nothynge but yll bysket & water but my trust ys yn
god to atayne to my contre & yff y may be harde I trust god
wyll gyve me the grase to acomply my wordes yff not stryke
of my hed as a trator I am in a galy cawlyd the stella
wother wyse cawlyd the sperra: in myzery I thanke god I
am hoole of my [illegible] all my body in clos pryzon hathe byn
for yor comen welthe: send me for godes love to pas thys yeer to com:
& bere to my vyage & bowerde maners I mervell you have not the
[illegible] ystande in the worlde you may yf you wyll put to yor hande

*'they have condemnyd me to the galys for fower yeeres'*

# 30 The galley slave's story

12 December 1579

Autograph letter by Thomas Cely of Bristol, to Queen Elizabeth, the letter smuggled out of the galleys in the port of Santa Maria, Andalucia, to where he had been sent by the Spanish Inquisition after having been racked, expressing gratitude that the Queen had already written in his favour, but begging that she do so again; headed 'In andalazia the 12 of desember yn porta santa marya – 1579' and subscribed 'your power obedyent servant Thomas Cely of brystowe of your garde extraordynare'

Thomas Cely was one of Queen Elizabeth's 'Guard Extraordinary', or Yeoman of the Guard. He had been sentenced by the Spanish Inquisition to a term as a galley slave, and thereafter to perpetual imprisonment. He afterward described his experiences to Lord Burghley: 'My good Lord, I am a poor man, and one that hath been brought up without learning, and one that hath but a patched carcass; for I had thirty-two sundry torments in the Inquisition with the apretados – you term them in English rackings; and eight years in prison lacking two months.' Accounts differ as to why he fell foul of the Inquisition. According to this letter, taken up by the official account, it was 'only for saying service in the churches of her Majesty's realm and saying it in ships at sea'; according to his wife, Dorothy, it was for striking a Spaniard who had insulted the Queen; according to Cely's boast after his release, it was for 'striking their secretary as I was before the Inquisidores, they sitting in judgement'. None of which touches on what one guesses was the real reason. Cely was both a spy – if rather a talkative one – as well as a henchman of Sir Francis Drake, 'el Drago'.

As befits the role, he was also something of a womaniser. In this letter he boasts that 'there is in the galley where I am a woman which woman is a courtesan & is daily in the company with the captain's where she doth hear much… This woman doth talk with me very often & I make fair weather with her & for such talk as passeth with the captain's I am sure to understand'. One wonders what the Virgin Queen made of this offer. On his return home, he offered to use much the same seduction technique to glean intelligence from a Spanish lady living in London. But, like James Bond, he was also a navy man. He sailed on Drake's expedition of 1586 as captain of the *Minion of Plymouth* and helped evacuate Ralegh's first colony from Roanoke. In July 1588 we find him empowered by the Lord Admiral to gain intelligence of the Spanish fleet. At the battle itself he commanded the *Elizabeth Drake.* That August we find a Captain 'Celie' relieving Spanish prisoners in Bridewell Gaol of their apparel, arms and ornaments. Afterwards, he continued to offer unsolicited advice to Lord Burghley – more often in the role of 'Q' than 007 – recommending a smoke-machine for use at sea, denouncing traitors and discussing the destruction of letters written with lemon juice.

[from end of line 4]*…I am wher I can not atteyn to Cownsell, nether wyll I that eny man shall understand that I wryte for that I am sworen by the Inquizision of spayne nether yet to speke nether to wryte nothynge tochyn the secretes of the ynquizision or ther howes wher I was thri yeer In cloes pryzon for godes cawes & youres & all my goodes taken frome me most unjustly for god I take to wytnes I never dyd eny thynge contrary to spayn In all the deyes of my lyffe not withstandyng thes grete ynjeryes they have condemnyd me to the galys for fower yeeres thrye of them within ii monethes be paste…*

That thinges concerning ye descrying of follie & faithlesse
harte to yor Matie: bee revealed nothing dislikes mee, but yt ye
crime should light upon some such as is nowe touched, pardon
I crave yf to sorrowe yt I cannot denye. The state of ye cause
at some length by a generall lre from us of yor Counsell here is
declared unto yor Highnes, wth such writinges & instrumentes by ye bearer
as conteyne ye grounde of or proceedinge in yt. The L. Chauncellor
his great pollicie & intollerable travaile, to ye great impairing
of his health and no lesse perill of his lif, hath chiefly yf not
onelye beaten out this matter. I therefore humbly beseche
yor Highnes. yt he maye have his deserved thankes; I feare the
indisposition of his bodye will enforce his licence for a monthe
or twoo; surelye Madame, yf it so fall out, as my self, I wisst
shall receive a cheif mayme in my assistaunce so will yor
Maties service here in diverse behalfe receive no small hinderaunce
I could therefore verye earnestly wish, & most humbly too
doe commend ye weighing thereof to yor Matie: that a skilfull
Physition were wth speed sent to Chester, ye lack whereof
is his undoing, and not possibly can he contynue here there
wthout seking remedy by better skill; to yor Maties gratious
care therefore I bequeathe yt. The Bish. of Dublin like
wise hath shewed no small trouthe and constancy in this cause
having not a litle endaungered him self by avouching his charge
against ye Earle. Delvin surely hath bene ye drawer of
ye Earle into this mischief, whose obstinate affection to
Poperie hath now approved him unsafe to him self, unsounde
to freinde, disloyall to Prince & false to God. such is the
yeild of such seede, wch, would to God, were not so plenty
in this land: yor Matie: I must be carefull therefore to roote
yt out, otherwise wthout hope of ease, masse of treasure &
continuall watche men are meinst to staye this governmt.
yor Highnes at my leave taking, gave me a warning for being
strict in dealing wth religion, I have observed yt, how
obediently soever, yett most unwillingly I confesse, and I
doubt

*'a warning for being strict in dealing with religion'*

# 31 Secrets that secretaries know

22 December 1580

Duplicate in the hand of the poet Edmund Spenser, secretary to the Lord Deputy of Ireland, Lord Grey de Wilton, of Grey's letter to Queen Elizabeth (forwarded by Grey to Sir Francis Walsingham), the letter providing a news bulletin of recent events in Ireland; docketed in Grey's hand: 'copie of my pryvate./to her majestie', 'Dublin this xxii$^{th}$ of December 1580'

Edmund Spenser stands at two extremes. On the one hand he was the poet of *The Faerie Queene,* that great epic dedicated to Elizabeth; and then there was his day job. In the sixteenth century, university sinecures were hard to come by and poets usually became clergymen or secretaries. In Spenser's case, he became secretary to Lord Grey de Wilton, the Queen's viceroy in Ireland, England's only colony (equivalent perhaps, in our time, to serving as a Chinese official in occupied Tibet). He took up the post in August 1580, and served with Grey through two sanguinary years, afterwards staying on in Ireland until, shortly before his death, his castle of Kilcolman was destroyed by the Earl of Tyrone (53). This letter is a duplicate in Spenser's handwriting of a dispatch Grey sent the Queen soon after his appointment. It was originally enclosed with one Grey sent at the same time to her Secretary of State, Sir Francis Walsingham.

It would have been good to include in this book part of the manuscript of *The Faerie Queene,* but unfortunately not a scrap of Spenser's literary work survives in his autograph. But this letter can be thought of – at a stretch – as an appendix to the poem. The Queen, to whom the letter is addressed, appears in the poem under many names including Gloriana, Belphoebe, Cynthia, and Britomart. Grey himself appears in the poem as Arthegall. From the evidence of another work, Spenser's *Vewe of the Present State of Ireland,* our poet greatly admired Grey, his employer. But it is this same work that provides some of the most damning – and haunting – accounts of the atrocities to which the Irish were subjected by Grey's regime. Nor is *The Faerie Queene* without its ambiguities. In the analysis of Douglas Brooks-Davies, a recent editor: 'from the considerable distance of Ireland, as one of the agents of Elizabeth's policy of colonial oppression there, Spenser paused from secretarial and other duties, over a period of many years, to write *The Faerie Queene.* He dedicated it to an empress. But in his daily life he saw (and, if he is a poet worth reading, he sympathised profoundly with) the wretched state of those over whom she ruled, and so he thought of secrets, those things that secretaries know but are not supposed officially to reveal. He thought of the Irish faith and of the queen's (and his) opposite, Protestant, one. He thought of things as they ought to be, and of things as they were: the Virgin Queen who had succeeded in usurping the place of the Virgin Mary in her people's affections... And as a result he wrote a double poem, a dream work of things as they might be; a nightmare of things as they were.'

[6 lines up] ...*your Majestie must be carefull therefore to roote yt out, otherwise without heapes of Care, masse of threasure & continuall warre never accoumpt to sway this governement. Your Highnes at my leave taking, gave me a warning for being strict in dealing with religion, I have observed yt, how obediently soever, yett most unwillingly I confesse, and I* [overleaf] *doubt as harmefullye to your & godes service, a Canker never receiving Cure without corrosive medicines...*

Vostre Ma.té d'adviser en quoy nous pourrons pardeça selon
nos petits moyens et facultés ayder a rompre les desseings
pernicieulx de nos communs ennemis, Je espere que nous
ferons tel debvoir de nostre part que V. M. en aura tout
contentement, et aura occasion de penser que les benefices dont
Il luy a pleu nous obliger par cydevant n'ont point esté
conferez a personnes qui retiennent la volonté Ingrate,
Et a tant apres avoir baisé treshumblement les mains de
Vostre Ma.té Je prieray Dieu

Madame luy donner en tresparfaicte santé treshereuse et
longue vie, Escrit a Delft ce [illegible] de febvrier
1581.

De vre Ma.té

Treshumble et tresobeissant
serviteur

Guille de Nassau

*'breaking the designs of the common enemy'*

## 32 25,000 crowns on his head

16 February 1581

Letter signed by William the Silent, Prince of Orange and Count of Nassau, to Queen Elizabeth, in French, warning her of the league formed against her by the Pope and Philip II of Spain, and that Philip would never regard the Netherlands conquered until England and Scotland were conquered also; signed and subscribed in his hand 'De vrs Ma$^{the}$ Tres humble et tres obeisant serviteur Guille de Nassau'

In William the Silent nineteenth-century America saw the precursor of George Washington. John Lothrop Motley, American historian of the Dutch Republic, asked, 'Was it necessary that an Alva should ravage a peaceful nation with sword and flame – that desolation should be spread over a happy land, in order that the pure and heroic character of a William of Orange should stand forth more conspicuously, like an antique statue of spotless marble against a stormy sky?' To his contemporaries, too, William possessed those republican virtues, which placed him in a very different sphere to that of Queen Elizabeth. Sidney's friend the poet Fulke Greville recollected his first encounter with William in 1579: 'His uppermost garment was a gown, yet such as (I dare confidently affirm) a mean-born student in our Inns of Court would not have been well-pleased to walk the streets in ... his waistcoat (which showed itself under it) not unlike the best sort of those woollen knit ones which our ordinary watermen row us in; his company about him the burgesses of that beer-brewing town, and he so fellow-encompassed with them as (had I not known his face) no exterior sign of degree of reservedness could have discovered the inequality of his worth or estate from that multitude'.

William the Silent 1568 by Adriaen Thomasz. Key

Philip II was sovereign of the Netherlands, and William in leading the revolt against him was rebelling against his lawful authority. This is something of which Elizabeth could not be expected to approve. But as a Protestant William was her ally, and furthermore she had no wish to see Spanish domination of the Netherlands. William did not claim sovereignty of Holland, a post that had been offered to Elizabeth and refused (the Dutch turning to her suitor the Duke of Anjou instead). Nevertheless in June 1580 Philip II declared William an enemy to the human race and placed 25,000 crowns on his head. In December William published in reply his famous 'Apology', a copy of which he sent to Elizabeth at the same time as this letter. On 26 July the Estates General published their Abjuration, or declaration of independence from Philip's rule. It cannot have been to Elizabeth's taste: 'All mankind knows', said the preamble, 'that a prince is appointed by God to cherish his subjects, even as a shepherd to guard his sheep. When, therefore, the prince does not fulfil his duty as protector; when he oppresses his subjects, destroys their ancient liberties, and treats them as slaves, he is to be considered, not a prince, but a tyrant. As such, the estates of the land may lawfully and reasonably depose him, and elect another in his room.'

[translation, from overleaf] *...I beg very humbly your Majesty to consider what we can do, according to our small powers, to aid in breaking the designs of the common enemy; and I hope that we shall so do our duty that you will have reason to deem that your benefits have not been conferred on ungrateful persons...*

8. No emb. 1582.

Madame. Sur ce qui est venu a ma congnoissance des dernieres conspirations executees en Escosse contre mon pauvre enfant, ayant toute occasion d'en creindre la consequence a l'example de moy mesmes, Il fault que J'employe si peu de vie & de force qui me reste, pour devant ma mort vous descharger plainement mon cœur de mes justes & lamantables plainctes, desquelles ie desire que ceste lre vous serve tant que vous viverez apres moy d'un perpetuel tesmoygnage & graveure en vostre consciance, tant a ma descharge pour la posterité qu'a la honte & confusion de tous ceulx qui soubz vostre adveu m'ont si cruellement & indignement traictee jusques icy & menee a lextremite ou ie suis. Mays d'aultant que leur desseingns pratiques actions & procedures pour detestables qu'elles puissent avoir esté, ont tousiours prevalleu en vostre endroict contre mes tres justes resmontrances & sinceres deportements, & que la force que vous avez en main vous a tousiours donne la raison entre les hommes, J'auray recours au Dieu vivant nostre seul Juge, qui nous a esgualement & Immediatement soubz luy establies au gouvernement de son peuple. Je l'invoqueray a lextremite de ceste mienne tresurgente affliction, pour retribuer a vous & a moy comme il fera a son dernier Jugement, la part de noz merites & demerites l'une vers l'autre. Et souvenez vous (Madame) qu'a luy nous ne scaurions rien deguiser par les fardz & polices de ce monde, ores que mes ennemys soubz vous, puissent pour un temps couvrir aux hommes & paradventure a vous mesmes, leurs subtilles & malicieuses inventions & dexteritez athees. En son nom doncques, & comme devant luy seant entre vous & moy, Je vous ramanteueray premierement que par les agentz, espyes & messagers secretz envoyez soubz vostre nom en Escosse durant que J'y estois, mes subiectz ont esté corompuz pratiquez & suscitez a se rebeller contre moy, a attempter contre ma personne propre & en un mot, a dire faire entreprendre & executer ce que durant mes troubles est advenu aud. pays. Dont ie ne veulx a present specifier aultre verification que celle que J'en tiray par la confession propre & tesmoyngs a luy confrontez d'un, qui depuis a esté des plus advancez en respect de ce sien bon service, auquel si ieusse dellors faict Justice, Il neust despuis par ses anciennes intelligences renouvellé les mesmes pratiques contre mon filz & n'eust moyenné a tous mes trahistres &

4 rebelles subiectz refugiez vers vous, l'ayde & support qu'ilz en ont eu, mesme depuis ma detention pardeca, sans lequel support Je panse que lesd. trahitres n'eussent dellors prevaleu ny depuis si longuement subsisté comme Ilz ont faict. Durant ma prison de Lochlevin

7 feu Throcmorton me conseilla de vostre part de signer ceste demission qu'il m'advertissoit me debvoir estre presentee, sur asseurance qu'elle ne pouvoit estre valable. Et depuis

*'this letter may serve for a perpetual testimony and engraving upon your conscience'*

# 33 De Profundis

8 November 1582

Autograph letter by Mary Queen of Scots, to Queen Elizabeth, in French, written as a final summary of the tribulations and sufferings she has endured at the hands of the English Queen, which may well result in her death; and begging Elizabeth at the very least to allow her 'to withdraw myself out of your realm, into some place of repose, to seek some comfort for my poor body, worn out as it is with continual sorrows, that, with liberty of conscience, I may prepare my soul for God'; subscribing herself, 'Your very disconsolate nearest kinswoman', dated 'At Sheffield, this 8th of November, one thousand, five hundred, eighty-two'

This letter, the product of the interminable leisure of the prisoner, runs to ten closely-written pages and in some ways resembles that other – even longer – example of the genre, Oscar Wilde's *De Profundis*. It is, as the opening makes clear, quite consciously written with posterity in mind, and projects into the future an image of Mary as a suffering queen held captive by the cousin she trusted, a martyr for the true faith. It makes no mention of Mary's political ambition or her hope of becoming Elizabeth's successor (let alone her replacement). If it sounds a valedictory note, it is because Mary thought she was dying. The letter was prompted by news of the seizure of her son James by the Ruthven family under the Earl of Gowrie. This placed the government of Scotland in pro-English hands, and threatened her hopes of the 'Association' (the proposal that she share the rule of Scotland with her son James). Less than five years later this 'celebrated letter', as Agnes Strickland calls it, had entered the Marian mythos. It is eulogised in Adam Blackwood's *Martyre de la Royne d'Ecosse*, published in 1587, the year of Mary's execution: 'The Queen, at the reported seizure of her son by Lord Gowry, having received an intimation of her son's captivity, fell so sick that she thought she should die, as the English physicians reported she would to their mistress, who wanted nothing better… the poor mother, being greatly agitated in her mind, after she had addressed her prayers to God, put her hand to the pen, thinking to obtain favour from her and to soften the heart of her cousin by this address.' Sir Francis Walsingham thought the letter proud and arrogant.

Mary Queen of Scots *c.*1559 after François Clouet

[translation] *Madam, – Upon that which has come to my knowledge of the last conspiracies executed in Scotland against my poor child, having reason to fear the consequence of it, from the example of myself, I must employ the very small remainder of my life and strength before my death to discharge my heart to you fully of my just and melancholy complaints; of which I desire that this letter may serve you as long as you live after me for a perpetual testimony and engraving upon your conscience, as much for my discharge to posterity as to the shame and confusion of all those who, under your approbation, have so cruelly and unworthily treated me to this time, and reduced me to the extremity in which I am. But as their designs, practices, actions, and proceedings, though as detestable as they could have been, have always prevailed with you against my just remonstrances and sincere deportment; and as the power which you have in your hands has always been a reason for you among mankind; I will have recourse to the living God, our only judge, who has established us equally and immediately under him for the government of his people…*

Nottez madame que je l'ay interrogue le plus qu'il m'a esté possible: et premierement sur les dix commandements de la loy laquelle chose c'est fort bien confessé hors mis sur / ne occides / car il a tousiours esté volont[illegible] vers vre Mate et luy ay faict les plus belles remonstrances du monde sur cela / mais il m'a respondu en somme que c'estoit pour la tranquillité de la vraye religion catholique apostolique et romaine et que resolument qu'il croyoit que son ame yroit tout droict en paradis quant il n'auroit faict aultre chose que cela: et estoit qu'il soit enragé en se confessant come il grinchoit les dentz et ne faisoit [illegible] en le disant: Notez qu'il m'a promis de me amener les aultres / mais il y a des qui viennent en brief d'espaigne ce qu'il attend / quant est des [illegible] pour tous les il ne vault les [illegible] que si d'espaigne a tel volonté / il doibvroient faire leur pasques de mercredi prochain en huit et leur [illegible]

Deus adiuvat te / et mandat tecu omnibus diebus vite tue Amen

Vre tres humble et affect. [illegible]
[illegible]
[illegible]

gardez mo[n] secret car je vous suis fidelle / et de continuer aultres choses

*'Keep my secret, because I am faithful to you and will discover other things'*

# 34 An Ash Wednesday supper

26 March 1584

Letter by an anonymous Roman Catholic priest, to Queen Elizabeth, in French, revealing that Pedro de Zubiaur, a Spanish agent, has made confession that he is plotting her assassination; subscribing himself 'Your humble affectionate/He whom you know', and in a Latin postscript urging her to 'Keep my secret, because I am faithful to you and will discover other things'

John Bossy, in his *Giordano Bruno and the Embassy Affair* (1991), has argued that this letter may have been written by the Italian philosopher Giordano Bruno, who was burnt as a heretic in 1600, and has been revered from the nineteenth century onwards as a prophet of free enquiry and a scientific, religiously tolerant age; someone who, in his own words, 'released the human spirit, and set knowledge at liberty'.

It belongs to a group of messages sent to Elizabeth's spymaster Sir Francis Walsingham from an agent in the French Embassy signing himself 'Henry Fagot'. Ours is the only one of the group addressed to the Queen. As a source of information Fagot's letters were valuable to Walsingham not just in terms of French intelligence, but because much correspondence with Mary Queen of Scots – and thus the plotting associated with her – was routed through the Embassy. The parallels between Bruno and Fagot are striking: Bruno was staying at the Embassy during the period when Fagot was writing his letters; Fagot wrote in French but was prone to make phonetic errors indicating that he was, like Bruno, an Italian; and both were in holy orders. Curiously though – for a scholar of international reputation – practically nothing survives in Bruno's hand, just one letter in Latin (an application to the University of Helmstedt), some pages of a draft treatise, and a couple of presentation inscriptions. There is, nevertheless, sufficient resemblance between the Helmstedt letter and ours to support an attribution to Bruno, even assuming – as seems likely – the Fagot hand to be disguised. Both letters share an underlying rhythm, an overall look, something that it is hard for the conscious mind to suppress (and which often betrays the forger); one of the characteristics of both being a Darwinian tendency for the writing to tumble down to the right.

Bossy argues that our letter was written at the same time as Bruno's masterpiece, his dialogue *La cena de le Ceneri* ('Ash Wednesday Supper'), published in England later that year, a tract advocating the Copernican system and where, *inter alia*, 'some vast, mystical universal empire is promised to the Queen of England'. Tract and letter have a curious detail in common. The Confessor's letter describes Elizabeth's would-be assassin as grinding his teeth in rage, which is what the pedant Torquato does when confronted by Bruno in *La cena*. This takes on greater significance if, as Bossy suggests, our letter – unlike other communications from Fagot – owes more to the literary impulse of *La cena* than sober fact. There is in any event no evidence that Walsingham thought it advisable to pass it on to the Queen.

[translation from line 15] *...he told me that he had the charge from M. de Mendoza, with four others whose names I do not know except for one called Courtois, to procure your death very shortly by arms, by poisons, bouquets, underclothes, smell, waters or by any other means; that it will be the greatest St Bartholomew's Day there has over been; and that neither God nor Devil will stand in the way of their doing it. This is an appalling thing, and in so much, Madame, as I have been the discoverer of many things which have become known to your good Council and found to be true, and would sooner die than tell you anything but the pure and sincere truth...*

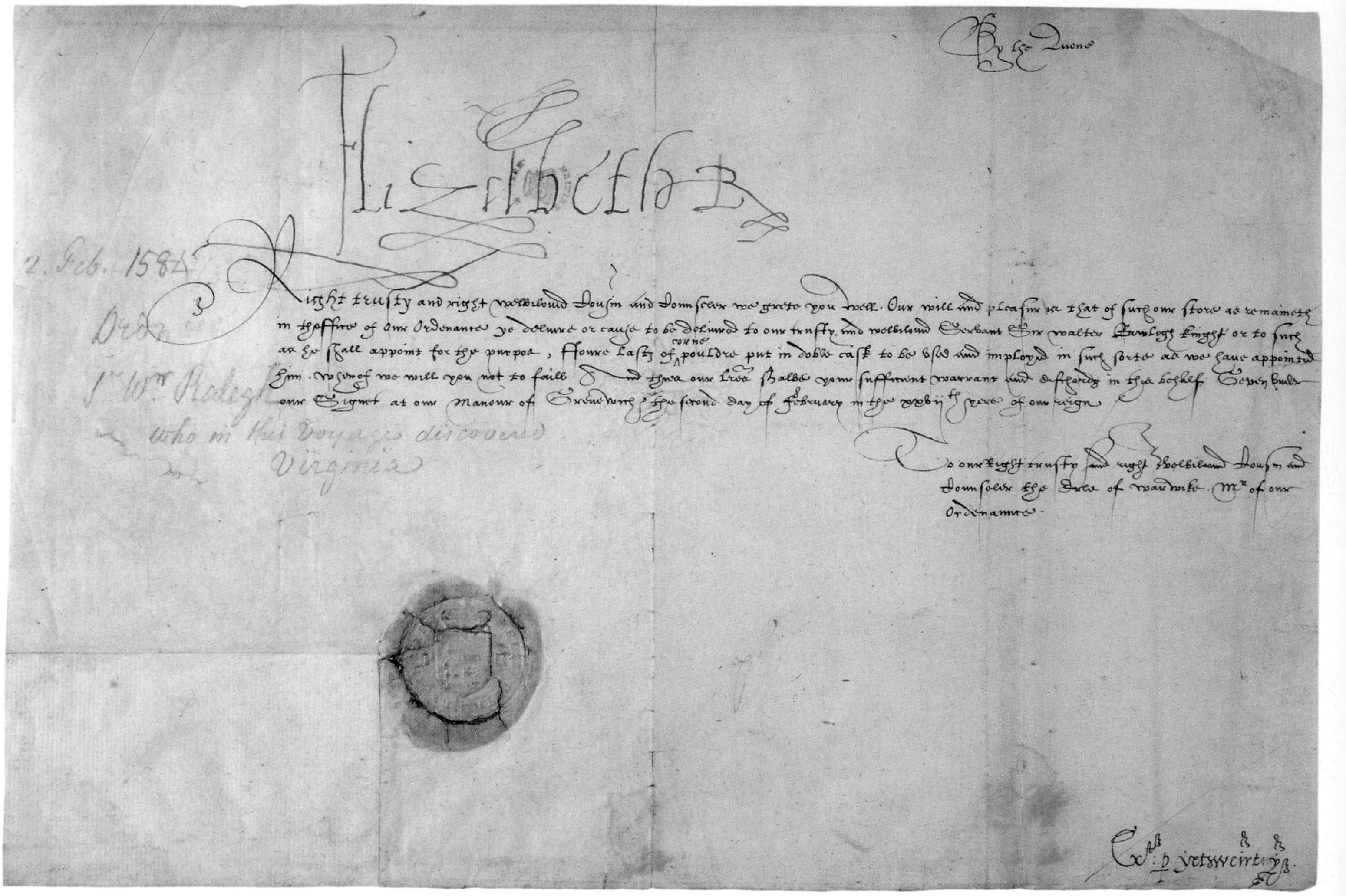
By the Queene
Elizabeth R
2. Feb. 1584
Sr Wm Ralegh
who in this voyage discovered
Virginia
Right trusty and right welbeloued Cousin and Counsellor we grete you well. Our will and pleasure is that of such our store as remaineth
in thoffice of our Ordenance ye deliuer or cause to be deliuered to our trusty and welbeloued Seruant Sir Walter Rawleigh knight or to such
as he shall appoint for that purpose, ffower Lastes of corne pouldre put in doble cask to be used and imployed in such sorte as we haue appointed
him. Whereof we will you not to faile. And these our lettres shalbe your sufficient warrant and discharge in that behalf. Geven under
our Signet at our Manour of Grenewich the second day of February in the xxvijth yere of our reign
To our right trusty and right welbeloued Cousin and
Counsellor the Erle of Warwike Mr of our
Ordenance.
Ex. p Yetsweirt

*'delivre to our trusty and welbilovid Servant Sir Walter Rawlegh knight'*

# 35 Sailing for Virginia

2 February 1585

Warrant signed by Queen Elizabeth, to the Earl of Warwick, Master of Ordnance in the Tower of London, ordering gunpowder to be supplied to Sir Walter Ralegh, 'Geven under our Signet at our Manour of Grenewich the second day of February in the xxvii^th^ yere of our reign'

Sir Walter Ralegh, inspiration, promoter and chief financial backer of the first attempt to settle English people in the New World, had been granted a patent 'for the discovering and planting of new lands and Countreis' in 1584. That same year he sent an exploratory expedition which landed at the outer banks of present-day North Carolina, and took possession of the area in the Queen's name. She allowed the new land to be named Virginia in her honour, and on 6 January 1585 rewarded him with a knighthood. This warrant for gunpowder was issued while the main colonising expedition was being fitted out. 'Corn' was the name for gunpowder that had been granulated into roundish particles; thus Sir Richard Grenville, Ralegh's cousin who led the Roanoke expedition, was to be described a few years later as defending the *Revenge* 'till he had not one corne of powder left'. Unusually for such a document no price is named, implying that the gunpowder was either a gift from the Queen or part of her investment in the project: other contemporary warrants put the value of four lasts of gunpowder (equivalent to 9,600lb) at no less than £400. This warrant is also evidence of the military character of the colony, intended as an outpost from which raids could be made on Spanish treasure fleets.

Ralegh's seal as Governor of Virginia, 1584

Suitably provisioned, the fleet sailed from Plymouth on 9 April 1585. In the rhapsodic words of Holinshed's *Chronicle*: 'In this yeare 1585, even in Aprill, at the pleasant prime, sir Walter Raleigh knight, being incouraged by the reports of his men of the goodnesse of the soile and fertilitie of the countrie, which they had discovered this yeare last past, and now by her majestie called Virginia... furnished to his great charges eight sailes of all sortes, and immediatlie set them to the sea, ordeining sir Richard Gréenfield [Grenville] his kinsman... his lieutenant, injoining him either to tarrie himselfe, or to leave some gentlemen of good worth with a competent number of soldiers in the countrie of Virginia, to begin an English colonie there'. It was from Roanoke that the first clay pipes were brought back to England, thus initiating the craze, soon inextricably linked in the public mind with Ralegh, for smoking (tobacco itself having possibly been brought back to England by Sir John Hawkins in 1565) (*16*). This first colony lasted a year, and was to be evacuated by Sir Francis Drake. A second – the famous 'lost' colony – was sent in 1587 and found abandoned three years later. A permanent colony in Virginia was not to be settled until 1607; but by then Ralegh's patent had reverted to the Crown.

[from line 1]... *Our will and pleasur is that of such oure store as remaineth in thoffice of our Ordenance ye delivre or cause to be delivred to our trusty and welbilovid Servant Sir Walter Rawlegh knight or to such as he shall appoint for the purpos, Foure lastes of corne pouldre put in doble cask to be used and imployid in such sorte as we have appointid him. Wherof we will you not to faill...*

10 Nov:

19 30

Most gratious souerein.



This rude peece of paper shall presume becaws of your Ma^{tes} commandement, most humbly to present such a cypher as little leysure cowld aford me. if there come any matter to my knowledg the importance whereof shall deseru to be so masked I will not fail (since your pleasure is my onely boldnes) to your own handes to recomend it. in the mean tyme I beseech your Ma^{tie} will voutchsafe legibly to reed my hart in the course of my lyfe, and though it self bee but of a mean worth yet to esteem it lyke a poor hows well sett. I most lowly kis your handes and prai to God your enemies mai then onely haue peace when thei are weery of knowing your force. At Grauesend This 10^{th} of Nouember.



Your Ma^{ties} most humble seruant

Ph. Sidnei

To the Quene's most excellent Majesty. 43

*'I beseech your Majestie will vouchsafe legibly to reed my hart in the cource of my lyfe'*

# 36 Our perfect man

10 November 1585

Autograph letter by Sir Philip Sidney, to Queen Elizabeth, written while preparing to sail to the Low Countries, to take up his post as Governor of Flushing, sending her a cipher with which he will 'mask' his letters and assuring her of his devotion, 'At Gravesend This 10th of November'

This, the quintessential letter of devotion from the quintessential poet-courtier of the Elizabethan age – Spenser's 'president of nobless and of chivalry' – was written on the eve of Sidney's departure for the Low Countries, where at the request of the Estates General the Queen had appointed him Governor of Flushing. He was part of the English expeditionary force under the command of his uncle the Earl of Leicester, sent to help England's Dutch co-religionists in their struggle against Philip II of Spain. Eleven months later, after being wounded near Zutphen, he was dead. Mourning was universal, and his state funeral at St Paul's Cathedral was one of the great events of the reign. William Camden's eulogy catches the tone: 'This is that Sidney, who as Providence seems to have sent him into the world to give the present a specimen of the ancients, so it did on a sudden recall him and snatch him from us as more worthy of heaven than of earth'. To later ages Sidney continued to embody the ideal of Elizabethan chivalry. To Shelley he was 'Sidney, as he fought/And as he fell and as he lived and loved/Sublimely mild, a Spirit without spot'; Yeats mourning the death of Robert Gregory called him 'our Sidney and our perfect man'.

Sir Philip Sydney *c.*1576 by an unknown artist

Sidney owed his exalted position both to his own attainments and to the fact that he was son of a viceroy of Ireland, Sir Henry Sidney, as well as nephew and heir to his uncles, the Earls of Leicester and Warwick. Abroad he achieved quasi-royal status, especially after his mission to the Emperor Rudolf (27). But at home his advancement was slower. Although he acted as deputy to his uncle Warwick, Master of the Ordnance (35), he was not officially appointed Joint Master until July 1585. It seems that Elizabeth never really liked him, nor he her. In 1579, he wrote the Queen a letter protesting at the Anjou match (John Stubbs had his right hand hacked off for doing as much). In his *New Arcadia* we catch a glimpse of Elizabeth as the Queen of Iberia, Andromana ('man-mad'), described as a well-preserved 'older woman', possessed of 'an exceeding red hair with small eyes'. Sidney looked to employment outside the court. He had purchased from Ralegh's stepbrother Sir Humphrey Gilbert three million acres in 'Norumberga', the future New England. He had long wanted to fight for the Protestant cause in Europe, but, finding his plans frustrated, decided instead to sail with Drake to America. He was actually on board Drake's flagship as it was setting out from Plymouth that September when he was ordered back to court. By way of compensation he was made Governor of Flushing; and so went to his death in the Old World, without setting eyes on the New.

[from line 8] *. . . I beseech your Majestie will vouchsafe legibly to reed my hart in the cource of my lyfe, and though it self bee but of a mean worth, yet to esteem it lyke a poor hows well sett. I most lowly kis your handes and prai to God your enemies mai then onely have peace when thei are weery of knowing your force. . .*

No. 35.

of this Realme, of the Judges and others of good account, whose sentence I must approue. 85

And all litle inowgh for wee Princes, I tell you are set on stages, in the sight and veiw, of al the worlde duly obserued, th' eyes of many behold our actions, a spott is sone spied in our garments, a blemish quickly noted in our doinges, It behoueth vs therefore to be carefull that our proceedings be just and honorable.

But I must tell you one thing further in this late Acte of Parliament you haue laied an hard hand on mee that I must giue direction for her death wch cannot be to mee but most greiuous and displeasant. And [illegible] you do not mistake mine absence frome this Parliament (wch I had almost forgotten) although there be no cawse why I should willinglie come amongst multitudes, for that amongest many, some nor be euill yet hath it [illegible] mee away but only the great greif to heare this cawse spoken of, especiallie that this nation sholde be so spotted with blotts of disloyaltie, wherein the lesse is my greife for that I hope the better part is myne, and those of the worse not much to be accounted of, for that in seeking my destruction, they spoiled theire owne sowles.

Her Matie referred the further knoledg hereof to some of the ll. there present whereof the L. Threr seemed to be one for yt he stood vp to verefy it.

And euen now cold I tell you that wch wold make you sorie, It is a secrett, and I will tell it you (although it be knowen I haue the propertie to keepe Counsaile but to well, often to mine owne perill) It is not long since mine eyes did see it written that an othe was taken wthin [illegible] daies, either to kill mee or to be hanged themselues, and that to be performed ere one moneth were ended.

Hereby I see youre daungr in mee, and neithr can or will be so vnthankfull or carelesse of yor consciences, as to take no care for youre safetie.

I am not vnmindfull of youre othe of association manifesting [illegible] goodwilles and affections taken and entered into for safegard of my person, donn (I protest to God) before I euer heard of it, or thought of such a matter, till a thowsand of obligations were shewed me at Hampton Court signed and subscribed wth handes and seales of the best of my Realme. wch neuerthelesse I acknowledge as an argument of youre loyall harts, and trew zeale to my safetie, for wch I thincke my self bounde carefully to consider of it, and respect you therein.

But for asmuch as this matter is verie rare, weightie, and of great consequence, and that I haue not yet perused youre petition, I thincke you do not looke for any present resolution, the rather for that as it is not my maner in matters of farre lesse moment, to giue speedie awnswere wthout due consideration, So in this of such importaunce, I thincke it verie requisite wth earnest praier to beseech his diuine Matie, so to illuminate myne vnderstanding and inspire mee wth his grace, as I may do and determine yt wch shall serue to the Establishment of his Church, Preseruacon of youre Estats and prosperitie of this Common wealth vnder my Charge. Wherein for that I know delay is daungerous, you shall haue wth all conueniency or Resolution deliuered by or message to you all. And what euer any Prince may meritt of theire subiects, for theire approued testimony of theire vnfained synceritie, eithr by gouerning iustly, voide of all partiality, or suffrance of any iniuries donn euen to the poorest, that do I assuredly promis inuiolablie to performe for requitall of youre so many desertes.

*'you have laied an hard hand on mee that I must give direction for her death'*

# 37 Condemned

12 November 1586

Scribal manuscript, partly in the hand of Robert Cecil, with autograph revisions and interlineations by Queen Elizabeth, of her answer to a parliamentary deputation demanding the immediate execution of Mary Queen of Scots

The House of Lords and Commons assembled on 29 October 1586, following the discovery of the Babington Plot which furnished proof that Mary had acquiesced with the plot to assassinate Elizabeth and take her place on the throne. After debate they unanimously petitioned for Mary's immediate execution, sending a deputation to Elizabeth on 12 November. This is Elizabeth's answer. In some respects it is her counterpart to Mary's *De Profundis* letter (*33*). With its anguished hand-wringing it is said to have drawn tears from many. In it Elizabeth expresses grief that one of her own sex and caste should consent, as Mary has, to her death. She reveals – playing what she calls 'the blab' – that she wrote a secret letter to Mary, promising to forgive her if she should confess; but owns that Mary has steadfastly denied her guilt, although even now Elizabeth is prepared to forgive her. She rues the fact that she and Mary are not 'but as two milkmaids with pails upon our arms', for more than her own life is at stake; indeed, princes such as her are 'set on stages in the sight and view of all the world'. She ends by asking the parliamentary deputation whether any solution other than execution is possible.

This manuscript was copied out after Elizabeth had delivered her speech and then marked up by both author and editor for publication, in a collection edited by Robert Cecil and published by the government in 1586. As such it is an excessively rare survival. 'Copy' for publication was nearly always thrown away once it had served its purpose. Here piety no doubt intervened. The main text is in the hand of an anonymous scribe, interlineations are in the hand of the author (Elizabeth), while the five-line note in the margin is in the hand of the editor (the young Robert Cecil, here clearly acting for his father). A final copy, deciphering Elizabeth's atrocious writing, was presumably then made for the printer to use (and throw away).

Queen Elizabeth *c.*1575, the 'Darnley' portrait, by an unknown artist

[from line 2, Elizabeth's interlineations indicated ^thus^] *. . . And all litle inowgh for wee Princes, I tell you are set on stages, in the sight and veiw, of al[l] the worlde duly observed, th'eyes of many behold our actions, a spott is sone spied in our garments, a blemish quickly noted in our doinges. It behoveth us therefore to be carefull that our proceedings be Just and honorable.*

*But I must tell you one thing ~~further~~* ^more^ *that in this late Acte of Parliament you have laied an hard hand on mee, that I must give direction for her death, which cannot be ~~to mee~~ but most grievous* ^*and an yrksome burdon to me*^. . .

[Robert Cecil's marginal note] *Her Majestie referred the further knoledg hereof to some of the lords there present wherof the lord Thesaurer* [*Burghley*] *seemed to be one for that he stood upp to verefy it.*

15

Elizab. by ye Grace of God Q. of Englad fraunce and Irland

defendor of the fayth &c. To our trusty and

wellbeloved Gentilmen ~~we grete you well greting~~

Sr Amyce parlett knight

Where you have had and yet have the custody and charg of

ye pson of ye Q. of Scott. ~~and as yet~~ hath ayenst whō Iudicēd and Iudgment

hath bene gyven ~~charg~~ ~~whereby she hath bene Iudged~~

~~to have attempted~~ ~~that she hath compassed and~~

~~Imagyned our deth~~ sondry thyngs ~~to ye [illegible] death~~

~~and destruction of our pson~~, as by our late proclamation

dated ye 4. of this month is to all psons published

And also that we have bene ~~contynually~~ by the states

of our Parlement most instantly moved urged and

pressed to cause further execution to be made of ye sayd

sentence ~~being of our naturall disposition~~ We ~~[illegible]~~ have psecutey delyvered our warrant

under our great seale of England to our Shyreve of

~~of~~ our county of Northampton, to repayre to you, and

have thereby willed and warranted hym to receyve ye pson of ye sayd Q.

into his charg, and without delaye to do execution

~~[illegible]~~ as by our sayd Comission may further appeare unto you. And

therefor we do will and comand you to delyver hir

unto his charg, as [illegible] our chef officer of yt County, so as he may without

delay shall [illegible] ye purpose of [illegible] our Comission, and of your

self ~~do execute~~ untill ye same shalbe do ~~[illegible]~~ by ye same

A much comes but as wont this same, it is by this all duty [illegible] [illegible] that they can by no devise and meanes to ye worke of our [illegible] [illegible] the speaker [illegible] [illegible] their [illegible] and therefore [illegible] [illegible] our [illegible] ~~[illegible]~~ delay *'the Q. of Scottes ageynst whom sentence & judgment hath bene gyven'*

# 38 Execution of sentence

10 December 1586

Autograph draft by Lord Burghley for the death warrant of Mary Queen of Scots, drawn up for signature by Queen Elizabeth, addressed to Sir Amyas Paulet, who has 'in Custody and Chardg of the person of the Q. of Scottes', instructing him to deliver Mary to the Sheriff of Northampton 'to cause further execution to be made of the said sentence' for which 'these our letres patent under our Great Seale of England shall be your sufficient discharg'; the sheet of paper torn in half, docketed 10 December, 'Gyven at our Manor of Rychmond the [*blank*] of December the xxix$^{th}$ of our reign'

After further parliamentary deputations (37) and further 'answers answerless', Elizabeth finally gave in. On 2 December she promised to publish sentence against Mary. London exploded with celebratory bell-ringing, bonfires and psalms. The next battle was to get her to sign the actual warrant. Her hesitations over the execution of the Duke of Norfolk (25) were as nothing compared to her hesitations over a sister queen. Early that December she told the French Ambassador that she had never shed so many tears over anything, not even at the deaths of her father, her brother or her sister, as over this 'unfortunate affair'. Elizabeth was horrified at the public killing of a sovereign anointed by God. At one point she even sank so low as to ask Sir Amyas Paulet, Mary's gaoler, to dispatch her on the quiet, but was rebuffed.

Eyewitness drawing of Mary's execution from the papers of Robert Beale (see p. 14)

The unprecedented nature of the act is reflected in the warrant itself. Those for Norfolk and Essex follow a set form (56), while this one is at pains to justify itself, as if in implicit acknowledgement of its legal dubiety. The final warrant – the original of which is no longer known to survive – is an amplified version of the draft. It too draws attention to the threat that Mary poses Elizabeth, her succession and the realm, and the fact that it was issued at the insistent urging of parliament (the passage added to ours in the margin). The main difference is that the final version is addressed to the Earls of Shrewsbury, Kent, Derby, Cumberland and Pembroke, rather than to the hapless Amyas Paulet alone. Elizabeth eventually signed the warrant, to which the Great Seal had been attached, on 1 February. Her Council then despatched it without further ado and Mary was executed at Fotheringhay – with Paulet and Thomas Andrews, Sheriff of Northamptonshire, in attendance – on the morning of Wednesday 8 February 1587.

[15 lines down] . . .*we have presently directed our Commission under our great seale of England to our shyrryve of our County of Northampton, to repayer to you, and have thereby willed and warranted hym to receave the person of the sayd Q. of into his chardg, and without delaye to do execution as by our sayd Commission may further appeare unto you, and therfor we do will and Command you to delyver hir unto his chardg, as to our shyrryf and chef publick officer chef officer of that our County so as he also without delay shall in the presence of sundry our Noble men and of your self within that our Castle do the same* [overleaf] *exequution*. . .

Madame & dearest sister ~~I have receaved~~ quhairas by youre lettir & bearare ~~hirde~~
youre seruand & ambassadoure ~~robert carey~~ robert carey, ~~& quhairas~~ ye purge
youre selfe of yone unhappy fact as on the one pairt
considdering youre rank, sexe, consanguinitie, & longe professed goode will to the defunct together with youre many
& solemne attestationis of youre innocentie I darr not
wronge you so farre as not to iudge honorablie of youre unspotted pairt thairin so on the other syde I wishe that
youre honorable behauioure in all tymes heirafter may
fully persuaide the quhole worlde of the same ~~of youre innocent~~
~~pairt thairin~~, & as for my pairt I looke that ye will
~~at this tyme quhile~~ geue me at this tyme suche a
full satisfaction in all respectis ~~proofe of youre honorable & kynde dealing towar-~~
~~dis me~~ as sall be a meane to strenthin & unite this
yle, establishe & maintaine the trew religion, & obleis
me to be as of befoire I was youre most louing

this bearare
hath sumquhat
to informe you
of in my name
quhom I neid not
desyre you to credit
for ye knou I loue him.

*'youre many & solemne attestationis of youre innocentie'*

# 39 His dead mother

March 1587

Autograph draft of a letter by James VI of Scotland, to Queen Elizabeth, replying to her protestations that she had no hand in 'that miserable accident' of the execution of his mother, Mary Queen of Scots

James VI was ambivalent about the death of his mother, Mary Queen of Scots. He had been taken from her as a baby, and so would have had no memory of her. She was deposed soon afterwards and – in a novel twist to the usual Freudian scenario – he was crowned in her place. In a will of 1577 Mary had disinherited him in favour of Philip II of Spain should James remain Protestant; she informed Mendoza, her Spanish intermediary, of this in 1586. James, for his part, early in 1585 repudiated the Association with his mother providing for their joint rule, and instead signed a treaty of friendship with Elizabeth. By now it was obvious to all that his first priority was the English succession. Hearing of his mother's plight, he sent ambassadors to England with instructions to bargain for two things: 'the one to deal very earnestly both with the Queen and her councillors for our sovereign mother's life, the other that our title to that Crown be not prejudged'. He wrote to Leicester in the same spirit: 'How fond and inconsistent were I if I should prefer my mother to the title, let all men judge'.

James VI 1586 by an unknown artist

As for Elizabeth, when news reached her of Mary's execution she was horrified, and angrier than she had ever been in her life. Although she had signed Mary's death warrant, she distanced herself from the act by means of what many (not faced by her terrible predicament) may regard as a moral sleight of hand. She expressly ordered her secretary, William Davison, not to send the warrant. Davison and the Council, desperate – as she knew – to see Mary executed, defied her. Elizabeth wrote James a letter apologising for 'that miserable accident which, far contrary to my meaning, hath befallen' and protesting 'how innocent I am in this case'. Ours is the letter that James drafted in reply. Elizabeth's letter was entrusted to her young cousin, Robert Carey (who many years later was to be the one who galloped up to Scotland to tell James of his accession). Carey later wrote how 'Her Majesty sent me to the King of Scots, to make known her innocence of her sister's death, with letters of credence from herself to assure all that I should affirm' and of how James had warned him not to enter Scotland for, such was the fury of the people, 'no power of his could warrant my life at that time'.

*Madame & dearest Sister quhairas by youre lettir & beararе robert carey youre servand & ambasadoure ye purge youre self of yone unhappy fact as on the one pairt considering youre rank & sexe, consanguinitie, & longe professed goode will to the defunct together with youre many & solemne attestationis of youre innocentie I darr not wronge you so farre as not to judge honorablie of youre unspotted pairt thairin so on the other syde I wishe that youre honorable behavioure in all tymes heir after may fully persuaide the quhole world of the same, & as for my pairt I looke that ye will geve me at this tyme suche a full satisfaction in all respectis as sall be a meane to strenthin & unite this yle, establishe & maintaine the trew religion, & obleig me to be as of befoire I was youre most lovi~*

them as theie neyther woolde nor durst but observe; and wth all that yf 77 [him Ma] woold not, I durst assuer that 79 [ye Ma] should never deliver to amie that wch 77 [she] delivered to me, but to her selfe, and farther that wheras some used some speeche to me in the beginning, and $ [Pinard] (the last daye that he came from 77 [him]) had cast out suche a worde that 79 [yr Mat] did make these offers nowe to 77 [him] to make proffit of 77 [his] deling wth 79 [yr Ma] nowe to advance the treatye of peace wth 100 [the Spaniards] that 79 [yr Ma] was in hand wth all, to make [cipher: your bargain better] that I did protest to 77 [F.K.] from 79 [E.Ma] that 79 never had suche a mening, not soe muche as suche a thought; that there were evill disposed people to breake the amitie betwene 109 [Fra.] 111 [Eng] that had those invencions, wch was their only drifte; that I durst assuer 77 [him] upon my soule that 79 [E.M.] never had suche a thought, 77 [he] toulde me upon that, that 77 [he] woolde assuer him selfe upon my promis that I and 79 [yr Ma] woolde performe ytt in all pointes, that 77 [he] woolde deale plainly wth me, and [cipher: lave this state] more [cipher: open] to 79 [E.M.] then ever he did to any; that he was verie well contented 79 [E] should take [cipher: advice] of amie 79 [she] [cipher: secretest] [cipher: counsellors] whome ytt pleased 79 [her], that he knowe 79 [sho] had them that 79 [sho] did assuer should doe nothing passing 79 [hor] comandement that 77 [he] wisshed wth all his hart to have given of his bloude that 77 [he] had the like that woolde depend upon noe bodie but upon 77 [his] will, [cipher: his affaires] should not (as he termed ytt) pendre a la balance as theie doe) That wheras the last daie 77 [he] sent me word by $ [Pinard] the awnswer that 77 did make, ytt was 74 [d. Mo.] and [cipher: his whole counsels] peremptorie advise, standinge upon ytt that ytt was not fitt that 77 [he] should [cipher: desire] 79 [yr Ma] to meddell betwene 77 [him] [cipher: and his subjects], that there upon he made the answer and desyred me to send ytt awaye, as I did by Jhon Fourier that nothing mought be suspected that I hooped of amie thing else from 77 [him], but that 77 [he] woolde deale more pleinly wth 79 [E.M.], beseching 79 [her] wth all his hart to doe ytt, and wthout making knowen to amie that amie request came from 77 [him] because [cipher: they for ye religion] as he said coulde kepe nothinge secret, and that 79 [she] woolde perswade 66 [K. of Na] to have a care of his estate, and to accomodate 66 [him selfe] wth 77 [F.K.] in suche sort as [cipher: the leage] mought have noe more pretence to ruine 109 [Fra-] and him bothe; wher upon I replyed to him the impossibilities that ytt was for 79 [E.Ma] to deale wth 66 [K. of Na] in [cipher: religion] for the reasons that I had bothe toulde 77 [him] the other daye, and after to $ [Pinard] and wch 77 [F.K.] by himselfe in this action mought verie well considar; that 79 [E.Ma] I durst answer woolde doe what 79 [she] coulde amie waie, but to [cipher: perswad] 66 [him] amie more [cipher: to chainge] then 79 [she] had perswaded 66 [K. Na] to take ytt, that ytt was a thing 79 [she] woold not meddel in, that yf his owne iudgment woolde make him doe ytt for the good of [cipher: his estate] that you woolde not [cipher: medel with] [cipher: conscience] nor wth [cipher: his soule] 77 [he] answered me that he woolde deale as plainly wth me as yf I were his ghostly father, that as in truthe 77 [he] was soe muche adicted to his religion, as wth all he woolde ytt had coste him a peece of his realme and part of 77 [his] bloude, that all the worlde, but specially 109 [Fra] were of ytt,

soe

*'nobody saw me nor I saw nobody, for that he brought me tarried not in the chamber'*

# 40 Treachery

25 February 1588

Autograph letter by Sir Edward Stafford, British Ambassador to France, to Queen Elizabeth, with words deciphered by Sir Francis Walsingham, describing a clandestine meeting with Henri III, King of France, 'From Paris 25° February 1587'

This letter dates from the anxious months between the execution of Mary Queen of Scots and the coming of the Spanish Armada. The writer, Sir Edward Stafford, was English Ambassador to Paris, where Mary's execution caused particular outrage. He tells the Queen of an extraordinary meeting held with Henri III, at a secret location, at the dead of night (cipher words in italics): 'I spake yesternight with *the King*, who sent for me by a man quite unknown, to a house that I think I can guess at again, though it were in the night, and that he brought me far out of the right way to it; where I found nobody in the chamber but *himself*. In the house I heard folks, but nobody saw me nor I saw nobody, for that he brought me tarried not in the chamber. *The King* began with me... that whatsoever *he* delivered me, I would send it directly to *your Majesty's* own hands, and that *you* would do what lay in *you* for the good of *France*, and keep it to *yourself*.' The King wanted Elizabeth to persuade his brother-in-law and heir to the throne, Henri of Navarre (the future Henri IV) to convert to Catholicism (something he had been attempting since 1584), and so cut the ground from beneath the feet of the hard-line Catholic League. That May the League mounted the 'Day of the Barricades', forcing Henri III to flee Paris. On 31 July 1589, while laying siege to Paris, he was assassinated by a fanatic friar.

Sir Francis Walsingham *c.*1585, attributed to John de Critz the Elder

As befits such a cloak-and-dagger letter, it is written with proper names hidden by a cipher, each letter being substituted by a symbol and the names by a number. Stafford explains that he is using Lord Burghley's cipher, fearing that Elizabeth might have lost the one he sent her. On a spare sheet a clerk has copied out the cipher, enabling Walsingham himself, in his neatest handwriting, to write in the decipher above each of the cipher words. In the margin Walsingham has entered trefoils to draw the Queen's attention to passages of particular importance.

There is a twist in the tail of this particular story. For it has since come to light that Stafford was actually in the pay of Spain. Early in 1587 he had promised Mendoza, the Spanish Ambassador to Paris, that not a single warship would be equipped in England without Spain's foreknowledge. The month before his meeting with Henri III, Stafford sent home the first of a series of totally erroneous intelligence reports on the Armada.

[from line 15, additions by Walsingham in roman] ...*uppon my promis that I and* your Majesty *woolde performe ytt in all points, that* he *woolde deale plainly with me, and* laye his state *more* open *to* Q M *then ever he did to any; that he was verie well contented* Q *should take* advice *of anie* the secretest cownselors *whome yt pleased* her, *that he knew* she *had them that* she *did assure should doe nothing passing* her *commandement, that* he *wisshed with all his hart to have given of his bloude that* he *had the like that woolde depend uppon noe bodie but uppon* his will, his affayres *should not (as he termed ytt) pendre a la balance as theie doe...*

The absence of my Lord Admiral, most gracious Sovereign,
hath emboldened me to put my pen
to the paper. On Friday last, upon good
consideration, we left the Army of Spain so
far to the northwards, as they could neither
recover England nor Scotland; and within
three days after, we were entertained with a
great storm, considering the time of the
year, the which storm, in many of our judgments,
hath not a little annoyed the enemy's army.
If the wind hinder it not, I think they
are forced to Denmark, and that for divers
causes; certain it is that many of their people
were sick, and not a few killed; their ships,
sails, ropes and masts needeth great reparations,
for that they had all felt of your Majesty's force.
If your Majesty thought it meet, it were not
amiss you sent presently to Denmark
to understand the truth, and to deal with that
King according to your Majesty's great wisdom. I have
not written this whereby your Majesty should
diminish any of your forces; your Highness's enemies
are many, yet God hath and will hear your
Majesty's prayers, putting your hand to the plough
for the defence of His truth, as your Majesty
hath begun. God for His Christ's sake bless
your sacred Majesty, now and ever.
Written aboard Her Majesty's good ship
the Revenge this 8th of August
1588.

Your Majesty's faithful
vassal
Fra. Drake

*'god hath & will heare your Majestie's prairs, putting your hand to the plough for the defence of his truth'*

# 41 The wind of God

8 August 1588

Autograph letter by Sir Francis Drake, to Queen Elizabeth, writing as Vice-Admiral of the English fleet, announcing the flight of the Spanish Armada; Drake advises her that on Friday last the English fleet had left the Spanish 'army' so far to the northwards that they could make neither England nor Scotland, and that 'a great storme' would have added to the damage already inflicted by her navy; pleading with her nevertheless not to lay up any of her forces; 'written abord your Majestie's verie good shipp the Reveng this 8th of August 1588'

With the defeat of the Spanish Armada, England emerged onto the world stage. For contemporaries abroad, as well as for posterity, Drake personified her navy, just as Elizabeth did her people. Two days after Drake wrote this letter, Pope Sixtus V exclaimed: 'Just look at Drake! who is he? What forces has he?… His reputation is so great that his countrymen flock to him to share his booty. We are sorry to say it, but we have a poor opinion of this Spanish Armada, and fear some disaster'. When his fears were met, the Pope added: 'Have you heard how Drake with his fleet has offered battle to the Armada? With what courage! Do you think he showed any fear? He is a great captain.' To the Spanish Drake was 'El Draque', the dragon, a thing of terror. Recent historians have demurred, pointing out that he was only second in command and showed more interest in capturing a rich prize, the *Rosario*, than acting in concert with fellow commanders.

Sir Francis Drake c.1580 by an unknown artist

Drake's handwriting was, at the best of times, atrocious. This letter is docketed as being a 'copy', and was probably made by Drake for Sir Francis Walsingham. It was no doubt enclosed with a letter sent to Walsingham on the same day, which has been water-stained in the same manner, and in which Drake apologises for being 'but now half sleeping'. In a letter written two days later, Drake tells Walsingham that he has no secretary with him and has had to do his copying himself. He wrote our letter from Margate Roads, having just returned from the latitude of the Firth of Forth; Howard of Effingham, the admiral in command, being away in Dover in search of food. The Spanish had been defeated ten days before at the Battle of Gravelines. At the time of writing they were flying northwards, driven by what the English liked to think were the providential winds of God. But – so it seemed at the time – Parma's army in the Netherlands still threatened invasion. The Queen's copy of our letter would have been one of the very last despatches received by her before addressing her army at Tilbury (*42*).

*The absence of my Lord Admirall most gratious Soverayne, hath enboldened me, to putt my penne to the paper. On fridaye last, upon good consideracion we lefte the army of Spagne so farre to the northewardes, as they could neither recover England nor Scotland. And within three daies after we were entertayned with a great storme, considering the tyme of the yere, the which storme, in many of our judgmentes hath not a litle annoyedd the enemies army. If the wind hinder it not, I think they are forced to Denmark, & that for diverce causes. certain it is that manie of their people were sick & not a fewe killed, there shippes, sailes ropes & mastes needeth great reperations for that they had all felt of your Majestie's force…*

87

My louinge people, I haue bin perswaded by
som, yt are carefull of my safty, to take heed
how I committed my selfe to armed multitudes for fear of treachery. Butt I tell you
that I would not desyre to liue to distrust
my faythfull and louinge people. Lett ty=
rants fear: ~~butt~~ I haue so behaued my
selfe, yt under god I haue placed my
chiefest strength and safegard in ye loyall
harts and goodwill of my subiects. wher=
for I am com amoungst you at this tyme butt for
my recreation and pleasure, being resolued
in ye middst and heate of ye battle to
liue and dye amoungst you all, to lay
down for my god, and for my kyng=
dom and for my people myn honor
and my blood euen in ye dust. I know
I haue ye body butt of a weake and feble
woman, butt I haue ye harte and sto=
mark of a kinge, and of a kynge of
England too. and take foule scorn yt par=
ma or any prince of Europe should dare
to inuade ye borders of my realm:

*'I know I have the body butt of a' weake and feble woman, butt I have the harte and stomack of a' king, and of a' king of England too'*

# 42 At Tilbury

9 August 1588

Original manuscript of the speech delivered by Queen Elizabeth to her troops, assembled at Tilbury Camp to defend the realm against the Spanish Armada and invasion by the Duke of Parma; taken down by the Rev Dr Lionel Sharpe (or Leonel Sharp), chaplain to the Queen's Lieutenant General, the Earl of Leicester

It has often been doubted whether Elizabeth in fact ever made what is her most famous speech, and, if she did, what it was she actually said. Nothing of it survives in her own handwriting. The speech was not published until 1654, when a copy sent many years later by Lionel Sharpe to the Duke of Buckingham was printed. Sharpe told Buckingham: 'I remember in 88 waiting upon the Earl of *Leicester* at *Tilbury* Camp... The Queen the next morning rode through all the Squadrons of her Army, as Armed *Pallas*, attended by Noble Footmen, *Leicester, Essex,* and *Norris,* then Lord Marshal, and divers other great Lords. Where she made an excellent Oration to her Army, which, the next day after her departure, I was commanded to re-deliver to all the Army together, to keep a Publick Fast'. He adds that 'no man hath it but my self, and such as I have given it to'.

The only other surviving text is this manuscript. An American scholar, Janet Green, recently identified it as being in the handwriting of the same Lionel Sharpe; a discovery which puts the authenticity of the speech beyond question. Sharpe has subscribed his copy as 'Gathered by on[e] that heard itt, and was commaunded to utter itt to the whole army the next day, to send itt gathered to the queen her selfe'. In other words, he not only took a copy as the Queen spoke, but also sent one on to her. This means that she was speaking extempore, without notes – as its refreshing lack of elaboration would suggest – and that no manuscript in her hand ever existed. Sharpe was the first person to commit her words to paper. Presumably his experience as a preacher, practised in both public oration and sermon-taking, would have equipped him for such a task. This particular manuscript is clearly a fair copy, rather than the original scribbled out as the Queen spoke. Nevertheless, the unusual use of apostrophes indicating where she pronounced the indefinite article as a short 'a', as opposed to the longer 'aye', indicates that it was prepared for public recitation rather than private study. It is in a sense a speaking score; an attempt to record the inflections of Elizabeth's voice as she was delivering the words by which – thanks to Dr Sharpe – she will always be remembered.

*My lovinge people, I have bin perswaded by som, that ar carefull of my safty, to take heed how I committed my selfe to armed multitudes for feare of treachery. Butt I tell you, that I would not desyre to live to distrust my faythfull and loving people. Lett tyrants feare: I have so behaved my selfe, that under god I have placed my chiefest strength and safegard in the loyall harts and goodwill of my subjects. wherfor I am com amounge you att this tym butt for my recreation and pleasure, being resolved in the middst and heate of the battle to Live and Dye amoungst you all, to lay down for my god, and for my kyngdom and for my people myn honor and my blood even in the dust. I know I have the body butt of a' weake and feble woman, butt I have the harte and stomack of a' king, and of a' king of England too. and take foule scorn that Parma or any prince of Europe should dare to invade the borders of my realm...*

65 114

I most ~~most~~ humbly beseche your ma[jes]tie to pardon your poor
old servant to be thus bold in sending to know how my
gracious lady doth, and what ease of her late paynes she
findes, being the chefest thing in the world I do
pray for, for hir to have good health and long lyfe.
For my own poor case, I continew still your medycyn
and find it amend much better than any other
thing that hath ben geven me. Thus hoping to
find perfect cure at the bathe, with the continewance
of my wonted prayer for your ma[jes]ties most happy
preservation, I humbly kiss your foote, from
your old lodging at Rycott this Thursday morning
redy to take on my Journey

29 Aug. 1588

by your ma[jes]ties most faythfull and
obedient servant

R. Leycester

Even as I had writt thus
much I receyved your ma[jes]ties token by
yong Tracey

148

(65)



To the Q. most excellent
ma[jes]tie

his last letter

1588

*'for your majesty's most happy preservacion I humbly kyss your foote'*

# 43 His last letter

[29] August 1588

Autograph letter by the Earl of Leicester, to Queen Elizabeth, from her 'poore old servant', enquiring after her health and assuring her that he continues to take the medicine she has sent; 'from your old lodging at Rycott this thursday morning reddy to take on my Jorney'

Although she refused to be mastered by him, Leicester was the man Elizabeth loved above all others. His finest hour – like his stepson, Essex, he was never much good as a commander in the field – came when he organized the Queen's reception at Tilbury (*42*). In her oration Elizabeth described him as 'my lieutenant general… than whom never prince commanded a more noble or worthy subject'. Her nickname for him was 'eyes', and in writing to her he was in the habit of adding little dashes above any double-o's (as in the first line here). When he wrote this letter, Leicester was on his way to Kenilworth, probably with the intention of travelling on to Bath to take the waters. He had broken his journey at Rycote, near Thame in Oxfordshire. This was the house at which Elizabeth had lodged when on her way to Woodstock after her imprisonment in the Tower, and at which she and Leicester had since stayed, as guests of Sir Henry and Lady Norris. Leicester then moved on to Cornbury House, nearby in Wychwood Forest, where he died on 4 September, of what William Camden describes as 'a continual burning fever, as 'twas said' (very probably a case – as with Oliver Cromwell and so many others – of malaria). Camden, not one of Leicester's greatest admirers, adds that festivities celebrating the defeat of the Spanish Armada were not 'anything abated by Leicester's death'. Mendoza, Spanish Ambassador in Paris, put about a story that when the Queen received the news she retired to her chamber, where she remained two days, until Burghley and the Council had the doors broken down. Years later, when Elizabeth died, Leicester's letter from Rycote was found in a casket by her bed. On it, in her handwriting, is written: 'his Last lettar'.

The Earl of Leicester *c.*1575 by an unknown artist

Three years later Edmund Spenser, the poet for whom Leicester had found employment in Ireland, provided another memorial in his poem 'The Ruins of Time':

> He now is dead and all his glory gone,
> And all his greatness vapoured to nought,
> That as a glass upon the water shone,
> Which vanished quite, so soon as it was sought.
> His name is worn already out of thought…

*I most humbly besech your majeste to pardon your poore old servant to be this bold in sending to know how my gratious lady doth and what ease of her late paine she findes, being the chefest thinge in this world I doe prey for & for hir to have good health and longe lyfe/for my none poore case, I contynue still your meddycyn and finde yt amended much better than with any other thinge that hath byn given me. Thus hoping to finde perfect cure at the bath, with the contynduance of my wontyd preyer for your majesty's most happy preservacion I humbly kyss your foote…*

~~180~~ 28

[illegible]

45

Most Gratious Soueraine Lady, The God of heauen and earth, (Who hath mightilie, and evidently, given unto your most excellent Royall Maiestie, this wunderfull Triumphant victorie, against your mortall enemies) be allwaies, thanked, praysed, and glorified: And the same God Almightie, euermore direct and defend your most Royall Highnes from all evill and encumbrance: and finish and confirme in your most excellent Maiestie Royall, the blessings, long since, both decreed and offred: yea, euen into your most gratious Royall bosom, and Lap. Happy are they, that can perceyue, and so obey the pleasant call, of the mightie Ladie, OPPORTVNITIE. And, therfore, finding our duetie concurrent with a most secret beck, of the said Gratious Princess Ladie OPPORTVNITIE, NOW to embrace, and enioye, your most excellent Royall Maiesties high favor, and gratious great Clemencie, of CALLING me, Mr. Kelley, and our families, hoame, into your Brytish Earthly Paradise, and Monarchie incomparable: (and, that, abowt an yere since: by Master Customer Yong, his letters,) I, and myne, (by God his favor and help, and after the most convenient manner, we can,) Will, from hencefurth, endeuour our selues, faithfully, loyally, carefully, warily, and diligently, to ryd and untangle our selues from hence: And, so, very devowtely, and sowndlie, at your Sacred Maiesties feet, to offer our selues, and all, wherein, we are, or may be hable, to serve God, and your most Excellent Royall Maiestie. The Lord of Hoasts, be our help, and Gwyde, therein: and graunt unto your most excellent Royall Maiestie, the Incomparablest Triumphant Raigne, and Monarchie, that euer was, since Mans Creation. Amen.

Trebon: in the kingdome of Boemia,
the 10th of Nouebre: A. Dni: 1588: stylo vete[re]

Your Sacred and most excellent
Royall Maiesties:
most humble and dutyfull
Subiect, and Servant:
John Dee

*'your Brytish Earthly Paradise, and Monarchie incomparable'*

# 44 A rhapsody from Bohemia

10 November 1588

Autograph letter by John Dee to Queen Elizabeth, congratulating her on the defeat of the Spanish Armada and promising that he and Edward Kelley are returning home, from 'Trevon. in the kingdome of Boemia the 10th of Novembre: A. Domini: 1588: stylo veteri [i.e. old style]'

John Dee – a figure that seems to fascinate our own times as much as his own – was many things, a mathematician, geographer, astrologer, Hermetic magus, antiquarian and propagandist for Elizabethan expansion. It was he who was called upon by the Queen to cast the date most propitious for her coronation, and thereafter he received her constant protection, if not very much money. According to Aubrey's *Brief Lives*: 'The vulgar did verily believe him to be a conjurer. He had a great many mathematical instruments and glasses in his chamber, which did confirm the ignorant in their opinion, and his servitor would tell them that sometimes he would meet the spirits coming up his stairs like bees.' As well as writing the standard mathematical treatise of the day, he gave practical instruction in navigation to Frobisher, the Gilbert brothers, Ralegh and others. Had Sir Humphrey Gilbert's American venture been successful, Dee would have been assigned all land north of the 50th parallel, putting him in possession of present-day Canada. His house at Mortlake, on the Thames – visited several times by the Queen and often by members of the Court – contained probably the largest library at that date in England. He was also one of the first to argue for a national collection of manuscripts.

Practical geographer and magus come together in his role as propagandist. He argued for the creation of a royal navy and was a tireless advocate for a British Empire, a term he may well have invented. By his antiquarian researches he sought to establish that the Welsh prince Mardoc had travelled to 'Atlantis' (as he dubbed America) in the twelfth century, thus giving Elizabeth a claim to sovereignty of the New World. The year 1588 was seen – for a mire of numerological and astrological reasons – to be one of portents, and the defeat of the Spanish Armada opened the way to the imperial greatness that Dee had so long advocated. A decade after the Queen's death, he and the martyred Ralegh, along with the Armada, came to be seen as emblematic of the vanished golden age; indeed it has been argued that many watching Prospero first take the stage in 1612 would have been reminded of the Queen's magus.

This letter was written from the Castle of Trebon in Bohemia, half way between Vienna and Prague, where Dee had been living in lieu of more generous patronage at home. The 'Mr Kelley' referred to is the notorious Edward Kelley, Dee's medium or 'skryer', who was at this time in Prague. On 23 November Dee noted in his diary 'I writ to the Queen's Majestie'. He was back home a year later, and visited her at Richmond on 9 December 1589.

*Most Gratious Soveraine Lady, The God of heaven and earth, (Who hath mightilie, and evidently, given unto your most excellent Royall Majestie, this Wunderfull Triumphant Victorie, against your mortall enemies) be allwaies, thanked, praysed, and glorified... finding our duetie concurrent with a most secret beck, of the said Gratious Princess, Ladie OPPORTUNITIE, NOW to embrace, and enjoye, your most excellent Royall Majesties high favor, and gratious great Clemencie, of CALLING me, Mr Kelley, and our families, hoame, into your Brytish Earthly Paradise, and Monarchie incomparable...*

A most wonderfull vision for all to repente and to feare God. heare it every tyme



This vision was seene by me Roberte Dickons in the yeare of ou Lorde 1579 wch betokneth the greate crueltie of Antechriste wth the deliverance of the people of Englande and the sudaine destruction of the childe of perdition

The Angell of the Lorde stode before me as a younge man but his countenance was like a flame of fier and he saied folowe me for the Lorde shall showe the greate thinges that hereafter shalbe fullfilled uppon earthe. But I beinge afrayed of his countenance and voyce fell downe as one deade at his feete so beinge in that trance for the space of foure houres both sawe and harde suche highe misteries as is not for man to expresse And in the vision I sawe a feilde wth many flockes of sheepe and there arose a Lion amonge them wth many wolfes and foxes folowinge him and the came at the sheepe and overthrewe manye of them and there beinge a pasture paled aboute wch was full of sheepe and when the Lyon had overthrowne moste of them aboute him he came to enter into the pasture, but there stoode a sheepe as he shoulde enter into the pasture wch woll as roughe as heckell teethe and the tounge of that shepe stoode oute like a two edged swearde so that the lion coulde not touche it of any syde and there was a man in the middest of the pasture wth a swearde in his hande and when he sawe the Lyon wth the sheepe he came and stroke him downe and when the wolfes and foxes sawe him they fled but he folowed and slewe many of them and some escaped and fled a waye and when they weare all vanquished awaye from that sheepe the man stoode and cryed wth a loude voyce and saied there is but one sheperd enter all into this pasture and be one flocke and after the Angell lefte me a scrole of paper wth six verses saienge this is the true worde of god turne not from it for to that doth agree the whole testemonie of the worde of God And he saied thou shalt crie repentaunce as John for thy voyce shall sounde as a trompet before the Lordes cominge to Judgement Then chardged he me sayenge yf thou showe not these thinges wch thou haste seene and harde there sinnes be uppon thy head But yf thou showe them and they will not heare the truth they shalbe destroyed but God will defend his faithfull people as a sheperd his flocke. Now understand these wordes by this vision you maye knowe who is the childe of perdition and who is the Lordes anoynted to governe his people for the feylde signifieth the whole earthe and the flocke of sheepe doe signefie manye nationes and countries The Lyone wch is kinge of all beastes of the feilde betokneth the bysshope of Rome wch hath exalted him selfe above all people and princes of the earth, the wolfes and foxes signefie the cruell magistrates and false teachers wch folowe the pope of Rome to overthrowe as many people as he can in everie countrie wth traditiones and strange delusiones to make them perishe in there owne sinnes the pasture signefieth England, the sheepe in that pasture signifieth the people that fled from the Lyon that is to saye from the traditiones of the pope and are come to the true faithe in Christe, the sheepe wch roughe woll signefieth the prince of England wch a fearce zeale & sharpe Justice againste all heretickes and Infideles that come as wolfes and foxes to overthrowe Godes gospell they man wth the swearde signefieth the Angell of God sent to defende his anoynted from the Lyones rage and to destroye him wth all other traytoures and Rebelles that pretende any treason againste her matie for some of them shalbe taken and put to deathe and the reste caused to flee awaye, his loude voyce betokeneth the loude voyce of the preachers wch testefie that there is but one true confession wch nowe is set fourth in England it is beste for all true Christianes to gather into that true confession and so to be in one true faith that hath any hope of salvation

Whilst the lyon kepte him from the pasture wch signefieth England he overthrewe many of them before him but when he came to that pasture he prospered no longer for the man was prepared wth a swearde to smite him downe with the word of god

read Daniell the 11 chapter 36 verse
2 to the Thessolonians
the 2 epistell ye
the 2 chapter 4
verse

These are the wordes of the verses wch I receaued as foloweth

Woe be to the earthe for malice and coveteousnes

1 Thou shalt crie repentance and bringe all sinners into his favoure againe trulie repenting and amending there evill lyffe

2 Thou shalt live chaste in wedlocke flee and abhorre all the filthie lustes of the fleshe and deale trulie wth all people

3 He shall geve thee his true spirite and heavenlie wisdome and thou shalt doe good after thy power to all men hurte no man

4 He shall inspire thy harte wth faith hope love and charitie and thou shalt be patient in adversitie and humble in troble

5 Thou shalte obedient unto thy rulers faithfull and Just unto them for ever that his name maye be glorified in thee during this life

Thou shalt obtaine everlasting life trusting in the merit and mercie of Christes passion

Praise thou him

The that have not kepte the sayinges of these six verses and the whole testement agreeing therto let them repent for god is righteous in iudgement

By me Robert dickones

the man with the sword sine in the vision
betokeneth the angell of god
that be reaye the false prophettes god sendeth to defend these
Elyas is come all redye as John did
the vi verse [illegible] mallachie the iiii chapter
the xi verse the [illegible] of mathew the xv verse of marke
 repent all ye for whoe can escape the iudgment seate of god

*'The Angell of the Lorde stoode before me as a younge man*
*But his countenance was like a flame of fier'*

## 45 What the glover saw

2 February 1589

Petition presented by Robert Dickons to Queen Elizabeth, headed 'Robert Dickon's a disgraced Glover, his Request to the Queen that he may preach Repentence with his Enthusiastical Vision' seen in 1579; evidently written out by a professional scribe with autograph additions by Dickons

Writing in the twelfth century, a Frenchman said to an Englishman: 'Your island is surrounded by water, and not unnaturally its inhabitants are affected by the nature of the elements in which they live. Unsubstantial fantasies slide easily into their minds.' The tradition seems to have held, as Peter Ackroyd argues in his *Albion: The Origins of the English Imagination* (2002), through the nineteenth century and beyond. Charles Dickens, for example, claimed that he always lived partly in a dream. It could be that the author of this petition, Robert Dickons, was an ancestor of the novelist. If so, Dickens would have been delighted at the pedigree, for Shakespeare, no less, had a disgraced glover for a father. But since Dickens could trace his ancestors no further back than his grandparents, this cannot be verified. Nor, of course, are such visions as that seen by the sixteenth-century Dickons uniquely English. One of the best-known befell an imprisoned philosopher in the last stages of the Roman Empire: 'While of all this alone in silence I bethought me... over my head to stand a woman did appear of stately face, with flaming eyes'. This describes Lady Philosophy as she appears to Boethius at the beginning of his *Consolation of Philosophy*. The translation is by Queen Elizabeth (49).

1588 was a good time to be preaching enthusiastical visions. The Armada year (which under the old calendar ran until 24 March), was one of tremendous significance to soothsayers. In Garrett Mattingly's account: 'Basically the prophecy of doom depended on the numerology of the Revelation of St John, clarified (if that is the right word) by hints in Daniel xii, and reinforced by a blood-curdling passage in Isaiah. To those who had sufficiently studied the question there seemed to be no doubt that all history since the first year of Our Lord was divided into a series of cycles... each cycle terminated by some gigantic event, and the whole series closing with awful finality in 1588'. The Queen's appearance, dressed 'as Armed *Pallas*', before her troops at Tilbury must have fitted in with this atmosphere of heightened expectation (42). Robert Dickons was there. Perhaps he heard her speech. In all events he had one of his visions ready which – so he tells us here – he 'Delivred to your Royale majestie at your comenge to the campe at Tilsberie'.

*This vision was seene By me Roberte Dickones In the yeare of our Lorde 1579 which betokeneth the greate crueltie of Antechriste, with the deliverance of the people of Englande and the sudaine destruction of the childe of perdition*

*The Angell of the Lorde stoode before me as a younge man But his countenance was like a flame of fier and he saied folowe me for the Lorde shall showe the greate thinges that hereafter shalbe fullfilled uppon earthe. But I beinge afrayed of his countenance and voyce fell downe as one deade at his feete so beinge in that trance for the space of foure houres both sawe and harde suche highe misteries as is not for man to expresse And in the vision I sawe a feilde with many flockes of sheepe and there arose a Lion amonge them with many wolfes and foxes folowinge...*

Madame
Jay lymage de vos byenfes tellemant ampreynte au coeur quyls me &
sont an obyet perpetuel & mes sans plus contynuellemant occupes an
la cousyderasyon de leur meryte & de vre magnanymyte & grande
bonte anvers moy avec souhet ordynere autre mes plus ardantes pry
eres de vous pouvoyr un jour temoygner par quelque bon cervyce
que ie nan veus lesser le fruyt anceuely au tombeau dyngratytude &
& comme an toutes qualytes ie les recoñoys & avoue sans esample &
aussy ie vous supplye Madame de crere que ie ne mes an compara
son avec nul autre lestyme que ie fays de vre mageste ny &
lhonneur & lobeyssance que ie desyre toute ma vye vous randre &
le cecours quyl vous a pleu a presant maccorder met an syngulyere
grace pour la qualyte de celluy auquel yl vous a pleu an donner
la pryncypale charge & pour la belle force dont yl est compose &
vous an remersye tresafectueusemant mes ie vous dyray & &
Madame que ie ne me suys de ryen tant resjouy de ce que le sr
de Reau ma rapporte a son retour que davoyr antandu que &
vous fesyes estat de venyr a porsemue lors que nous serons vers
la coste de normandye ce que avenant ie vous supplye trouver &
bon que ie vous y aylle beser les meyns come Roy de navarre &
& estre aupres de vous deus heures afyn que jaye ce byen davoyr
veu au moyns une foys an ma vye celle a quy jay consacre & corps &
& tout ce que jauray james & que jayme & revere plus que &
chose quy soyt an ce monde & des ceste heure ie recoys un grand
contantemant an moy mesmes de lesperance que jay que vous &
ne me desnyeres ce bon heur duquel ie massure que la jouyssance

063

Vre plus afectyonne frere & cervyteur

Henry

*'her whom I love and revere more than anything in this world'*

# 46 Five days at Portsmouth

15 August 1591

Autograph letter by Henri IV of France, to Queen Elizabeth, in French, thanking her for sending him the Earl of Essex and his fine force, and suggesting that, were she to come to Portsmouth ('Porsemue') while he was in Normandy, they could meet; meanwhile assuring her that his servant de Reaux (Henri's ambassador to Elizabeth) would stay with Essex and his forces to make sure that they received the best possible treatment, 'Au camp devant noyon ce xv$^{me}$ daust'

In Henri IV, Elizabeth met her match: which is as it should be, for he is as much a hero to the French as she is to the English. As King of Navarre, he had been champion of the Protestant cause in France, and when he succeeded to the French throne as the first Bourbon king in 1589 he found Catholic Paris and much of France ranged against him. He was penniless and uncrowned. Elizabeth, ever anxious not to spend money or waste lives, was eventually prompted to come to his aid by the threat of a Spanish invasion and the possibility of the Normandy ports being used for another armada. She sent a force out to France under Lord Willoughby in 1589, which suffered heavy losses. She then sent a further force under the Earl of Essex, writing to Henri on 27 July: 'According to the promise which I have always kept in your behalf, my dearest brother, I send 4,000 men to your aid, with a Lieutenant who appears very competent. His quality, and the place he holds about me, are such, that it is not customary to permit him to be absent from me'; although she warns him that Essex 'is too impetuous to be given the reigns' and that 'the rashness of his youth' might make him 'too precipitate'. On his arrival at Dieppe, Essex was invited to meet Henri at Compiègne and made the hundred-mile journey through hostile territory with a resplendent troop of cavalry, attired in Devereux tangerine. Essex and Henri feasted, staged a leaping competition (which the tall athletic Earl won); and then Henri rode off eastward, leaving Essex to make the dangerous journey back to rejoin his main army.

Henri's avowal of single-minded devotion to Elizabeth in this letter was not strictly speaking true; for the year before he had met the most famous of all his mistresses, Gabrielle d'Estrées. Elizabeth, meanwhile, was making her annual progress in Sussex and Hampshire. She arrived at Portsmouth on 26 August. There she waited five days for her French admirer. There was no sign of him. She was not best pleased. That November she wrote him a blistering letter: 'Can you imagine that the softness of my sex deprives me of the courage to resent a public affront? The royal blood I boast could not brook, from the mightiest Prince in Christendom, such treatment as you have within the last three months offered to me'.

*...But I will tell you Madam that never have I been so delighted as to hear from M de Reau[x] on his return that you were intending to come to Portsmouth when we are on the coast of Normandy. If such be the case I beg you to permit me to go and kiss your hand as King of Navarre and to spend two hours with you so that at least once in my life I may have the honour of seeing her to whom I have dedicated my time and my life and whom I love and revere more than anything in this world...*

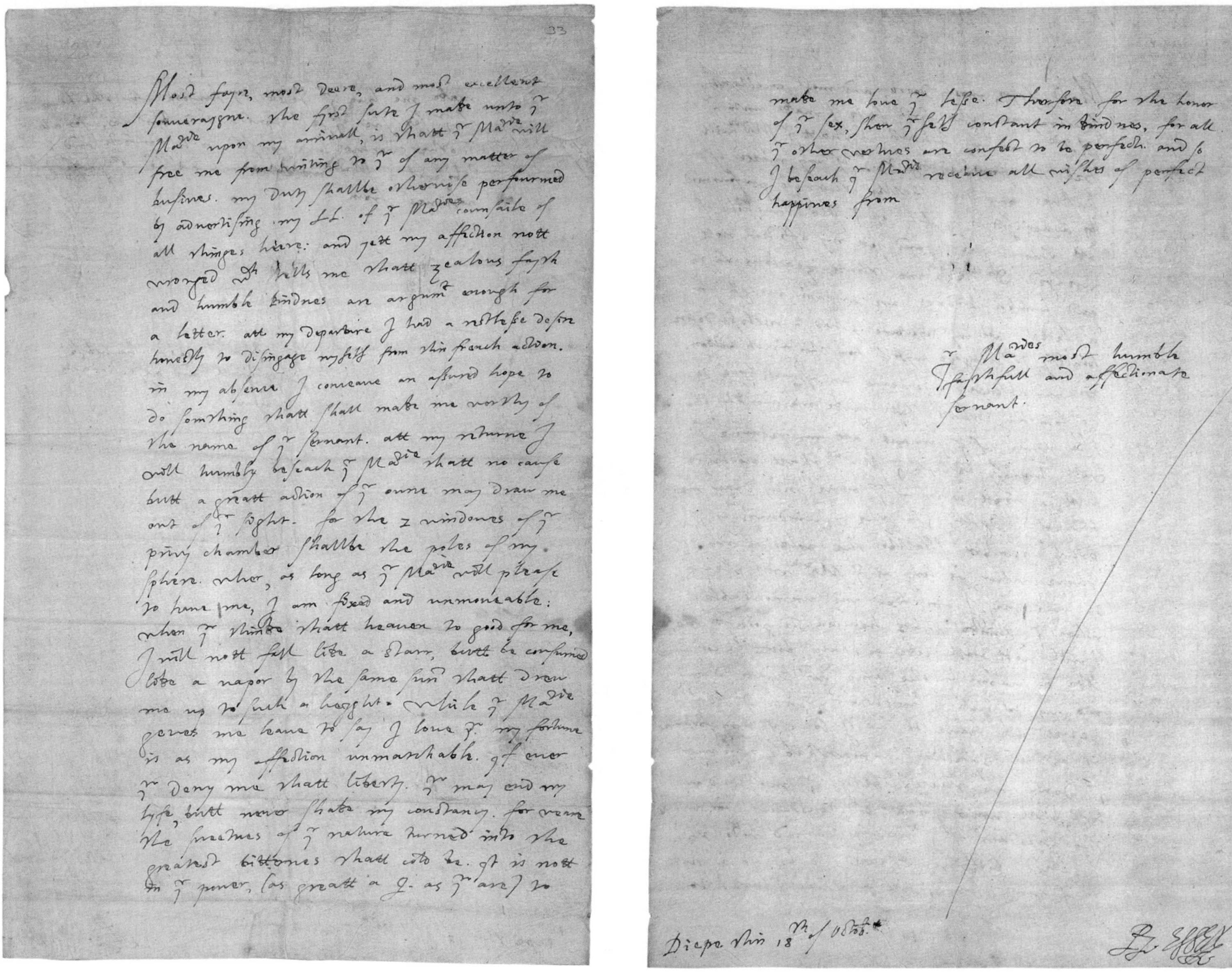
33

Most fayr, most deere, and most excellent
soueraygne. the first sute I make unto yr
Matie upon my arrivall, is that yr Matie will
free me from writing to yr of any matter of
busines. my duty shallbe otherwise performed
by advertising my LL. of yr Maties counsaile of
all thinges here: and yett my affection nott
wronged wch tells me that zealous fayth
and humble kindnes are argumt enough for
a letter. att my departure I had a restlesse desire
honestly to disingage myself from this french action.
in my absence I conceaue an assured hope to
do somthing that shall make me worthy of
the name of yr seruant. att my returne I
will humbly beseach yr Matie that no cause
butt a greatt action of yr owne may draw me
out of yr sight. for the 2 windowes of yr
priuy chamber shallbe the poles of my
sphere. wher, as long as yr Matie will please
to haue me, I am fixed and unmoueable:
when yr thinke that heauen to good for me,
I will nott fall like a starr, butt be consumed
like a vapor by the same sun that drew
me up to such a heyght. while yr Matie
geues me leaue to say I loue yr, my fortune
is as my affection unmatchable. yf euer
yr deny me that liberty, yr may end my
lyfe, butt neuer shake my constancy. for were
the swetnes of yr nature turned into the
greatest bitternes that could be. yt is nott
in yr power, (as greatt a Q. as yr are) to

make me loue yr lesse. Therfore for the honor
of yr sex, shew yr self constant in kindnes, for all
yr other vertues are confest to be perfect. and so
I beseach yr Matie receiue all wishes of perfect
happines from

Yr Maties most humble
faythfull and affectionate
seruant.

Diepe this 18th of Octob.

R. Essex

*'for the 2 windowes of your privy chamber shallbe the poles of my sphere'*

## 47 Consumed like a vapour

18 October 1591

Autograph letter by the Earl of Essex, to Queen Elizabeth, pledging her his love, written while serving with Henri IV in France, 'Diepe this 18th of Octob~'

The twenty-four-year-old Earl of Essex had been the Queen's favourite for some four years, but the expeditionary force sent to aid Henri IV in Normandy was his first major command (*46*). In this role he saw himself as heir not only to his stepfather the Earl of Leicester, but also to Sir Philip Sidney, beau idéal of Protestant chivalry. Sidney had bequeathed Essex his 'best swoord' and Essex had returned the compliment by marrying his widow. He was 'a man that did affect nothing in the world so much as Fame, and to be reputed matchlesse of magnanimitie, and undertaking'.

The Earl of Essex, possibly attired for the Accession Day tilt of 1595 (*51*), by Nicholas Hilliard

After making his dash to meet Henri IV at Compiègne, Essex's campaign had not gone well; which is perhaps not surprising given the incompatible strategic goals of Elizabeth and Henri. Added to which his only brother Walter had been killed while leading a sally on Rouen. The Queen wrote highly critical letters and demanded his return, which 'put his honour in suche an extreme agony and passion that he sownded often and did so swell that, castyng hem selfe upon his bed, all his bottons of his doblett brake away as thoth they had ben cut with a kneffe'. In order to save the campaign, he dashed home, and managed to placate his mistress. She reappointed him to his command, this time with greater authority than before (his latest biographer believes that this marks the moment that Essex finally became a power to be reckoned with). Arriving back at Dieppe, he wrote her this extraordinary letter. But, as with Henri, his protestations are not all that they seem. Elizabeth of course was old enough to be his mother. Furthermore, not only had Essex recently married Frances Sidney and had a son that January; but he was a notorious court Lothario: Elizabeth Southwell, one of the Queen's Maids of Honour, was, at the time of writing, heavily pregnant with his child. But whatever its ambiguities, this letter gives some inkling of what it was that gave such a conspicuously unsuccessful commander such sway over the Queen.

[from line 14] *. . . att my returne I will humbly beseach your Majestie thatt no cause butt a greatt action of your owne may draw me out of your sight. for the 2 windowes of your privy chamber shallbe the poles of my sphere. wher, as long as your Majestie will please to have me, I am fixed and unmoveable: when yow thinke thatt heaven to good for me, I will nott fall like a starr, butt be consumed like a vapor by the same sunn thatt drew me up to such a heyght. While your Majestie geves me leave to say I love yow my fortune is as my affection unmatchable. yf ever yow deny me thatt liberty. yow may end my lyfe, butt never shake my constancy. for ware the sweetnes of your nature turned into the greatest bitternes thatt cold be. yt is nott in your power, (as greatt a Queen as yow are) to make me love yow lesse. Therfore for the honor of your sex, shew yourself constant in kindnes, for all your other vertues are confest to be perfect. . .*

I presumed to present your Maiestye with a paper contayninge the dangers wch might grow by
the Spanish faction in Skotlande, how it pleased your Maiestye to accept therof I know not, I have
since harde yt divers ill disposed have a purpose to speake of succession if the same be suppressed
I am gladd of it, yet fearinge the worst I sett down sume reasons to shew the motive utterly
vayne, dangerous and unnecessarye, and because I durst not my sealf speake in any matter
without warrant, I have sent your Maiestye thes arguments wch may perhaps put others
in minde of sumewhat not impertinent, who beinge graced by your Maiesties favor may if
need requyre use them amonge others more worthye, without glory I speake it, that
I durst ether by writinge or speach satisfye the worlde in that poynct and in every part
of their foolishe conseytes, wch for shortnes of tyme I could not so amplely insert, this
beinge after one houres warninge, but one houres worke, I humble desire your Maiestye
not to acquaynt any withall unles occasion be offred to use them, your Maiestye may
perhaps speake herof to thes seeminge my great frinds but I finde poore effects
of it or any other supposed amitye, for your Ma: havinge left mee I am left all alone
in the worlde and am sorry that ever I was att all, what I have done was out of zeale
and love and not by any incoragement, for I am only forgotten in all rights, and in all
affaires, & myne enemis have their wills and desires over mee, ther ar many other
things concerninge your Ma: present service wch mee thinke ar not as they ought
remembred, and the tymes pass away unmesured of wch more proffett might be taken
but I feare I have allreddy presumed to much, wch love stronger then reason
hath incoraged, for my errors ar eternal and thos of other mortall, and my labors
thankless, & mean unacceptable, for thanks belongeth not to vassalls, if your Maiestye
pardon it, it is more then to great a rewarde, & so most humbly in kissinge & admiringe the memory of thos celestiall bewtes (wch with the people is denied mee to
renew) I pray god your Maiestie may be eternall [illegible]ioyes and happines.



Your Maiesties most humble
slave.

*'your Majestie havinge left mee I am left all alone in the worlde'*

# 48 The sorrow of this world

23 February 1593

Autograph letter by Sir Walter Ralegh, to Queen Elizabeth, presenting her with a paper 'contayninge the dangers which might groe by the Spanish faction in Skotlande', and deploring 'ill-disposed' attempts in Parliament [by the puritan MP Peter Wentworth] to bring up the subject of her succession; he ends the letter by begging to be readmitted to her favour and praising her celestial beauty, subscribing himself 'Your Majesties most humble slave/WR:'

This is the only letter, original or otherwise, that survives from Ralegh to the Queen. Nor is there any evidence that she ever read it. Ralegh's rise from comparatively humble origins, in contrast to those of his rival Essex, had been spectacular, but so was his fall; in the words of the antiquary Anthony à Wood: 'He was one that fortune had pickt up out of purpose, of whom to make an example, or to use as her Tennis-Ball.' All the Queen's favourites, excepting Sir Christopher Hatton, had at some time risked marriage and felt her wrath: but Ralegh, in marrying her Lady of the Bedchamber Bess Throckmorton, compounded matters by brazenly denying the fact, even after the birth of their child. Nevertheless many, including Essex, managed to get away with more, as Ralegh complains in this letter. It was probably during this period – although the matter is by no means certain – that the disgraced favourite wrote that strange, beautiful fragment 'The 11th: and last booke of the Ocean to Scinthia', in which Ralegh casts himself as the 'Shepherd of the Ocean' and Elizabeth as 'Cynthia', the Virgin Moon that governs the tides; the Queen's nickname for him being 'Water' (60).

Sir Walter Ralegh c.1585 by Nicholas Hilliard

Ralegh had been placed under house arrest when his marriage came to light in May 1592. That July he asked Sir Robert Cecil to intercede with the Queen, lamenting that 'My hart was never broken till this day' and, in hopes that she would see the letter, sighed: 'I that was wont to behold her riding like Alexander, hunting like Diana, walking like Venus, the gentle wind blowing her fair hair about her pure cheeks like a nymph, sometime sitting in that shade like a goddess, sometime singing like an angel, sometime playing like Orpheus. Behold the sorrow of this world, once amiss hath bereaved me of all'.

[from line 14] *...your Majestie havinge left mee I am left all alone in the worlde and am sorry that ever I was att all. what I have dunn is out of zeale and love and not by any incoragement, for I am only forgotten in all rights, and in all affaires & myne enemis have their wills and desires over mee. ther ar many other things concerninge your Majesties present service which mee thincke ar not as the ought* [to be] *remembred and the tymes pass away unmesured of which more profett might be taken. but I feare I have allreddy presumed too mich, which love stronger then reason hath incoraged, for my errors ar eternal, and thos of other mortall, and my labors thanckless; I mean unacceptable, for thancks belongeth not to vassalls. if your Majestye pardun it it is more then to great a rewarde. & so most humble imbracinge & admiringe the memory of thos celestiall bewtes (which with the people is denied mee to renew) I pray god your Majesties may be eternall in joyes and happines./Your Majesties most humble slave./WR:*

disputest ~~that~~ god was he that ruled the universalitie by the raynes of goodnes, & all thinges willingly did obey, And so ther was no ill in nature. And didst show how all thinges not by outward but our own homebred thinking beleefe had unwrapt provaunce and them obey. These we do not sport, ~~any~~ nor yet ~~great~~ the greatest gifte ~~do~~ requier, that thing that of late we so much disired. For such is the shape of divine substance that neither is skipping to outward causes, nor inwardly doth take for him self any thing wont him. But as ~~[illegible]~~ Parmenides sayth, A lyke ~~[illegible]~~ to passe in Roundnes in Circle turnes, This if we have so well to past, that we have not gathered our reasons out of the matter, but agreing with that that we have treated, ther is no cause why thou shuldst doute, whan thou hast lernt by Plato, that all ~~[illegible]~~ talk should agree all mener of kyn to matter that we speake of.

12. M. Blist that may of Good
The fountaine clire behold
Happy that can of waighty
Erthe the bondes to breake
The Tracian profit wons
his wives funeralz wailing
Wha with ~~wail~~ sorowes noti
The wandring trees he moved
And steady rivers made
And hind ~~...~~ joind
Unfearing sides to Lion fierce
Nor hare did feare the looki
Of cruel dog so plised with song
Wha fervent dier the inward
brist more burnt
Nor could the notes that al subdued
~~[illegible]~~ pacifie thir Lord
Of ireful godz complaining
~~the~~ The hilly housi went to

*'with sorows note the wavering trees he moved'*

# 49 Descent into the underworld

October and November 1593

Working draft of Queen Elizabeth's translation of Boethius' *De Consolatione Philosophiæ* (the *Consolation of Philosophy*), the verse 'Meters' in her hand, the alternating prose sections dictated to her secretary Thomas Windebank, begun at Windsor Castle on 10 October and finished on 5 or 8 November 1593

Elizabeth made this translation at Windsor Castle in the autumn of 1593, shortly after her sixtieth birthday. She began by writing it all in her own hand, but after a few pages started dictating the prose sections to a secretary, Thomas Windebank, while continuing to write the verse herself. According to a set of calculations found with the manuscript, it took her some twenty-four hours, spread out over a month, to complete the work. There is no evidence that it was ever circulated. In the words of her nineteenth-century editor, Caroline Pemberton: 'We cannot... but admire the intelligence and industry of a Queen, who, at the age of sixty, occupied as she must have been with state affairs and the multifarious other duties pertaining to her position, could yet find inclination to undertake such tasks and time to devote to them. Even the incentive of literary fame was wanting, for her translations, not being printed, were probably read only by the secretaries who copied some of them, so that it is evident that Elizabeth loved learning for its own sake.'

Boethius' work, written from prison during the closing years of the Roman Empire, had already been 'Englished' by authors such as King Alfred, Chaucer and Caxton. In her version Elizabeth opts for a deliberately 'antique' style. The prose sections of *De Consolatione* seek to puzzle out the ways of providence and God to man; while the verse, adapted in the main from Virgil and Ovid, furnish us with examples. In the page reproduced here, the prose section (in Windebank's hand) seeks to demonstrate the existence of God, ending with quotation from Parmenides and Plato. The verse, in Elizabeth's hand, takes the example of Orpheus to show that even after attaining the light of truth it may be lost by returning to darkness: Orpheus – the archetypal poet-musician – was able to move the stones and trees by his music (in Elizabeth's translation 'with sorrow's note/The wavering trees he moved') and descended to hell ('The helly house went to'), where he persuaded Hades to restore to him his wife Eurydice; but, returning to earth, loses her by ignoring the injunction not to look back. It is through Boethius' version that the myth first attained wide circulation, and it holds its own to this day. Ted Hughes, the second Elizabeth's Laureate, incorporated the story into his last work, an adaptation of *Alcestis*, in a passage evoking the shade of his first wife Sylvia Plath, telling 'How he went down there,/Into the underworld, the dead land,/With his guitar and his voice –/He rode the dark road...'; the story might also have had resonance for the first Elizabeth, sixty years old, with the two men she came closest to marrying in the grave.

[verse section]: *blist that may of Good/The fontaine Clire behold/happy that Can Of waighty/Erthe the bondes to breake/The Tracian profit wons/his wives funeralz wailing/Whan with sorows note/The wavering trees he moved/And stedy rivers made/And hind caused Join/Unfearing Sides to Lion fierce/Nor hare did feare the Looke/Of Cruel dog so plised with Song/Whan ferventur desir the inward/brest more burnt,/Nor Could the notes that al subdued/Pacefie ther Lord/Of Ireful Godz Complaining/The helly house went to...*

Most gracious Ladye & Mistres whom (next under allmightie god) I love & adore wth all duetie
and reverence, I acknowledge my selfe so muche bounden unto your sacred matie as I thinke no subiecte in
the worlde more infinitely beholden unto his Soveraigne, in that in these my olde aged & extreme or
last dayes of my life it pleaseth your highnes so favourablye to respecte the weake & sicke estate of so poore
& base a vassale at this present weakened in bodye wth infirmities & sicknes, but somuche revived in harte
& mynde wth your gracious remembraunce & regarde of mee, that I truste in the allmightie god will
lengthen my dayes & strengthen my bodye to proceede & goe forwarde in your maties service for the safetie
of your most royall parson (wch I beseeche the Lord for ever to defende) & for the advauncement of yor highnes
proffitt & revenues accordinge to my othe & bounden duetye; But feelinge my selfe allogether unable to sett
downe in writinge the depth & profunditye of my harte & meaninge, nor to expresse in wordes how muche in
duetie I am indebted to your maties desertes, I will feede & nourishe my selfe wth the memory thereof, And doe
hereby signifie unto yor highnes, that accordinge to yor commaundement I have made collection of such examinacons &
matters as concerne your maties service, & have putt them into a cheste safely sealed up, the key whereof I doe here
withall presente unto yor highnes wth this briefe notice of some of the speciall matters conteyned therein.
~~First~~ (because the matter is now in question) there are examinacons notes & lres touchinge Mr Willm Wiseman
~~ww~~ of Bradockes, now prisoner in Woodstreete Compter & Mrs Jane Wiseman his mother for the harbouringe
receyvinge & mainteyninge of Jesuites, Seminarie priestes & other dangerous psons to your matie & the State
viz John Gerarde als Tanfeilde als Staunton a Jesuite now prisoner in the Clinke sonne to Sr Thomas Gerarde
Sudamore als John Wiseman the priest sonne to Sr John Sudamore, Brewster & Chapman priestes, and Robert
Barrowes priest now prisoner in the Clinke, All which confessed by Frauncis servaunt to Mr Wiseman & sufficientlye
proved by many other circumstances, his brother Thomas is a Jesuite at Rome, iiij of his sisters sent over beyonde
the Seas to be nonnes, of whom two went over wth Sudamore, & all his other brethren & familie most obstinate
papistes, all wch appeare by their severall examinacons, wch I have made knowen to some of yor maties most hono=
rable privy Counsaile & to your Counsell learned in the lawes who were determyned to have proceeded by lawe
in this laste terme if god had bene pleased to contynue my healthe, it appeareth allso by the confession of one
Wallpoole now prison in the Tower that all psons cominge from beyonde the Seas for any evill purpose were
directed to Mr Wiseman by whom they shoulde be furnished wth horses, men & money to goe whether they woulde
And now of late I have upon searche made founde divers lres wch Mrs Wiseman written to him here & others
from Gerarde the Jesuite since his imprisonment, & allso other notes & lres manifestinge what greate
somes of money have bene offered & woulde have bene payed for the libertie & release of Mr Wiseman
There are allso examinacons & other matters concerninge Mrs Jane Shelley prison in the Fleete who hath
gone aboute to Sorcerers witches & Charmers to knowe the tyme of your maties deathe and what
shall become of this state, Allso the confession of Roger Dykand priest prison in Wisbiche touchinge
the conspiracie of Rebell now prison in the Tower, wth Doctor Parry against yor highnes wth two psons
receyved the Sacrament upon it at the handes of Thomson als Blackborne priest executed aboute xx or
xx yeares paste & were dissuaded from their purpose by the said Dykand, together allso wth certeine other
examinacons concerninge Sheldon had of reedie since his beinge in the Tower, the copy whereof I lately
delivered to my Lord Threasorer, And allso matters touchinge Mr Ballarde of Kenworthe & moste of the
papistes in the severall shires of this lande, the confessions & examinacons of many other priestes, some of wch
have bene executed, some others remayne prisoners in Wisbiche & some others are reformed, manifestinge the
names & dwellinges of such as are your maties mortall enemies & the practises & conspiracies of such as
are abroade in forreyne countries, There are allso examinacons of a practise in breakinge the seales & contentes of
Custome in Mr Birdes tyme wth many other notes writinges & papers wch to recite particulerly woulde bee
tedious to mee (& I feare me) over longe for your maties to heare, Such as they bee, gotten wth my greate
paynes & expences I leave them to yor highnes as the laste frutes of all myne endevours & travailles (yf it
please not god to restore me to healthe) and will not cease duringe this mortall life to praye unto allmightie
god for the longe & happy preservacon of your highnes most royall pson for the settinge forthe of his glorye & the
comforte of all your subiectes

Written the laste of November 1594

Your maties most bounden & humble servaunt for ever to be commaunded

Ric: Younge

*'John Gerarde alias Tanfield alias Staunton a Jhesuite now prisoner in the Clinke'*

# 50 The devil's confessor

30 November 1594

Autograph letter by Richard Young, a London Justice of the Peace, to Queen Elizabeth, written 'in these my olde aged & extreme or laste dayes of my life', sending 'as the last frutes of all myne endevours' details of Catholics he has hunted down (plus 'm[rs] Jane Shelley prisoner in the fleete who hath gone aboute to Sorcerers witches & Charmers to knowe the time of your majesties deathe'), which he has put 'into a cheste safely sealed up, the key whereof I doe here withall presente unto your highnes', 'Written the laste of November 1594'

Heading the list of Catholic priests in this memorandum is Father John Gerard SJ, apprehended, along with those who had harboured him, following the confession of Father Henry Walpole SJ 'now prisoner in the Tower' (a victim of Richard Topcliffe's tortures and to be martyred the following year). Gerard, too, was later transferred to the Tower where he suffered appalling torture, but from where he managed a spectacular escape. He was to remain in England, undetected, until 1606.

In all 183 Catholics were executed during Elizabeth's reign, of whom 123 were priests. Richard Young, writer of this letter, ranks second only to his colleague Topcliffe in notoriety as priest-hunter and torturer. One complainant described him in 1590 as a thief 'who lived by robbing papists'. Understandably, Gerard shared this low opinion of him. In his famous *Autobiography* he describes the circumstances in which this, Young's last testimony to the Queen, was written: 'In his life he was the devil's confessor and in his death the devil's martyr. Not merely did he die in the devil's service, but it was the actual cause of his death. Day and night he toiled to bring more and more pressure on Catholics, drawing up lists of names, giving instructions, listening to reports'; bringing about his death through overwork. Nor, Gerard tells us, did the Queen pay off his debts: 'All she did was to send one of her courtiers to visit him when he lay sick and dying. He was so pleased by this favour that he was ready to sing his *Nunc Dimittis*... he was bidden not to a banquet but to eternal doom. With the Queen's praises on his lips and singing his own indebtedness to Her Majesty he died miserably'. Young also makes an appearance in the French Embassy Affair, having to be warned off from arresting two of Walsingham's most successful undercover agents (34). Less expectedly, he receives frequent mention in the diaries of John Dee, who calls him his 'brother'; and was the first person Dee called upon after getting back from Trebon (44).

[from line 15] *...there are examinacons notes & letters touchinge m[r] William Wiseman of Braddockes now prisoner in Woodstreet Comnpter & m[rs] Jane Wiseman his mother for harbouringe receyvinge & mainteyninge of Jhesuites, Seminarie priestes & other daungerous persons to your majestie & the State viz. John Gerarde alias Tanfield alias Staunton a Jhesuite now prisoner in the Clinke sonne to Sir Thomas Gerarde, Scudamore alias John Wiseman the prieste sonne to Sir John Scudamore, Brewster & Chapman priestes, and Robert Barrowes prieste nowe prisoner in the Clinke, All wich is confessed by Franke servaunte to m[r] Wiseman & sufficiently proved by many other circumstances, his brother Thomas is a Jhesuite at Rome, iiii of his sisters sent over beyonde the Seas to bee nonnes, of whom two went over with Scudamore, & all his other brethren & familie most obstinate papistes, all which appeare by their severall examinacons, which I have made knowen to some of your majesties moste honorable prevy Counsaile & your Counsell learned in the lawes who were determyned to have proceeded by law in this laste terme if god had bene pleased to continue my health...*

3 spi. – payn. – disc. c different spirits & the Engl. 274

M. 17. The persons to be three one dressed
like an Heremite or philosopher
representing Contemplation; the
second like a Captayne representing fame and ye third like
a Counsellor of Estate representing Experience, ye
third to begynne to ye Sqr.
as being ye man of ye best
behavior or Complement though
he speake less.

Squire Sr. Philautia, whose servaunt
though you you cannot but remember
what tyme the opposition against the
force of his argumts was like the
opposition of the Raynebowe against
the Sonne, pretty colours but easily
scattered, Then he & hath since taken
some course towardes the mr Knightes
his frendes these he hath changed
with his humor and so made his Endevors
more unequall, he taketh his self bound
in honor to not to leave his whole defendaunce
tyme and therefore hath sent to
treat with you for his own grace.

*'dressed like an Heremite or philosopher representing Contemplative life'*

# 51 The playwright of St Albans

17 November 1595

Autograph draft by Francis Bacon for 'A Device to Entertain the Queen at Essex House 17 November 1595', written on behalf of the Earl of Essex, for performance before Queen Elizabeth at the Accession Day tilt of 1595

Sir Francis Bacon first came to prominence as a playwright in 1857. This was the year his namesake Delia published *The Philosophy of the Plays of Shakespere Unfolded,* in which she announced that he had written the plays previously attributed to Shakespeare (52). Since then, of course, it has been discovered that he was really the son of Queen Elizabeth, England's chief Rosicrucian and many other things besides. Such claims may be, in some eyes, as mad as they are boring, but the truth is that Bacon did indeed write plays of a sort; although they failed in their avowed intent, which was to amuse the Queen.

The play-writing phase of Bacon's career belongs to his early days, when he was seeking advancement under the Earl of Essex. Essex – in one of those gestures that reveal both his generosity and his political ineptitude – pushed Bacon's cause with such enthusiasm that all doors were closed to him; at one point Essex even went so far as to insist that 'the attorneyship for ffrances ys that I must have, and in that will I spend all my power, might, autorytie and amytie, and with toothe and nayle deffende and procuer the same for hym agaynst whomesoever'. It was only when Essex himself was in trouble that the Crown found a use for his protégé: Bacon was to appear as one of the most damning witnesses at Essex's trial (55).

In happier days Bacon had acted as Essex's in-house philosopher; and it was in this capacity that he helped flesh out the 'device' which Essex staged before the Queen on the occasion of the Accession Day tournament of 1595: of which only fragments, some in Bacon's hand, survive. Accession Day was the high-point of the Elizabethan secular calendar, marking the anniversary of 17 November 1558, the day on which she came to the throne and 'married' her people. The mock-mediaeval tournaments were held at Whitehall, with the Queen sitting in the tilt gallery where she received the homage of her knights, while large crowds of the public looked on. The actual fighting became more and more overlaid with theatre, anticipating the masques of the Jacobean era (a tradition distinct from that of the public commercial theatre nurturing Shakespeare). The Accession Day tilts met their apogee in that of 1595, of which a contemporary wrote: 'My Lord Essex's device is much commended in these late triumphs. Some pretty while before he came in himself to the tilt, he sent his page with some pretty speech to the Queen, who returned with her Majesty's glove. And when he came in himself, he was met with an old Hermit, a Secretary of State, a brave Soldier, and an Esquire… the Queen said that if she had thought there had been so much said of her, she would not have been there that night, and so went to bed.'

*The persons to be three one dressed like an Heremite or philosopher representing Contemplation, the second like a Capitayne representing fame, and the third like a Counsellor of estate representing Experience, the third to beyginne to the Squire as being the master of the best behavier or complent though he speake last…*

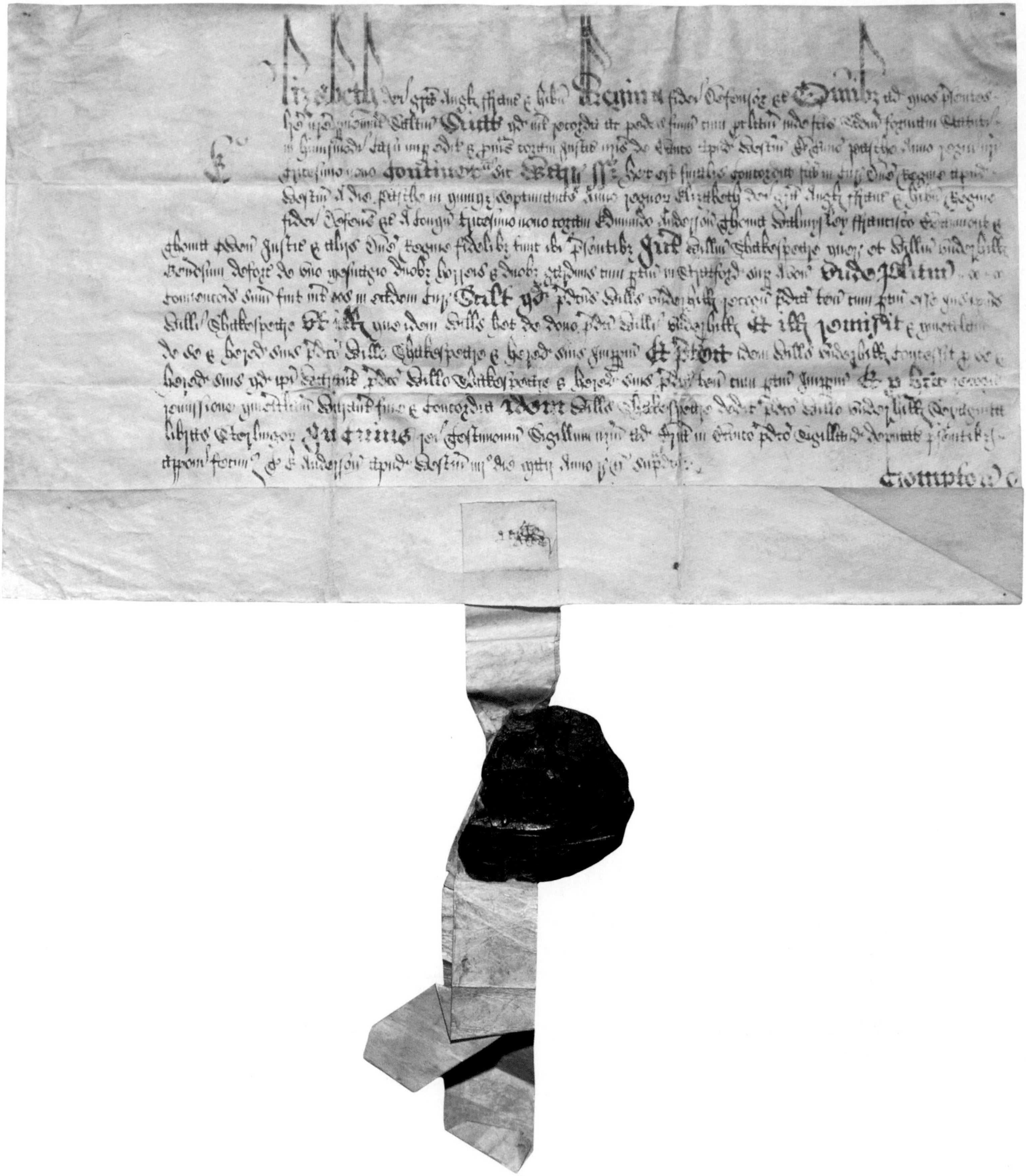

*'to the aforesaid William Shakespeare & his heirs forever'*

## 52 A subtle covetous and crafty man

4 May 1597

Exemplification of a fine, issued in the name of Queen Elizabeth, in Latin, which records the purchase by William Shakespeare from William Underhill of New Place, Stratford-upon-Avon, comprising one messuage, two granaries plus two gardens, and recording that Underhill recognises the aforesaid tenement with appurtenances to be the right of Shakespeare and his heirs for ever; on vellum, with a blank space left for the initial 'E' of 'Elizabeth' to be engrossed (indicating its status as a royal document), seal of the Court of Common Pleas, 'at Westminster the fourth day of May in the year and reign above written'

New Place, pulled down in the eighteenth century, was 'a praty house of brike and tymbar' and the second largest in Stratford. Shakespeare's purchase would originally have been effected by means of a deed of conveyance. In order to record the transaction, a fictional action would be brought before the courts, which would rule out any further litigation (hence the 'fine' in the sense of finality). Three copies of the fine would be made from one sheet of vellum: two written lengthways (for buyer and seller), the third copy written crossways at the 'foot' (for the court). Finally – to use Hamlet's pun – an 'exemplification' (certified copy) of the foot of fine, issued in the Queen's name and bearing the court's seal, could be secured. Which is what we have here. But an exemplification was an optional extra; in the words of Robert Bearman: 'Most people were evidently satisfied to receive just the standard copies and only too ready to forgo the more costly process of securing an exemplification. Certainly an exemplification was a more impressive document to produce if a dispute did ensue, but we know of no reason, when Shakespeare made the purchase, to anticipate trouble and, even if there had been, his deed and his purchaser's fine would have been sufficient to prove title. It could be, however, that Shakespeare, like the other "new" gentry of his time, was indulging in a little harmless snobbery'.

William Shakespeare, engraved by Martin Droeshout for the First Folio (1623)

But perhaps he had cause to feel jittery. For in 1563 the then owner of New Place, William Bott, was accused of poisoning his daughter with ratsbane and of forging property deeds, although the case never came to court. Bott, the putative forger and murderer, then sold the house to William Underhill, 'a subtle, covetous, and crafty man'. Underhill sold it to Shakespeare. Two months after the sale, Underhill was in his turn poisoned by his eldest son, Fulke, who was hanged for the murder in 1599. This put Shakespeare's right to the property in doubt and the question was not settled until 1602, when Underhill's second son came of age and could confirm the sale.

In the autumn of 1599 – the year of Fulke's hanging – *Hamlet* received its first performance. Park Honan explores the affinities between purchase and play: 'In buying the property, Shakespeare thus got in the strange bargain a father's alleged murder of a daughter, and the murder of a father by his son... He knew Underhill, just as his father knew Bott; and the murders in *Hamlet* are not like pictures out of Ovid... but intimately known happenings based in part on real, acutely judged events.' Or as the Prince says to the skull: 'hum. This fellow might be in's time a great buyer of Land, with his Statutes, his Recognizances, his Fines... Is this the fine of his Fines... to have his fine Pate full of fine Dirt?'

Elizabeth R

Right trustie and right welbeloved Cousin and Councellor we greet you well.
By the letter and the jornall which we have receaved from you, we see a quicke
end made of a slowe proceeding, for any thing which yor forces shall undertake
in those quarters which you pretended to visite, And therefore doubt not but
before this time you have ended the charge of the last two thowsand which we
yealded for other purposes, and of the three hundred horse onely destined for
Ulster services. It remaineth therefore that we returne you somewhat of our conceipt
upon this late accident of yor enterview with the Rebell. We never doubted
but that Tyrone whensoever he sawe any force approache, either himselfe or
any of his principall partisans wold instantly offer a parley, specially with
our supreme governors of that kingdome having often don it to those who had
but subalterne authority, alwayes seeking these dilatories with like wordes,
like protestations, and upon such contingents, as we gather these will prove
by yor advertisment of his purpose to goe consult with Odonnell. Herein
we must confesse to you that we are doubtfull least the successe wilbe
suitable with yor owne opinion heretofore when the same Rebells held like
course with others that preceaded you And therefore to come to some answeare
for the present. It appeareth to us by yor jornall that you and the traitor
spake togither halfe an howre alone, and without any bodyes hearinge, wherein
though we that truste you with our kingdome are farre from mistrusting you
with a Traitor, yet both for comelinesse example, and for yor owne discharge
we mervaile you wold carry it no better, especially when you have seemed
in all thinges since yor arrivall to be so precise to have good testimony for
yor actions as whensoever there was any thinge to be don to which our commandement tyed you, it seemed sufficient warrant for you if yor fellowe
counsellors allowed better of other wayes, though yor owne reason carryed you
to have pursued our directions against their opinions. to whose conduct if
we had meant that Irelande (after all the calamities in which they have wrapped it) should still have been abandoned (to whose courses never any joyned take
more exceptions then your selfe) Then was it very superfluous to have
sent over such a personage as you are who had deciphered so well the errors

of

*'we see a quicke end made of a slowe proceadinge'*

# 53 The Ford of Bellaclinthe

17 September 1599

Letter signed by Queen Elizabeth, to the Earl of Essex, as Lieutenant and Governor General of Ireland, venting her fury after his conclusion of a truce with the rebel Earl of Tyrone, 'Given under our Signet at Nonsuch the xvii$^{th}$ day of September, 1599, in the xli$^{th}$ yeare of our Raigne'

Hugh O'Neill, Earl of Tyrone, elected the O'Neill (Prince of Ulster), had inflicted a devastating defeat on the English forces in 1598, prompting the despatch of the largest army yet sent to Ireland, under the Earl of Essex. Essex knew that in accepting the appointment he was running a terrible risk; but he had so run down the capabilities of rival candidates (as the Queen acidly reminds him in this letter) that he had little choice, lest he lose face altogether. Furthermore he was, with his dreams of chivalry, temperamentally unsuited for a guerrilla war fought in the country known as 'the Englishman's grave'. But expectations of the hero hailed by Shakespeare as 'General of our gracious Empress' ran high. Arriving in Ireland that April, Essex spent most of the summer – contrary to instructions – engaged in minor forays to the south and west. Only in late August did he set off to confront Tyrone in the north. But instead of fighting, he talked. On 6 September, he met Tyrone at the Ford of Bellaclinthe on the Lagan. The meeting was held without witnesses – as the Queen sarcastically notes – with Tyrone bareheaded on his horse in mid-stream and Essex on the bank. Tyrone tendered his submission. By the terms of the truce, the Irish surrendered nothing at all and the English suspended operations. Essex informed the Queen of this triumph in a letter delivered by Captain Lawson on 16 September. She gave Lawson this reply for Essex; but it never reached him, as he had by then deserted his command and was on his way home. This, the original, is fuller than the text published in Harrison's *Letters of Queen Elizabeth* (1935) which derives from a copy and leaves out some of Elizabeth's choicer invective, such as her comment 'we cannot but muse that you shoulde recite that circumstance of his beinge sometime uncovvered as if that were much in a Rebell when our person is so represented'.

*Right trustie and right welbeloved Cousin and Councellor we greet you well. By the letre and the jornall which we have receaved from you, we see a quicke end made of a slowe proceadinge...* [from line 7] *It remaineth therefore that we return you somewhat of our Conceiptes uppon this late accident of your enterviewe with the Rebels. We never doubted but that Tyrone whensoever he sawe anie force approache, ether himselfe or anie of his principall partisans wold instantly offer a parley specially with our supreme gouvernor of that kingdome having often don it to those who had but subalterne authority...* [from line 18] *It appeareth to us by your jornall that you and the Traitor spake togither halfe an houre neare, and without anie bodyes hearinge, wherein though we that truste you with our kingdome are farre from mistrusting you with a Traitor; yet both for comelines, example, and for your owne discharge we mervaile you wolde cary it no better, especially when you have seemed in all thinges since your arrivall to be so precise to have good testimony for your actions...* [end of line 27] *if we had meant that Irlande (after all the Calamities in which they have wrapped it) should still have been abandoned (to whose Coorses never any could take more exceptions then your selfe) Then was it very superfluous to have sent over such a personage as you are who had decyphred so well the errors of* [overleaf] *their proceadinges beinge still at hande with us and of our secreatest councell... To trust this Traytor uppon oath is to truste a divell uppon his religion...*

292 561 568

May itt please youre Matye. In this greate
game wheare one equall hazarde you ventire
golde agaynst leed, though you winn more, yett youre
losses wilbe more famus; and the best recompenses
wee can make you, will seem shorte, till you vouch=
safe to looke uppon the whole summe. Iff since my
comminge over, I should give you an accounte
unto this day, I will presume to speake itt with
assurance, youre Matye hathe wonn muche more
then you have lost, and you have lost nothinge
thatt the providence off youre minister coulde
prevente; youre army hathe recovered harte
and reputation, and the estate hope beyonde theire
owne expectation, wch I esteem so great a degree
unto good successe, as thatt by compassinge so muche
I have allreddy stepped over the greatest barr
to doo you servis. The Earle off Ormonds parley
I bore one my allegeance to god and you was wont
my privitye; and so muche have I distasted the lyke
in others thatt before this accidente I have forbidden
itt to private captaynes, and no rebell hathe ever yet
spoken to my sellfe but uppon his knees. But iff I
may presume to yeeld unto youre Matye a iust excuse
for the presence off Mountgarret, as itt was nott in
his power to hinder the earles parley, so his intente
to be present was to doo you servis, by discoveringe
in his manner many ielousyes conceaved uppon good
grownde, and off great consequence to youre Matye;
neither was he able to give him any further ayde,
when the earles owne men had forsaken him.
Youre Matye in youre heavenly nature may be moved
wth this great example humanæ fragilitatis;
but I hope you shall nott heere off any dangerous
consequence thereoff to youre servis; I fear nott
his countrye, though itt were all oute. for neither the
place nor people have any great strengthe, but my
mynde dothe labor wth the estate off no province

*'ether to bowe or to breake the crooked humors off theas People'*

# 54 The Great Game

2 April 1600

Autograph letter by Lord Mountjoy, Lord Deputy of Ireland, to Queen Elizabeth, assuring her that, in 'the great game' in which they were both engaged, they must keep an eye to the long-term result, and that her army in Ireland has recovered heart and reputation; assuring her also that the parley recently held with the rebels, at which the Earl of Ormonde had been captured, had taken place without his authority; and trusting that 'itt willbe in your power ether to bowe or to breake the crooked humors off theas People'

Before Essex's appointment, his younger contemporary Lord Mountjoy had been the Queen's choice for the command of the army going into Ireland; but Essex had been so vociferous in his criticism – he was too young, too inexperienced, too bookish – that Mountjoy was passed over; only to be given the job after Essex's spectacular desertion, and to succeed where Essex had failed. Despite this, the two had become firm friends. Mountjoy was the lover of Essex's sister, Lady Penelope Rich (the 'Stella' of Sidney's sonnets); and during Essex's disgrace was, with the Earl of Southampton, entrusted with his financial affairs. Nor was beating the Irish the only 'great game' afoot. At Essex's trial, it was to emerge that, before going to Ireland, Mountjoy had promised Essex and James VI that he would send soldiers, if need be, to support James in his claim to the succession. But, with Mountjoy's successful campaign against Tyrone under way, the promise was forgotten; nor did the government look too closely into the matter.

Mountjoy's appointment marked a decisive shift in English policy towards Ireland, hitherto divided as to whether Gaelic Ireland should be anglicised by a policy of assimilation or by one of coercion. The English now finally opted for the latter, a policy of conquest which was to lead to the destruction of the Gaelic order. Mountjoy arrived in Ireland in February 1600, and completed his task in three years. With theatrical appropriateness he received the final surrender of Tyrone only a few days after Elizabeth's death (of which he kept the Irish in ignorance until after they had signed away everything). In the words of Wallace MacCaffrey: 'It was the greatest of Tudor enterprises and (apart from the Reformation) the most long-lasting in its consequences. It was achieved in agony and pain through the misery and deaths of countless of the Queen's subjects. It was altogether unheroic... It evoked on both sides a venomous outpouring of hatred which would permanently poison relations between the two islands. It bequeathed to the Queen's successors a problem of granite-like intractability'.

*May itt please youre Majestye In this greate game wheare on equall hazarde you venture gollde agaynst led, though you winn more, yett youre losses willbe more famus; and the best reconynges wee can make you, will seem shorte, till you voutsafe to looke uppon the whole somme. Iff since my comminge over, I should give you an accounte unto this day, I will presume to speake itt withe assurance, youre Majestye hathe wonn muche more then you have lost, and you have lost nothing thatt the providence off your minister coullde prevente; youre army hathe reccovered harte and reputation, and the estate hope beyonde ther owne expectation, which I esteem so great a degree unto good success, as thatt by compassinge so muche I have allreddy stepped over the greatest barr to doo you servis; The Earle off Ormonds Parley I vowe one my aleageance to god and you was without my privitye; and so muche have I distasted the lyke in others thatt before this accidente I have forbidden itt to private captaynes, and no rebel hathe ever yet spoken to my sellfe but uppon his knees...*

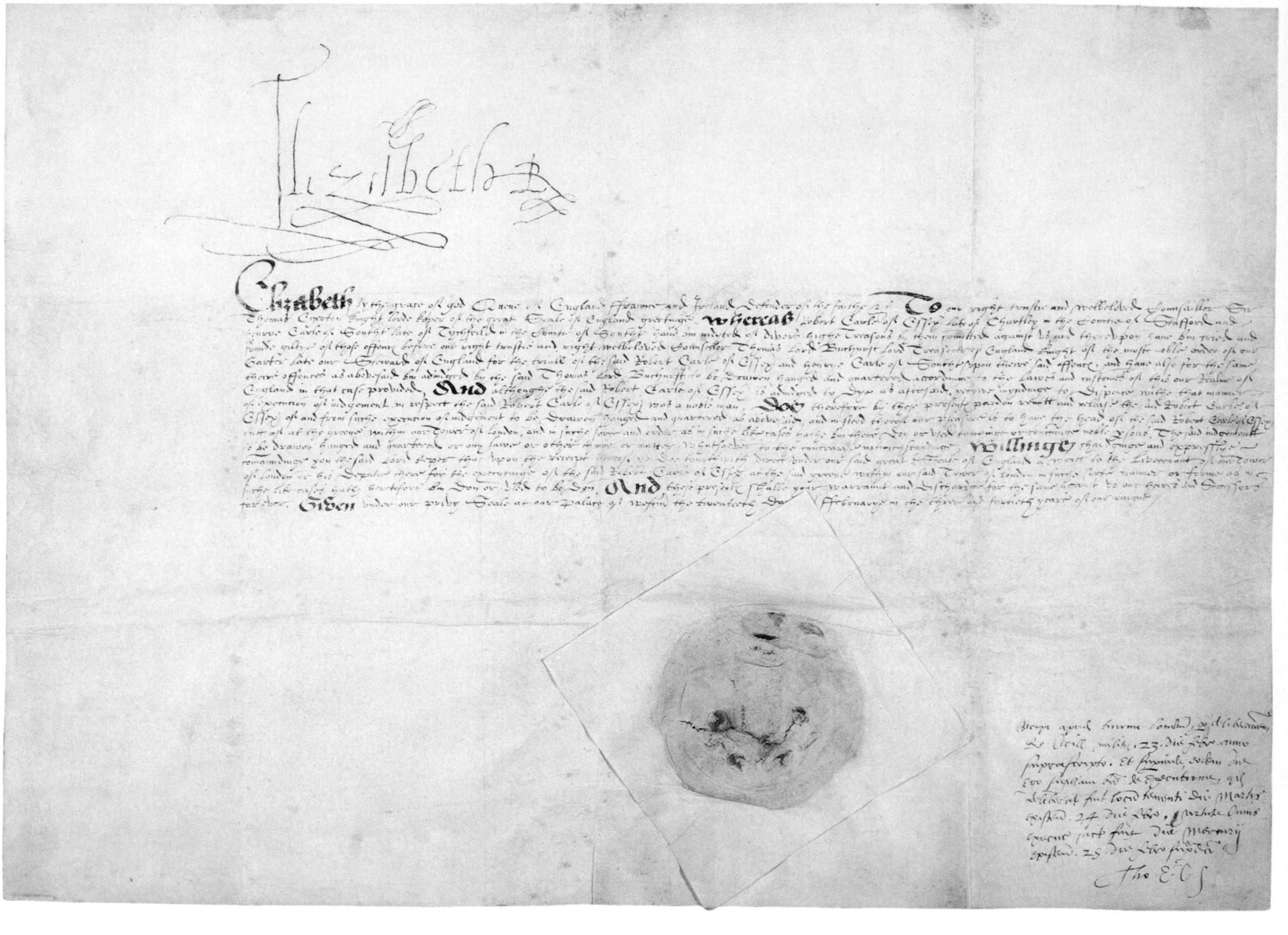

Elizabeth R

Elizabeth by the grace of god Quene of England ffrance and Ireland Defender of the faythe &c. To our right trustie and welbeloved Counsellor Sir Thomas Egerton knight lorde keper of the great Seale of England greetinge. Whereas Robert Earle of Essex late of Chartley in the Countie of Stafford and Henrye Earle of Southt late of Tychfeild in the Countie of Southt have ben indicted of diverse highe treasons by them comitted against us and thereupon have ben tried and founde giltye of those offences before our right trustie and right welbeloved Counsellor Thomas Lord Buckhurst Lord Treasorer of England knight of the most noble order of our Garter late our Steward of England for the triall of the said Robert Earle of Essex and Henrye Earle of Southt upon theire said offence, and have also for the same theire offences as abovesaid ben adiudged by the said Thomas Lord Buckhurst to be drawen hanged and quartered accordinge to the lawes and customes of this our Realme of England in that case provided, And although the said Robert Earle of Essex is adiudged to dye as aforesaid, yet we myndinge to dispence with that maner of execution of iudgement in respect the said Robert Earle of Essex was a noble man, Doe therefore by these presents pardon remitt and release the said Robert Earle of Essex of and from suche execution of iudgement to be drawen hanged and quartered as abovesaid, and instead thereof our pleasure is to have the head of the said Robert Earle of Essex cut of at the greene within our Tower of London, and in suche forme and order as in suche like cases hathe ben there [illegible] ... The said iudgement to be drawen hanged and quartered or any lawe or other thinge or matter whatsoever to the contrary notwithstandinge, Willinge and commandinge you the said Lord keper that upon the receipt hereof ye doe forthwith direct under our said great Seale of England a writt to the Lieutenant of our Tower of London or his Deputie there for the executinge of the said Robert Earle of Essex at the said greene within our said Tower of London in suche forte maner or forme as in suche like cases hathe heretofore ben don or used to be don, And these presents shalbe your warraunt and discharge for the same against us our heires and successors forever. Given under our privy Seale at our Palace of Westm the twentieth day of ffebruarye in the three and fortieth yeare of our raigne

... 23 die ... anno ... 24 die ... 25 die ...

Tho. E. C. S.

*'our pleasure is to have the head of the said Robert Earle of Essex cutt of at the greene within our Tower of london'*

# 55 Nemesis

20 February 1601

Warrant signed by Queen Elizabeth, to Sir Thomas Egerton, Lord Keeper of the Great Seal, for the execution of the Earl of Essex and the Earl of Southampton, found guilty of high treason, 'Given under our privy Seale at our Palace of Westminster the twenteeth Day of ffebruarye in the three and fortieth yeare of our raigne'

On his return from Ireland and the Ford of Belladinthe (53), Essex hoped that, once again, personal magnetism would save the day. He galloped to Nonsuch Palace, and burst unannounced into the Queen's bedchamber on the morning of 28 September 1599. Unfortunately she had only just got up and had on neither wig nor makeup. There followed nearly a year and a half of house arrest and exile from court, under supervision of the not unsympathetic Lord Keeper Egerton. Eventually he was allowed back to live at Essex House. Round him gathered a rump of followers, soldiers of fortune with nowhere else to go. Their enemy, they claimed, was not the Queen's Majesty but rather her advisors, men like the hated Sir Robert Cecil and Essex's other great rival, Sir Walter Ralegh. The conspirators' hand was forced by the arrival of Egerton and a party of senior officials at Essex House on the morning of 8 February 1601, demanding entry in the Queen's name. They were admitted, and then locked up in the Earl's study. Upon which Essex and his followers streamed out of Essex House. But instead of making for the court – which lay unprotected – they headed towards the City, where it was hoped the citizens would rise in their favour. Essex was immensely popular, especially with Londoners, but on this occasion his adoring public showed no inclination to risk their lives on his behalf. They stayed indoors. By the evening the rising had fizzled out. The inevitable trial and sentence followed, with Essex's erstwhile protégé Francis Bacon appearing as counsel for the Crown.

By this warrant, Essex, as a peer of the realm, is spared the usual penalty reserved for traitors of being hung, drawn and quartered; and instead of being executed in public at Tower Hill, he is to be beheaded in private on Tower Green, as had been the Queen's mother Anne Boleyn and Lady Jane Grey. The warrant is inscribed in the right-hand corner by Egerton himself: 'I received this at the Tower of London by delivery of Sir Robert Cecil 23 February in the year written above. And thereupon on the same day I signed the warrant of execution, which was delivered to the holder of the post [Lieutenant of the Tower] on the present Tuesday 24 February by virtue of which the execution was carried out the present Wednesday 25 February above written' (translated from the Latin). This warrant also condemns the young Earl of Southampton (Shakespeare's patron). He was however spared on account of his age and imprisoned in the Tower instead, being let out as soon as James ascended the throne.

*[*from line 2*] . . . whereas Robert Earle of Essex late of Chartley in the County of Stafford and henry Earle of Southampton late of Tichfeild in the Countie of Southampton have bin indyted of divers highe Treasons by them comitted against us, and thereupon have bin tried and founde guiltie of those offences . . . [*from line 8*] DOE therefore by these presentes pardon remitt and release the said Robert Earle of Essex of and from suche execucion of judgement to be Drawen hanged and quartered as abovesaid, and in steed therof our pleasure is to have the head of the said Robert Earle of Essex cutt of at the greene within our Tower of london . . .*

97

Your most obedient and loueing subiects dooe with greuous sightes and teares beholde the dayngerous staye and standing both of your person and Comon wealth wee perceaue playnly the wholle weight of vs all to rest uppon hallow brittle sticks how cann this vniuerse prosper when venomus wormes haue perced the tender rootes of the cheefest plants wherby for a season they could not spring and now lyke caterpillers dooe clime haueing brought them In despayre to bring both bodyes and all to the grounde a wofull and a dayngerous tyme is this for vs poore sheepe to lyue In when wolues and foxes shall thus praye uppon our Cheefest shepherds were yt not greatly In regarde of our allegence and care of your maiestyes quiet wee woulde adventure to smoke those caterpillers and to Chase such wolues and foxes thus praying for your maiestyes longe and prosperous raigne wee Conclude most earnestly and most humbly Intreating your grace with speede mercifully to Consider least wee all perish together

Your maiesties poor distresed Comon wealth full of bleeding harts

*'Your majesties poor distresed Common Wealth full of bleeding harts'*

# 56 No season for fooling

20 February 1601

Anonymous letter to Queen Elizabeth, from 'Your majesties poor distresed Common Wealth full of bleeding harts', inscribed on the address-leaf: 'Into the handes of our most noble and gracious Queene of Englande delyver me', endorsed by a member of Sir Robert Cecil's office: '1600 20 February Coppie of a Sedyciouse Lybell found in the market-place at Sarum [Salisbury]'

With the death of the Earl of Essex in February 1601 (55), Elizabethan England seemed to slip into the past tense; living out a sort of posthumous life. Although the citizens of London were relieved that their Queen was spared, they mourned their hero too. The song of the day was 'Essex's Last Good Night', lamenting 'the valiant Knight of Chivalry'; another ballad mourned 'Sweet England's pride', killed by 'Envy, that foul fiend'. For the balladeers, Envy was personified by the 'Fox' Sir Robert Cecil, the competent, conscientious but unromantic son of old Lord Burghley, who had died in 1598: 'Little Cecil trips up and down,/He rules both Court and Crown'. They were later to grace him with the epitaph: 'But now in Hatfield lies the Fox/Who stank while he lived and died of the Pox'.

At about this time the Queen's godson, Sir John Harington, paid her a visit, only to be given the message: 'Go tell that witty fellow, my godson, to get home; it is no season now to fool it here'. Harrington complained – perhaps somewhat fancifully – that 'The many evil plots and designs have overcome all her Highness' sweet temper. She walks much in her Privy Chamber, and stamps with her feet at ill news, and thrusts her rusty sword at times into the arras in great rage'. Of all the great heroes of the age, only Sir Walter Ralegh remained: but he had been Essex's rival, and was no more loved than Cecil.

Nor of course was the sombre mood just a question of Essex's demise. It is perhaps to be expected of any regime that has been in power for so long: in Christopher Haigh's influential analysis, 'her reign had been 30 years of illusion, followed by fifteen of disillusion'. The 1590s saw an economic downturn after a long period of prosperity, brought on partly by a succession of failed harvests in 1592-6. Foreign wars – above all in Ireland – had drained the treasury of money, forcing the Queen to sell lands and jewels. The ranks of the unemployed were swelled with discharged veterans. Corruption, too, was on the increase: for example when the excoriated priest-hunter Richard Young (50) died in December 1594, it was found he owed the customs £10,000, shocking Lord Burghley so much that he was unable to write for some days.

*Your most obedient and loveing subjects dooe with grevous sightes and teares beholde the dayngerous staye and standing both of your person and Common Wealth wee perceave playnly the wholle weight of us all to rest uppon hallow brittle stickses how cann this viniorde prosper when venomus wormes have perced the tender rootes of the cheefest plants wherby for a season they could not spring and now lyke caterpillers dooe clime haveing brought them In despayre to bring both bodyes and all to the grounde a wofull and a dayngerous tyme is this for us poore sheepe to lyve In when wolves and foxes shall thus praye uppon our Cheefest shepherds were yt not greatly In regarde of our allegence and care of your majestyes quiet wee woulde adventure to smoke those caterpillers and to Chase such wolves and foxes thus praying for your majestyes longe and prosperous raigne wee Conclude most earnestly and most humbly Intreating your grace with speede mercifully to Consider least we all perish together/Your majesties poor distresed Common Wealth full of bleeding harts*

Suche a prelate if he came shuld be
taught a bittar lesson than play
so presumtius and bold a part afor
he knewe your good liking therof
which as I hope is far fro your
intent so wyl his coming verifie
to muche good measur sprinkled
asseverations of kinges of which
you haue or now be warned that
thus you se how to fulfil your
trust reposed in [illegible] which to
infringe I neuer suspected
haue scantly made patente
my securitie and not trust
wt muche wisdom yet stuffed
wt great good wyl I hope you
wyl beare wt this blistering
you to long wt my scratting
hand as proceding fro a hart
that shal euer be filled wt the
sure affection of your
louing and ~~[illegible]~~ frendely
sistar
Elizabeth R

*'I hope you wyl beare with my molesting you to long with my skrating hand'*

# 57 The grasping heir

6 January 1603

Autograph letter by Queen Elizabeth, to James VI of Scotland, expressing pleasure at his readiness to take frank advice, which she offers in good measure: she warns him against opening diplomatic relations with Spain, treats him to a brief history of how badly the Spanish have behaved in the face of her always friendly behaviour, and winds up by telling him how he should conduct himself when dealing with Henri IV and the Vatican

On 7 September 1602 Elizabeth reached her seventieth year, but her health remained remarkably good. It was only with the onset of cold weather in the new year that she began to show signs of frailty; as William Camden, chronicler of her reign, records: 'The Queen, who had hitherto enjoyed her health without impairment, by reason of her abstinence from wine, and observing a temperate diet... now being in her Climacterical year, to wit, the seventieth year of her age, began to be sensible of some weakness and indisposition, both of health and old age, which the badness of weather increased'. The death of her old friend the Countess of Nottingham on 27 January is also said to have precipitated her decline. Her 'witty godson' Sir John Harington came to court at this time and wrote home to his wife: 'Our dear Queen doth now bear show of human infirmity'. He read her some of his witty verses, at which she smiled but said, 'When thou dost feel creeping time at thy gate, these fooleries will please thee less: I am past relish with such matters'. She had for some years found writing increasingly difficult, suffering from either rheumatism or gout in her fingers. In 1597 Sir Robert Cecil wrote to a friend: 'The Queen hath a desperate ache in her right thumb, but will not be known of it, for the gout it *cannot* be, nor *dare* not be'.

Elizabeth *c.*1592 by Isaac Oliver

According to the not-always-reliable Harington, Elizabeth once exclaimed that 'they were great fools that did not know that the line of Scotland must needs be next heirs'. But generally she kept silent on the matter and, as always, refused to nominate a successor (*14*). All the same, James VI of Scotland was the obvious candidate, even if in his more gloomy moments he thought she would 'endure as long as the sun and moon'. It was only when Cecil himself opened a secret correspondence with him that James's mind was put at ease. Elizabeth must have guessed what was going on, and at the opening of this letter comes close to gloating on his tractability: 'It pleaseth me not a little that my true intents without glosses or guiles are by you so gratefully taken'.

[from line 10] ...*Thus you Se how to fulfil your trust reposed in me wiche to infring I never mynde I have Sincereley made patente my Sinceritie and thogh not fraught with muche wisedome yet stuffed with great good wyl I hope you wyl beare with my molesting you to long with my skrating hand, as proceding from a hart that shall ever be filled with the/Sure affection of your/Loving and ~~Sure~~ frendely sistar /Elizabeth R*

146

189

May it please your most Excellent Maiesty. Sr. Henry Brunker hath charged me with many thinges in your Maties the most whearof I aknowledge to be true. and am hartily sory that I haue guien your Maiesty the least cause of offence. The particulers and the manner of handling I haue to auoide your Maiesties trouble deliuered to Sr. Henry Brunker. I humbly prostrate my selfe at your Maiesties feete crauing pardon for what is passed and of your Princely clemency to signify your Maiesties most gratious remission to me by your Highnesse letter to my La: my Grandmother whose discomfort I shall be till then. The Almighty encrease and for euer continue your Maiesties diuine vertues and prosperity whearwt you blessed blesse vs all.

Your Maiesties most



humble and dutifull handmaid

Arbella Stuart.

*'hartily sory that I have given your Majesty the least cause of offence'*

# 58 The prisoner of Hardwick

Early January 1603

Autograph letter by Lady Arabella (or Arbella) Stuart, to Queen Elizabeth, apologising for her attempt to escape from Hardwick Hall and for the offence caused both to the Queen and her grandmother, the Countess of Shrewsbury (Bess of Hardwick); subscribing herself 'Your Majesties most humble and dutifull handmaid'

Arabella Stuart – like her aunt by marriage Mary Queen of Scots – made a success of one thing at which their mutual cousin Elizabeth proved a complete failure, which was playing the part of the doomed romantic heroine. Arabella was doomed both by blood, and by love. She stood second in line to the succession, after her first cousin James VI of Scotland (28). Indeed she was believed by some to have a preferable title since she had been born on English soil, whereas James was an alien, and theoretically disqualified from possessing land in England and wearing the crown. Late in 1602 she made approaches to her cousin the Earl of Hertford, seeking to marry his grandson, William Seymour. Hertford and Seymour were descended from Henry VIII's younger sister, Mary. The proposed match would thus have fused two of the existing claims to the throne. Hertford warned the Council of what was being planned. Elizabeth took the matter very seriously, and despatched Sir Henry Brounker to Hardwick Hall where Arabella was kept by her grandmother, the redoubtable Bess of Hardwick (28). Arabella tearfully confessed all and wrote a confession which Brounker described as 'confused, obscure and somewhat ridiculous'. He thought 'her wits were somewhat distracted either through fear of her own grandmother or conceit of her own folly' and reported that Bess took the business 'so ill as with much ado she refrained her hands'. Arabella wrote the Queen this contrite letter, which Brounker took with him when he left Hardwick on 9 January.

Arabella felt herself a prisoner – heir almost to Mary Queen of Scots – at Hardwick. She complained that her grandmother subjected her to 'despiteful and disgraceful words' and that she was 'bobbed and her nose played withal'. She may also have been suffering from the hereditary Stuart disease, porphyria. This, as well as producing physical symptoms, induced extreme mood-changes. Certainly some of the letters she wrote at this time are incoherent, and her handwriting changes – sometimes within the space of the same letter – from the calligraphically formal and elegant (as here) to something like a scrawl, although this may be, as the editor of her *Letters* suggests, merely alternation between formal and informal hands. In all events, Bess begged the Queen to take her off her hands. The Queen refused. In 1610, after the Queen's death, Arabella became engaged to Seymour. They were discovered and promised not to marry, but broke their promise. Arabella was put under house arrest but, after attempting escape to the Continent, was sent to the Tower, where she died in 1615.

*May it please your most Excellent Majesty./Sir Henry Brunker hath charged me with many thinges in your Majesties* [sic] *the most whearof I aknowledge to be true, and am hartily sory that I have given your Majesty the least cause of offence. The particulers and the manner of handling I have to avoide your Majesties trouble delivered to Sir Henry Brunker. I humbly prostrate my selfe at your Majesties feete craving pardon for what is passed and of your Princely clemency to signify your Majesties most gratious remission to me by your Highnesse letter to my Lady my Grandmother whose discomfort I shall be till then…*

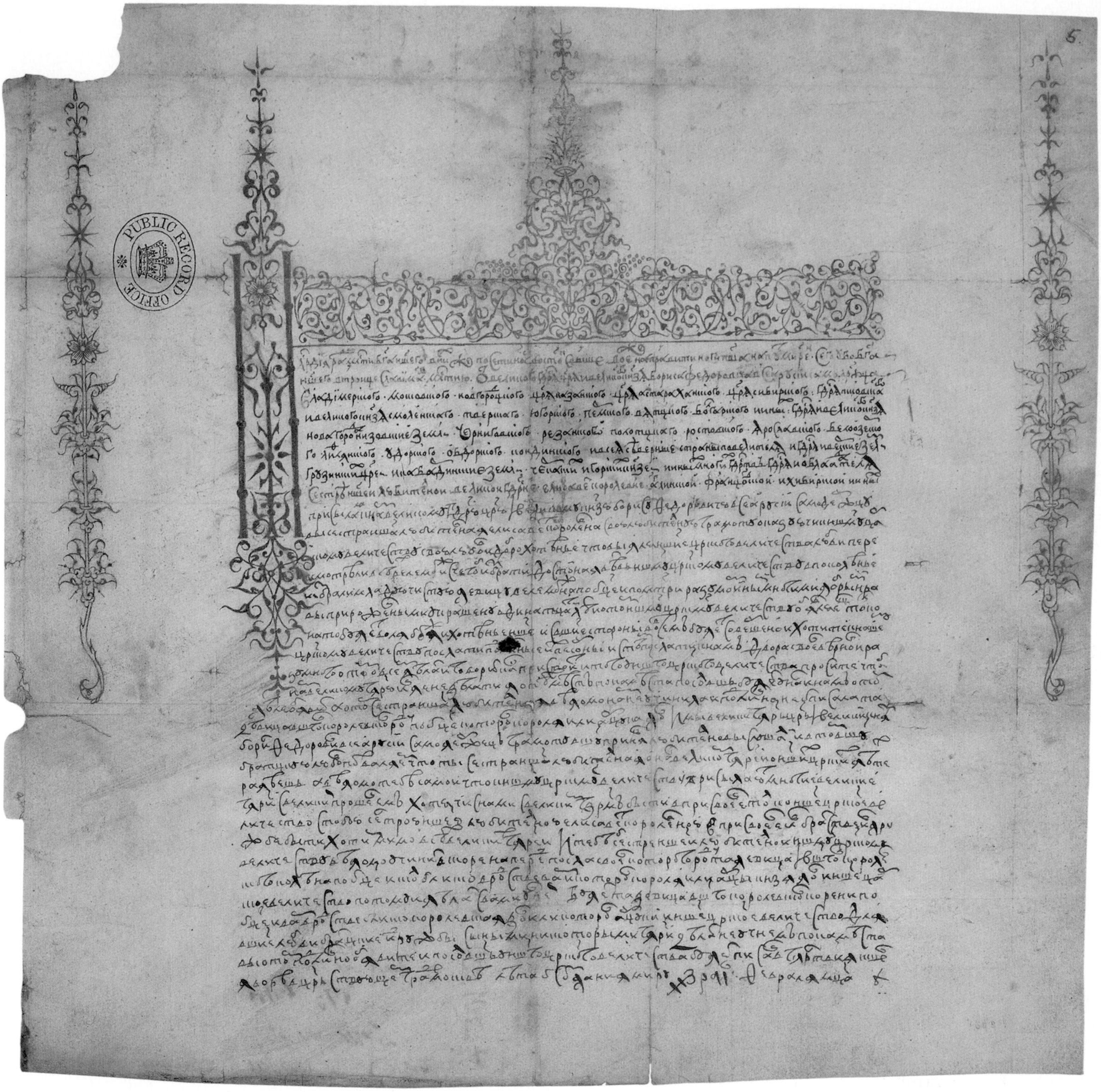
PUBLIC RECORD OFFICE
5

*'the matching and bestowing of them in your owne line and race'*

# 59 A dead queen gives away the bride

February 1603

Letter by Tsar Boris (Godunov), to Queen Elizabeth, expressing his pleasure at her willingness to bestow an English bride on his son, the Tsarevich Fyodor, and asking for further details of the girl's parentage and her relationship to the Queen, 'Written in our Princly Pallace in the citty of Mosco, in the year since the begenning of the world 7111 and in the month of Aprill'

Boris Godunov had been elected Tsar on the death of Ivan the Terrible's son Tsar Fyodor I in 1598. He was popularly believed to have cleared the way to the throne by arranging for the death, in a knife accident, of Fyodor I's half brother, Dmitry (this is the mainspring of Musorgsky's opera). Like Henry VII, Boris was much under threat from pretenders, notably the so-called 'False Dmitry'. Neither was he in good health. He was therefore anxious to secure his newly established dynasty by finding a bride for his son, Fyodor II, born in 1598 and – like Henry Prince of Wales – a youth of great promise.

The English were worried that Boris might find a match for the Tsarevich from one of their European commercial rivals. So marriage negotiations were set in train. The aim was not so much to secure a union, with its attendant danger of embroiling England in Moscow's wars, but rather to frustrate other offers. There was thus a good deal of vagueness and circumlocution, and what was indubitably the last of Elizabeth's wooings ran true to form. Our letter was written by Boris in reply to one from Elizabeth dated 5 October 1602 in which she offers the Tsarevich a 'young lady, being a pure maiden, noble descended by father and mother, adorned with graces and extraordinary gifts of nature, of convenient years between eleven and twelve'. The marriage never took place, nor is the identity of the girl known. English fears were to prove baseless and their commercial privileges were confirmed after James I's accession. When Boris died in 1605, Fyodor II was murdered with his family by the False Dmitry. A period of civil war followed, eventually leading to the election in 1613 of Michael Romanoff, son of Boris's bitterest boyar rival.

The illumination of the letter is typical of such diplomatic exchanges. The heading and opening salutations would have been prepared by a professional illuminator or limner, and the rest written out by a more senior official (the script can be seen changing at line 9). A memorandum survives from the Muscovy Company to Sir Robert Cecil which shows that Elizabeth's letters were prepared in much the same way. One of her letters to Boris is described as 'limned by him that was wont to do other letters of Her Majesty; who shall only begin the style thereof and limn the border', the rest being entrusted to one 'able to contain a matter of this nature without imparting it to any'. Our quotation is taken from a contemporary translation among the state papers. It is dated April. The Queen meanwhile had died at Richmond Palace in the early hours of the morning of 24 March 1603.

*. . . yt cannot but geve us an extraordenary contentment, we finding therin your majesties love and affectyone towards us and our children, carefully endevoring the matching and bestowing of them in your owne lyne and race. By which your letters your highnes made knowen unto to us that, amongste others, you have made choyse of a young lady, being a pure mayden, nobly discended by father & mother, adorned with graces & extraordenary guiftes of nature, abowt xi yeares of age, of whom you make an offer unto us that, yf it be the plesuer of god to incline the hartes of the two young couple to like one of the other, all sercumstances shall be accomodated on your part . . .*

The seat of ioyes, and loves abundance
Out of that mass of mirakells, my Muse,
gathered thos flowres, to her pure sences pleasinge
Out of her eyes (the store of ioyes) did chuse
equall delights, my sorrowes counterpoysinge
Her regall lookes, my rigarus sythes suppressed
Small droppes of ioies, sweetned great worlds of woes,
one gladsume day a thowsand cares redressed.
Whom love defends, what fortune overthrowes?
When shee did well, what did ther elce amiss.
when shee did ill what empires could have pleased
no other poure effectinge wo, or bliss.
Shee gave, shee tooke, shee wounded, shee apeased.

The honor of her love, love still devisinge
woundinge my mind with contrary conceyte
~~[illegible]~~ transferde it sealf sumetyme to her aspiringe
sumetyme the trumpett of her thoughts retrayt
To seeke new worlds, for golde, for prayse, for glory,
to try desire, to try love severed farr
when I was gonn shee sent her memory
more stronge then weare ten thowsand shipps of warr
to call mee back, to leve great honors thought
to leve my frinds, my fortune, my attempte
to leve the purpose I so longe had sought
and holde both cares, and cumforts in contempt,
Such heat in Ize, such fier in frost remaynde
such trust in doubt, such cumfort in dispaire
mich like the gentell Lame, though lately waynde
playes with the dug though finds no cumfort ther,
But as a boddy violently slayne
retayneath warmth although the spirit be gonn.
and by a poure in nature moves agayne
till it be layd below the fatall stone
Or as the earth yeven in cold winter dayes
left for a tyme by her life gevinge soonn.
douth by the poure remayninge of his rayes
produce sume green, though not as it hath donn.
Or as a wheele forst by the fallinge streame
although the course be turnde sume other way
douth for a tyme go rownde uppon the beame
till wantinge strength to move, it stands att stay,

*'when I was gonn shee sent her memory'*

# 60 Postscript

undated

Autograph manuscript by Sir Walter Ralegh of his poem 'The 11th: and last booke of the Ocean to Scinthia', addressed to Cynthia (Queen Elizabeth) by the Shepherd of the Ocean (Ralegh), undated, in a notebook seized with Ralegh's papers after the Queen's death

*To seeke new worlds, for golde, for prayse, for glory,*
*to try desire, to try love severed farr*
*when I was gonn shee sent her memory*
*more stronge then weare tenthowsand shipps of warr*
*to call me back, to leve great honors thought*
*to leve my frinds, my fortune, my attempte*
*to leve the purpose I so longe had sought*
*and holde both cares, and cumforts in contempt,*
*Such heat in Ize, such fier in frost remaynde*
*such trust in doubt, such cumfort in dispaire*
*mich like the gentell Lamm, though lately waynde*
*playes with the dug though finds no cumfort ther,*
*But as a boddy violently slayne*
*retayneath warmth although the spirrit be gonn*
*and by a poure in nature moves agayne*
*till it be layd below the fatall stone*
*Or as the yearth yeven in cold winter dayes*
*left for a tyme by her life gevinge soonn*
*douth by the poure remayninge of his rayes*
*produce some green, though not as it hath dunn*
*Or as a wheele forst by the fallinge streame*
*although the course be turnde some other way*
*douth for a tyme go rounde uppon the beame*
*till wantinge strenght to move, it stands att stay...*

# Further reading

In order of date of publication


### Writings by Elizabeth:

*The Letters of Queen Elizabeth I*, edited by G. B. Harrison (1935)

Maria Perry, *Elizabeth I: The Word of a Prince: A Life from Contemporary Documents* (Folio Society 1990)

*Elizabeth I: Collected Works*, edited by Leah S. Marcus, Janel Mueller, and Mary Beth Rose (1999)

*Elizabeth I: Autograph Compositions and Foreign Language Originals*, edited by Janel Mueller and Leah S. Marcus (2003)

### Biographies of Elizabeth:

J. E. Neale, *Queen Elizabeth* (1934)

Joel Hurstfield, *Elizabeth I and the Unity of England* (1960)

Neville Williams, *Elizabeth: Queen of England* (1967)

Anne Somerset, *Elizabeth I* (1991)

Wallace MacCaffrey, *Elizabeth I* (1993)

David Starkey, *Elizabeth I: Apprenticeship* or *The Struggle for the Throne* (2000)

### Studies of Elizabeth and her reign:

A.L. Rowse, *The England of Elizabeth* (1950)

Wallace MacCaffrey, *The Shaping of the Elizabethan Regime* (1969), *Queen Elizabeth and the Making of Policy 1570-1588* (1981), and *Elizabeth I: War and Politics 1588-1603* (1992)

Christopher Haigh, *Elizabeth I* (1988)

*Elizabeth: The Exhibition at the National Maritime Museum*, edited by Susan Doran (2003)

### Histories of the Tudor period:

G. R. Elton, *England under the Tudors* (1955, 1962)

John Guy, *Tudor England* (1988)

Susan Brigden, *New Worlds, Lost Worlds: The Rule of the Tudors 1485-1603* (2000)

### Manuscript Facsimiles and Guides to Scripts:

W. W. Greg, *English Literary Autographs 1550-1650* (1932)

L. C. Hector, *The Handwriting of English Documents* (1958)

Giles E. Dawson and Laetitia Kennedy-Skipton, *Elizabethan Handwriting 1500-1650* (1968)

P. J. Croft, *Autograph Poetry in the English Language: Facsimiles of original manuscripts from the Fourteenth to the Twentieth Century* (1973)

Anthony G. Petti, *English Literary Hands from Chaucer to Dryden* (1977)

*British Literary Manuscripts: Series I From 800 to 1800*, catalogue by Verlyn Klinkenborg (Pierpont Morgan Library, 1981)

*Index of English Literary Manuscripts*, vol.i: *1450-1625*, part 1, edited by Peter Beal (1987)

Jean F. Preston and Laetitia Yeandle, *English Handwriting 1400-1650: An Introductory Manual* (1992)


# Abbreviations

| | |
|---|---|
| BL | British Library |
| *CSP* | *Calendar of State Papers* |
| *DNB* | *Dictionary of National Biography* |
| HMC | Historical Manuscript Commission |
| Harrison | *The Letters of Queen Elizabeth I*, edited by G. B. Harrison (1935) |
| Marcus | *Elizabeth I: Collected Works*, edited by Leah S. Marcus, Janel Mueller, and Mary Beth Rose (1999) |
| Mueller | *Elizabeth I: Autograph Compositions and Foreign Language Originals*, edited by Janel Mueller and Leah S. Marcus (2003) |
| *OED* | *Oxford English Dictionary* |
| Perry | Maria Perry, *Elizabeth I: The Word of a Prince: A Life from Contemporary Documents* (1990) |
| PRO | Public Record Office |
| Starkey | David Starkey, *Elizabeth I: Apprenticeship* or *The Struggle for the Throne* (2000) |

# Notes and references

INTRODUCTION. The opening quotation is from John Simpson, *News from No Man's Land: Reporting the World* (2002), p.150. The quotation from Keats is from his 'Fall of Hyperion', line 18 ('When this warm scribe my hand is in the grave'). The remark by MacCulloch is taken from his review of Brian Moynahan's biography of Tyndale, in the *Guardian*, 1 June 2002. The quotation from Larkin's 'Aubade' is from his *Collected Poems*, edited by Anthony Thwaite (1988): it is possible (*pace* MacCulloch) to download a recording of Larkin reading the poem from the Albion College website (martinamis.albion.edu/larkina.htm). David Hockney places the first use of proto-photography to the 1430s (during the same decade that Gutenberg was experimenting with opaque lenses and the latent image) in his *Secret Knowledge* (2001). The early history of the Public Record Office (PRO) is given by F. S. Thomas, *A History of the State Paper Office* (1849); further details supplied courtesy of Simon Adams. The Essex letters were lot 249 in the book and manuscripts sale at Phillips, London, 11 June 1999; see also HMC, *Twelfth Report, Appendix, Part IX* (1891), pp.165-78. For the migrations of state papers now at Hatfield, the Pepys Library and Longleat, see the respective HMC reports, which have been supplemented by Simon Adams, 'The Papers of Robert Dudley, Earl of Leicester: I-III', *Archives*, xxx (1992), pp.63-85, xx (1993), pp.131-44, xxii (1996), pp.1-26; for the Lauderdale MSS (from which the draft of James VI's letter to Elizabeth derives), see Adams, 'The Lauderdale Papers, 1561-1570: The Maitland of Lethington State Papers and the Leicester Correspondence' and 'Two "Missing" Lauderdale Letters', *Scottish Historical Review*, lxxvii (1988), pp.28-55 and lxx (1991), pp.55-7. Information on John Spilman and his watermarked paper I owe to Henry Woudhuysen, 'The Queen's Own Hand', delivered at a PERDITA conference, 'Standards of Manuscript Description', 14 July 2001. The recipe for ink comes from Anthony G. Petti, *English Literary Hands from Chaucer to Dryden* (1977), p.7. The quote by Lytton Strachey is from *Elizabeth and Essex* (1928), p.36. The discussion of Elizabeth's pronunciation is based on Mueller, p.xxiv: I owe the note on Burghley and Leicester's usage to Simon Adams. Essex's complaint about signing letters is quoted by Paul E. J. Hammer, *The Polarisation of Elizabethan Politics: The Political Career of Robert Devereaux, 2nd Earl of Essex, 1585-1597* (1999), p.293. For analysis of Elizabeth's mature hand, with transcripts and sample letter-formations, see Preston and Yeandle, *English Handwriting*, no.21. The contemporary observation on Elizabeth's arthritic hand comes from *Elizabeth of England: Certain Observations Concerning the Life and Reign of Queen Elizabeth by John Clapham*, ed. Evelyn Plummer Read and Conyers Read (1951), p.292, quoted in Woudhuysen's paper on Elizabeth's handwriting. The quotation by Dianne Tillotson is from her *Medieval Writing* website, where a summary and glossary of relevant terms is given (http://medievalwriting.50megs.com/writing.htm). The description of Elizabeth's signature as 'queenly trademark' is from Mueller, p.xvii. My account of Henry VIII's dry stamp leans heavily on David Starkey, *The Reign of Henry VIII: Personalities and Politics* (1985), and John Guy, *Tudor England*, 1988 (references are indexed in both books under the name of the respective monarch). As regards Mary, Guy states that 'despite commissioning a "dry stamp", Mary does not appear to have used it, signing state papers with her own hand until the day of her death' (p.228). But in fact Mary's wet stamp is fairly commonly encountered (see for example the auction records listed by *American Book Prices Current*), and I have encountered signed documents which seem problematical and which might well indicate the use of a dry stamp. For a discussion of Levina Teerlinc's opus and the Great Seal, see the note to 22 below. For Elizabeth's stamped signature, see *CSP Domestic*, lxvii, no.9; the document quoted is SP 12/67, fol.30v. I am grateful to Peter Beal for pointing out to me his namesake's note on Mary Queen of Scots's death warrant, BL Add. MS 48027, ff.645-6; to be discussed in his forthcoming paper on the Queen's execution warrants.

1. For translation and discussion of this letter, see Harrison, pp.4-5; Perry, p.30; Starkey, *Elizabeth: Apprenticeship*, pp.35-6 (where letter-writing etiquette is discussed); and Marcus, pp.5-6. The original Italian, with missing words supplied from a Bodleian Library transcript, is given by Mueller, pp.5-6. For Giovanni Battista Castiglione, see the *Dizionario biografico degli Italiani*; a memoir at Yale states that he served in Henry's Boulogne campaign and afterwards was preferred to Elizabeth's service; she may have also been tutored by a John Picton, about whom very little is known (information courtesy Simon Adams).

2. For translation and discussion of this dedication, see Perry, pp.34-9; Starkey, *Elizabeth: Apprenticeship*, pp.51-3; and Marcus, pp.9-10. The original Latin is given by Mueller, pp.8-9. For the conflicting views of Elizabeth's attitude to Henry, see Philippa Berry, *Of Chastity and Power: Elizabeth Literature and the Unmarried Queen* (1989), pp.72-3 and Starkey, *Elizabeth: Apprenticeship*, p.23: I owe this comparison – which perhaps overplays Starkey's remark about Elizabeth's dresses – to Michael Dobson and Nicola J. Watson's *England's Elizabeth: An Afterlife in Fame and Fantasy* (2002), p.6.

3. This letter is printed and discussed by Harrison, p.16; Perry, pp.51-66; Starkey, *Elizabeth: Apprenticeship*, pp.65-80; and Marcus, who prints the dispositions made by Kat Ashley, pp.25-30 as well as the letter, pp.31-33. A diplomatic transcript is given by Mueller, pp.28-9. Elizabeth's famous remark on Seymour derives from the thoroughly unreliable seventeenth-century biographer Grigorio Leti, see the discussion by Perry, p.65. The historian quoted is J. B. Black, *The Reign of Elizabeth* (1936), p.2.

4. For the 'Like as the richman' letter, see Harrison, p.15; Marcus, pp.35-6; Mueller, pp.24-6. Elizabeth invokes fickle Fortune in her first letter. (Incidentally, the rather opaque reference in this letter to 'my Lorde Marques' in line 11 may allude either to Lord Winchester or, most likely, Lord Northampton. He could not, as Marcus suggests, have been Lord Dorset, as he became Duke of Suffolk

in November 1551: information courtesy Simon Adams). The historian quoted is Joel Hurstfield, *Elizabeth I and the Unity of England* (1960), p.11.

5. This letter is printed by Harrison, pp.19-21; Perry, pp.91-4; Marcus, pp.41-2: all erroneously date the letter to 16 March; this, and a minor mistranscription, are corrected by Mueller, pp.29-32. The letter is also discussed by Starkey, *Elizabeth: Apprenticeship*, pp.141-2, where the right date is given, and reproduced in *Elizabeth: The Exhibition at the National Maritime Museum*, edited by Susan Doran (2003), pp.23-4, where the erroneous date is given. Analysis of the tide was undertaken by the Public Record Office with the Navy Hydrographic Office and the Proudman Oceanographic Laboratory, Bridston, and is discussed at fascinating length in the new edition of *CSP Domestic, Mary I*, edited by C. S. Knighton (1998), p.53, n.3. For another example of (considerably less vigorous) slashes entered between text and signature, see Norfolk's letter to Elizabeth, also from the Tower (24).

6. This letter is discussed by Starkey, *Elizabeth: Apprenticeship*, pp.233-6.

7. The translation is based on that given in *CSP Foreign 1558-1559*, pp.154-5.

8. For Feria's correspondence with Philip, see *CSP Simancas 1558-1567*.

9. The description of Gresham as 'the Wealthiest Citizen...', is taken from Thomas Fuller's *Worthies*. The discussion of Elizabethan finances is based on Neale, *Elizabeth*, pp.284-5. I owe the suggestion that Fugger may have been one of the lenders to Thomas G. Barnes. For further details of Gresham's career, see J. W. Burgon, *The Life and Times of Sir Thomas Gresham* (1839); a useful summary is to be found in A. L. Rowse, *The England of Elizabeth* (1950), pp.143-49 and in the *DNB*.

11. This letter was published by Knox himself in his *History of the Reformation of Religion within the Realme of Scotland*. His handwriting shows two interesting usages, in 'travaleht earnestlie to have' the tick over the letter 'u' (modernised here to 'v') is made to differentiate it from 'n' and is to be found in contemporary Scottish hands; in 'the writar And because' the terminal 's' is a legal letter-form (Knox, besides being a former galley slave, was also a lawyer).

12. For a summary of the siege of Malta, see Ernle Bradford, *The Great Siege: Malta 1565* (1961). The German traveller who saw the picture of the siege in the Queen's apartment was Paul Hentzner in his *Travels in England* (web text available under the Gutenberg Project): it is tempting to think that this was one of the set of eight by Matteo Perez d'Aleccio, later in the collection of Charles I and now in the National Maritime Museum (at the Queens House).

13. Ascham was tutor to Princess Elizabeth between Midsummer 1548 and January 1550, with an absence beginning in January 1549 and ending sometime in the spring. For Ascham's tutelage of Elizabeth, see Lawrence V. Ryan, *Roger Ascham* (1963). As the Latin Secretary, he seems to have been the last (along with her French Secretary Nicasius Yetsweirt) of the secretaries to have counter-signed letters, a practice carried over from his predecessor, Peter Vannes: John Milton and Georg Rudolph Weckherlin, Latin Secretaries in the next century, left their letters unsigned, and the only counter-signature to appear would be that of the secretary of state. What appears to be Ascham's personal register of state correspondence between 26 November 1558 and 8 October 1568, comprising copies of over two hundred letters, is BL Royal MS 13.B.I, most transcripts being by scribes, but fols.1-6, 10r and 16-24 being autograph, as are a number of marginal notes and additions; other official letters are preserved in BL Lansdowne 98, fols.49-101; and among the state papers for the decade 1558-68 in the PRO (see Ryan, pp.326-7, n.7). A further letterbook of Ascham as Latin Secretary is to be found in the Bodleian Library, Oxford, Clarendon MS 1. Examples of Ascham's various hands can be found in the Pierpont Morgan Library's *British Literary Manuscripts*, Series I, no.14 (a presentation inscription in a book in a regular unelaborated hand); Alfred Fairbank, *A Book of Scripts* (Pelican edition, 1968), pl. 41 (for an elaborate letter written on behalf of the University of Cambridge); W.W. Greg, *English Literary Autographs 1550-1650* (1932), pl.lxiii (for samples of his ordinary hand in both Secretary and Italic scripts); and Anthony G. Petti, *English Literary Hands from Dryden to Chaucer* (1977), pl.23 (his formal Italic) and 24 (Secretary). For details of gunrunning for Ivan the Terrible, see Benson Bobrick, *Ivan the Terrible* (Canongate edition 1990), p.258 (originally published in the US as *Fearful Majesty: The Life and Times of Ivan the Terrible*, 1987); the denial is in a letter dated 6 May 1561.

14. Printed by Marcus, pp.79-80; with a diplomatic transcript given by Mueller, pp.34-7. Marcus misleadingly describes the speech as written in answer to the Lords' petition: there were in all three speeches addressed by Elizabeth to Parliament, namely her answer to the Commons, her answer to the Lords and finally this, her answer to both Houses: a useful summary is given in Neale's *Elizabeth*, pp.125-6, and fuller details in his *Elizabeth I and her Parliaments* (1953). Elizabeth's conversations with Maitland are printed by Marcus, pp.60-70. The quotation by Elton is from *England under the Tudors* (1955, 1962), p.284.

15. Frobisher also found a narwhal tusk which he presented to the Queen; another was owned by Rudolf II. For an illustration of one, see the , p.162. The description of Ivan's last days is by the English Ambassador, Sir Jerome Horsey, printed in *Russia at the Close of the Sixteenth Century*, edited by Edward A. Bond, Hakluyt Society (1856), p.200. The full text of Jenkinson's petition is taken from the BL MS with damaged readings supplied from the PRO copy printed in *Early Voyages and Travels in Russia and Persia by Anthony Jenkinson and other Englishmen*, edited by E. Delmar Morgan and C. H. Coote, Hakluyt Society (1886), i, pp.159-166.

16. For Hawkins and the reform of the navy, see Simon Adams, 'New Light on the "Reformation" of John Hawkins: the Ellesmere Naval Survey of January 1584', in the *English Historical Review* 105 (1990), pp. 96ff: the Survey dispels the myth 'that Hawkins was uniquely responsible for designing the new type of galleon' (p.106).

18. The linen story is related and speculated upon, but without attribution, by Elizabeth Jenkins, *Elizabeth the Great* (U.S. edition, 1958), pp.139-140. I am grateful to Simon Adams for pointing out its source. The translation of the

letter is by Agnes Strickland, *Letters of Mary Queen of Scots* (1844) i, pp.67-71.

19. Printed by Harrison, pp.54-5. Regarding the Casket Letters, reading the account by Antonia Fraser, one is left in no doubt that they are such a mishmash of the genuine, the fake, the falsely-attributed, the tampered-with, that they are worthless as evidence; reading the account by Jenny Wormold one is equally convinced that they are basically trustworthy; see Fraser, *Mary Queen of Scots* (1969), Chap.20 and Appendix; and Wormald, *Mary, Queen of Scots* (revised edition 2001), pp.179-182. For the two contrasting opinions of this letter, see Strickland, *Letters of Mary, Queen of Scots*, i, p.143; and Perry, p.205.

20. The contemporary translation, BL Cotton Nero B.VIII, fol.4, is printed in *Early Voyages and Travels in Russia and Persia by Anthony Jenkinson and other Englishmen*, edited by E. Delmar Morgan and C. H. Coote, Hakluyt Society (1886), ii, pp.280-3. The analysis of Ivan's nickname is given by Benson Bobrick, *Ivan the Terrible* (Canongate edition 1990), p.344. For Jenkinson's secret memorandum on the asylum exchange, and a discussion of this and of the marriage proposal, see Morgan and Coote, i, pp.236-39; also *Russia at the Close of the Sixteenth Century*, edited by Edward A. Bond, Hakluyt Society (1856), p.173: 'It is believed that Anthony Jenkinson was, in the year 1567, entrusted by Ivan with secret orders to negotiate a marriage with Queen Elizabeth. See Hamel, [*England and Russia*] p.179 *et seq*', see also pp.187, 196 and the Preface. For a further account of Ivan's courtship of Lady Mary Hastings, see the *DNB*, under the entry for her father, Francis Hastings, second Earl of Huntingdon.

21. The contemporary translation, BL Cotton Nero B.XI, fol.347, is printed in Morgan and Coote, *Early Voyages and Travels in Russia*, ii, pp.292-7. Ivan's letter is quoted and discussed by Bobrick, *Ivan the Terrible*, pp.261-2. For Elizabeth's letters of 18 May which prompted the outburst, see Morgan and Coote, pp.287-92; for her reply of May or June 1571, pp.297-8.

22. The standard discussion of the initial letter portrait is Erna Auerbach, *Tudor Artists* (1954), although many of her illustrations are untypical in that they come from the Plea Rolls and so do not follow the Great Seal format. Generally, coloured initial letter portraits were commissioned by corporations and similar institutions, a good example being those granted to Boston, in Lincolnshire, which although illuminated closely resemble the monochrome type and differ sharply from Burghley's grant. Hilliard's earliest mature miniature is dated 1571 and earliest dated picture of the Queen 1572. For an outline of Teerlinc's career, see Roy Strong's entry in *DNB: Missing Persons*; for a discussion of the canon, Roy Strong and V.J. Murrell, *The Portrait Miniature Rediscovered 1520-1620* (V&A Exhibition catalogue, 1983) and Roy Strong, *The English Renaissance Miniature* (1983): to which the miniature of Lord Darnley, formerly in the Charles E. Lees Collection, sold at Bonhams, 20 November 1997, should be added (here illustrated facing 17). If our deed is by Teerlinc, it adds support to Strong's suggestion that the body of work centring around the Maundy Ceremony miniature is by Teerlinc: for by 1571 the two other recorded miniaturists who might otherwise be candidates, John Shute and John Bettes, were both dead (for a reproduction of the Maundy miniature, see *Elizabeth: The Exhibition at the National Maritime Museum*, edited by Susan Doran, 2003, p.74). On the other hand, the secondary body of work which Strong attributes to Teerlinc, namely the Westminster Cathedral Cramp Ring Manuscript (V&A no.39) and the indenture establishing the Poor Knights of Windsor (V&A no.47) can be ruled out as not being by her; for the initial letter portrait in the Windsor MS shows none of Teerlinc's peculiarities. I am also doubtful of the theory that Teerlinc was responsible for designing Elizabeth's first Great Seal, given her difficulty in producing a conventional likeness of the seal's obverse in the present document; as I am of the attribution to her of the coronation miniature, reproduced as frontispiece to *Elizabeth: The Exhibition at the National Maritime Museum*, and discussed pp.42-3. The youthful self-portrait of Hilliard shown in the same exhibition (pp.198-9) would suggest that he was indeed taught by Teerlinc. A panel at Burghley House sometimes identified as being of Mary Queen of Scots (illustrated by Christopher Hibbert, *The Virgin Queen: The Personal History of Elizabeth I*, Penguin edition 1992, plate 21) could be based on a Teerlinc original, if not one by Hans Eworth, whose compositions she mimicked.

23. Printed by Marcus, p.127. For another case of clerk-confidentiality see the letter from Boris Godunov of 1603. A list of torture warrants is given by J. H. Langbein, *Torture and the Law of Proof* (1977), Chapter 6. The quotation is from *John Gerard: The Autobiography of an Elizabethan*, translated from the Latin by Philip Caraman (1951), p.107-8. The various biographies of Elizabeth give conflicting accounts of who was, and who was not, tortured, and what they said: I have here relied upon Neville Williams, *A Tudor Tragedy: Thomas Howard Fourth Duke of Norfolk* (1964). Barker, Smith and Wilson have their own entries in the *DNB*.

24. A third nobleman to be executed was the 7th Earl of Northumberland, beheaded at York in August 1572 for his participation in the Rebellion of the Northern Earls (I am grateful to Simon Adams for pointing this out).

25. Printed by Marcus, p.131 (with minor mistranscriptions not noted in the errata listed by Mueller, p.xxxiv). The quotation is from Jenkins, *Elizabeth the Great*, p.186.

26. For Catherine de' Medici, see R. J. Knecht, *Catherine de' Medici* (1998); Ivan Cloulas, Catherine de Médici (1979); J.E. Neale, *The Age of Catherine de Medici* (1943); for the marriage negotiations see Susan Doran, *Monarchy and Matrimony: The Courtships of Elizabeth I* (1996).

27. The quotations are taken from R. J. W. Evans, *Rudolf II and his World* (1973), pp.121-2. An account of Sidney's embassy is given by Katharine Duncan-Jones, *Sir Philip Sidney* (1991), pp.127-8.

31. For full diplomatic transcripts of this and other letters written by Spenser for Grey, see Andrew Zurcher's internet *Edmund Spenser's Home Page*
(via www.english.cam.ac.uk/spenser/main.htm).
The final quotation is from the introduction to *The Faerie Queene Books I-III*, edited by Douglas Brooks-Davies (1993), p.xxii.

32. Fulke Greville's description of William the Silent is quoted by Katharine Duncan-Jones, *Sir Philip Sidney*, p.131:

Simon Adams has pointed out to me that Greville's meeting with William was in 1579 and his account written much later, in 1613, when William's legend was already fully established.

33. The extract from Blackwood is quoted by Agnes Strickland, *Letters of Mary, Queen of Scots* (1844), ii, p.39. The translation is also from Strickland, pp.39-40.

34. This entry owes everything to John Bossy, *Giordano Bruno and the Embassy Affair* (1991); see especially the 2002 reprint (third edition), where Bossy introduces some qualifying remarks. I have also consulted his *Under the Molehill: An Elizabethan Spy Story* (2001). For Giordano Bruno in general, see Frances A. Yates, *The Art of Memory* (1966), *Giordano Bruno and the Hermetic Tradition* (1964) and other works; the quotation from Bruno's *La cena de le Cenere* is taken from Yates, *Giordano Bruno and the Hermetic Tradition*, p.236. Illustrations of MSS with transcripts and full translations are given by Bossy. My subjective impression is that Bossy's 'Hand FA' could well be Bruno's but, equally, Bossy's 'Hand FB' seems to have a different overall look and rhythm. Our translation is taken from Bossy, pp.217-8.

35. This warrant, and other documentation relating to the voyage, is quoted and discussed by David B. Quinn, *The Roanoke Voyages 1584-1590* (the Hakluyt Society, 1955), i. pp.173-4.

36. For further details of Sidney's appointment, see Simon Adams, *Household Accounts and Disbursement Books of Robert Dudley, Earl of Leicester, 1558-1561, 1584-1586* (Camden Society, 1995), Appendix II.

37. A diplomatic transcript of this MS is printed by Mueller, pp.67-72; with variant texts given by Marcus, pp.186-196. The possibility of Robert Cecil's hand being found in this manuscript was first raised, so far as I am aware, by Marcus, p.190n, although Cecil is not as they suggest the main scribe. The published text for which this MS was prepared is in R. C., *The Copy of a Letter to the Earl of Leicester... with a Report of Certain Petitions and Declarations Made to the Queen's Majesty at Two Several Times... and Her Majesty's Answers Thereunto by Herself Delivered* (1586), STC 6052. Elizabeth's famous theatrical simile was well-timed: 1587, the year of Mary's execution, marks the beginning of the golden age of English drama, with first performances of Marlowe's *Tamburlaine* and Kyd's *Spanish Tragedy*.

38. The unprecedented nature of the warrant was kindly pointed out to me by Peter Beal, who is currently studying Elizabeth's death warrants. The final version is known from several contemporary copies and the text printed by Strickland, *Letters of Mary, Queen of Scots* (1844), ii, pp.239-41. The original of the document signed by the Privy Council which enforced execution of the warrant was sold at Sotheby's, London, on 16 December 1996 (lot 40) and is now in the Lambeth Palace Library.

39. This letter is published by Marcus, p.297, and in the *Letters of Queen Elizabeth and King James VI of Scotland*, edited by John Bruce (Camden Society, 1849); my quotation from Carey is taken from Marcus, following Bruce, following Sir Walter Scott, although the memoirs have been edited more recently by F. H. Mares, *The Memoirs of Robert Carey* (1972).

40. For a summary of Stafford's spying career, see Colin Martin and Geoffrey Parker, *The Spanish Armada* (1999), pp. 106-8.

41. For a full transcription, see J.K. Laughton, *State Papers Relating to the Defeat of the Spanish Armada, Anno 1588* (1895); for analysis of the documentary and archaeological records, see Colin Martin and Geoffrey Parker, *The Spanish Armada* (1999).

42. This MS printed by Marcus, pp.325-6, who also give excerpts from the version printed in *Cabala, Mysteries of State, in Letters of the Great Ministers of K. James and K. Charles* (1654, our excerpts are taken from the reprint of 1663). The Cabala version, taken from a letter written by Sharpe to Buckingham in 1623, shows a degree of literary polish and is clearly a later version than the MS (for example the MS reading 'take foul scorn that Parma' is expanded into the less cogent 'take foul scorn that Parma or Spain'). Doubts as to the speech's authenticity are discussed by Susan Frye, 'The Myth of Elizabeth at Tilbury', *Sixteenth Century Journal*, 23 (1992), pp.95-114. These doubts are echoed in *Elizabeth: The Exhibition at the National Maritime Museum*, edited by Susan Doran (2003), pp.235-6. Sharpe's hand was identified by Janet M. Green, following a suggestion by Laetitia Yeandle of the Folger Library, in '"I My Self": Queen Elizabeth I's Oration at Tilbury Camp' in *Sixteenth Century Journal*, 28 (1997), pp.421-45. From further comparison of Sharpe's handwriting with other documents in the British Library (e.g. Sloane 3826, f.134, Lansdowne 61, f.44), Green's identification seems to me to be beyond question; as also does her additional suggestion that the explanatory note is likewise in his hand. The transcript given by Green should however be read in conjunction with the more accurate one given by Marcus (where, however, it is not noted that the manuscript is in Sharpe's hand). The apostrophes which I here suggest indicate that Sharpe had prepared this manuscript as a reading copy are not an invariable feature of his hand: for example, indefinite articles appear in the rest of the manuscript (overleaf) without such marks; nor, from the small sample that I have taken, does Sharpe make use of them in his letters.

44. For a discussion of Dee in terms of the Hermetic tradition and in context of his time, see Frances Yates, *The Occult Philosophy in the Elizabethan Age* (1979, reprinted 2002); for biographies see Peter French, *John Dee: The World of an Elizabethan Magus* (1972), Benjamin Woolley, *The Queen's Conjuror: The Life and Magic of Dr Dee* (2001). The quotation from Aubrey is from *Brief Lives*, ed. A. Clark, i, p.27. For a recent account of Dee's relations with Mercator, see Nicholas Crane, *Mercator* (2002). Dee's 'standard mathematical treatise' is his 'Mathematicall Preface' to the English *Euclide* of 1570. The phrase 'Incomparable BRYTISH IMPIRE' is in *General and Rare Memorials* (1570); the earliest instance of the phrase 'British Empire' cited by the *OED* occurs in a 1604 petition addressed by Dee to James I. The association (in the minds of the audience at any rate) between Dee and Prospero, is suggested by Frances Yates, *The Occult Philosophy in the Elizabethan Age* (1979, reprint 2002), pp.187-8. For a recent edition of Dee's diaries, see *The Diaries of John Dee*, edited by Edward Fenton (1998), p.237.

45. Peter Ackroyd, *Albion: The Origins of the English Imagination* (2002), p.47; for Dickens as a dreamer, see p.53. The quotation by Garrett Mattingly is from *The Defeat of the Spanish Armada* (Pimlico edition, 2000), p.166.

47. The most recent analysis of Essex's career is Paul E. J. Hammer, *The Polarisation of Elizabethan Politics: The Political Career of Robert Devereaux, 2nd Earl of Essex, 1585-1597* (1999), see especially pp.106 (Essex's bursting doublet), and 107. Elizabeth was, in fact, even older that Essex's mother, who was born in about 1540.

48. This letter is published and discussed in *The Letters of Sir Walter Ralegh*, edited by Agnes Latham and Joyce Youings (1999), no.58, where it is stated that 'There is no evidence that the letter was ever read by the Queen'. For the famous letter to Sir Robert Cecil (here modernised), see *Letters*, no. 46. The tennis ball quotation is from Anthony à Wood's *Athenes Oxoniensis*.

49. The full text of Elizabeth's translation of Boethius is printed and discussed by Caroline Pemberton, *Elizabeth's Englishings of Boethius De Consolatione Philosophiae, 1593, Plutarch De Curiositate, 1598, Horace De Arte Poetica, 1598* (Early English Text Society, 1899). Further discussion is to be found in Perry, pp.297-8. The only original English verse surviving in Elizabeth's autograph known to me is the cryptic five-line entry made in a French Psalter, now in the Royal Library, Windsor, beginning 'No crooked leg…'. Marcus, p.132, and Mueller, p.37, mistranscribe it as signed 'Elizabeth R' and date it to c.1565, whereas it is signed plain 'Elizabeth' and clearly dates from the period before she came to the throne. The handwriting is more consistent with a date of c.1549, and it could well refer to doubts about Elizabeth's conduct raised during the Seymour scandal (3): see the reproduction given in *Elizabeth: The Exhibition at the National Maritime Museum*, edited by Susan Doran (2003), p.201. For the discussion of Ted Hughes, I am indebted to Keith Sagar's *'Alcestis': Introductory Talk on 'Alcestis' for the Performance at the Lowry in Salford* (Northern Broadsides 2000).

50. For Young's relations with Dee, see Edward Fenton, *The Diaries of John Dee* (1998), p.246; and for his with Gerard, see *John Gerard: The Autobiography of an Elizabethan*, translated from the Latin by Philip Caraman (1951), pp.92-3.

51. A useful summary of the extremely wearisome Baconian controversy is given by Samuel Schoenbaum, *Shakespeare's Lives* (1991), Part VI. For Essex's advocacy of Bacon, see Hammer, *Polarisation of Elizabethan Politics*, p.297. The surviving text of the 'device' and the contemporary report, is printed by James Spedding, *The Letters and the Life of Francis Bacon*, vol.i (1861), pp.374-92 (376). My account of the Accession Day tilts is based upon Roy Strong, *The Cult of Elizabeth* (1977, new edition 1999), Chapter V 'Fair England's Knights: The Accession Day Tournaments', and Appendix I 'Sources for the Accession Day Tilts'.

52. For this document, see B. Roland Lewis, *The Shakespeare Documents* (1940), i, pp.238-9, where Latin and English texts are printed; Robert Bearman, *Shakespeare in the Stratford Records* (1994), pp.16-19, 67; Samuel Schoenbaum, *William Shakespeare: A Documentary Life* (1975), pp.173-5; E.K. Chambers, *William Shakespeare: A Study of Facts and Problems* (1930), ii, pp.95-99; and Park Honan, *Shakespeare: A Life* (1998), p.237-8. For the date of *Hamlet* see Harold Jenkins's Arden edition (1982), supplemented by my own study *The Mirror and the Globe* (1992). The quotation from *Hamlet* is from the First Folio, V.i., in the Nonesuch Coronation edition (1953), p.648.

53. The text, from a contemporary copy rather than the original, is printed by Harrison, pp.274-6.

54. Wallace MacCaffrey, *Elizabeth I* (1993), p.432.

56. Christopher Haigh, *Elizabeth I* (1988), p.202. For an analysis of the unchecked corruption in the Cecils' later administration, see Hammer, *Polarisation of Elizabethan Politics*, pp.354-5, n.72.

57. Printed by Harrison, pp.295-6. For Elizabeth's epistolary relations with James, see MacCaffrey, *Elizabeth*, p.441.

58. Printed in *The Letters of Lady Arbella Stuart*, edited by Sara Jayne Steen (1994), no.4. For a recent account of Arabella, see Sarah Gristwood, *Arbella: England's Lost Queen* (2003).

59. Printed and discussed by Norman Evans, 'Queen Elizabeth I and Tsar Boris: Five Letters, 1597-1603' in *Oxford Slavonic Papers*, vol.xii, 1965, pp.49-68. See also W. E. D. Allen, 'The Georgian Marriage Projects of Boris Godunov', in the same volume, p.69; and Ian Gray, *Boris Godunov: The Tragic Tsar* (1973). Another copy of the contemporary translation is BL Cotton MS Nero B.XI, fol.392.

60. 'The 11th: and last booke of the Ocean to Scinthia' and 'The end of the bookes, of the Oceans love to Scinthia, and the beginninge of the 12 Boock, entreatinge of Sorrow', with other shorter pieces, come from a notebook in Ralegh's handwriting discovered among the Salisbury Papers at Hatfield House and first published in 1870. Whether the other books ever existed is open to doubt. In *Colin Clouts Come Home Againe*, Spenser praises the 'Shepheard of the Ocean' whose song 'was all a lamentable lay,/Of great unkindnesse, and of usage hard,/Of *Cynthia*, the Ladie of the Sea': he is known to have met Ralegh when in temporary exile from the Court in 1589. Spenser also makes several references to Ralegh's 'Cynthia' in *The Faerie Queene*. The date of the Hatfield fragment however remains uncertain. Most commentators think it was written during Ralegh's disgrace following his marriage in 1592. Simon Adams has pointed out to me that it would have been among the papers confiscated from Ralegh when James I came to the throne. The most recent scholarly edition of Ralegh's poems is *The Poems of Sir Walter Ralegh: A Historical Edition*, edited by Michael Rudick (2000).

# Picture credits

Numbers in this list refer to the reproductions of the letters and documents.
Abbreviations: BL = The British Library; PRO = Public Record Office

Endpapers: Watermarks in BL Cotton MS Caligula E VIII f.119 (Garter arms) and f.131 (crowned cypher), from autograph letters by Sir Robert Cecil to Sir Henry Unton, Ambassador to France, 13 September 1591 and 14 March 1592

Frontispiece: Walker Art Gallery, Liverpool

Introduction: p.10 Secretary alphabet BL C.44.a.2; p.11 second Great Seal BL Detached Seal XXXVI.19; pp.12-13 stamped signature (1570) PRO SP 12/67 f.30, other signatures BL Add. MS 5756 ff.263 (1559), 271 (1568), 239 (1580), 273 (1588), 274 (1602)

1 BL Cotton MS Otho C X f.235
Portrait: Royal Collection © 2003 Her Majesty Queen Elizabeth
2 BL Royal MS 7 D X f.2 & lower cover
Portrait: Palazzo Barberini/Bridgeman Art Library
3 BL Lansdowne MS 1236 f.33
Portrait: National Portrait Gallery, London
4 BL Harley MS 6986 f.23
Portrait: National Portrait Gallery, London
5 PRO SP 11/4/2 f.3, 3v
Portrait: National Portrait Gallery, London
6 BL Vespasian MS F.III f.28
7 PRO SP 70/3 f.10v
Portrait: National Portrait Gallery, London
8 Hatfield House, Cecil Papers 2/18
9 PRO SP 70/11 f.78
10 BL Cotton MS Caligula B X f.106
Portrait: National Portrait Gallery, London
11 PRO SP 52/6, f.119
12 PRO SP 70/30 f.75
Painting: National Maritime Museum
13 BL Cotton Titus MS B II f.184
14 BL Lansdowne MS 94 f.30
Portrait: National Portrait Gallery, London
15 BL Cotton MS Galba D IX f.5
Drawing: Department of Prints and Drawings, British Museum
16 Pepys Library, Magdalene College, Cambridge, Papers of State, I f.427
17 PRO SP 52/12 f.77v
Portrait: Bonhams, London
18 BL Cotton MS Caligula C.I f. 94v
19 BL Cotton MS Caligula C.I f.367
20 BL MS Cotton Nero B.XI ff.316-7
Portrait: National Museet, Copenhagen/Bridgeman Art Library
21 PRO SP 102/49 f.1
22 Burghley House, MS 18518
23 BL Cotton MS Caligula C III f.242
24 Hatfield House, Cecil Papers 5/70 f.70v
25 Bodleian Library, MS Ashmole 1729 f.13
26 BL Cotton MS Vespasian F.VI f.86
Portrait: Victoria and Albert Museum/Bridgeman Art Library
27 PRO SP 70/144 f.161v
Portrait: Skokloster Palace Stockholm/LSH photo Samuel Uhrdin
28 Hatfield House, Cecil Papers 9/62
Portrait: Hardwick Hall, National Trust
29 Hatfield House, Cecil Papers 135/18
30 PRO SP 94/1 f.89
31 PRO SP 63/79 f.51
32 PRO SP 83/14 f.60v
Portrait: Rijksmuseum, Amsterdam
33 BL MS Cotton Caligula C.VII f.77
Scottish National Portrait Gallery/Bridgeman Art Library
34 BL Harley MS 1582 f.390v
35 BL Add. MS 5752 f.39
Seal: The British Museum
36 Hatfield House, Cecil Papers 14/19
Portrait: National Portrait Gallery, London
37 BL Lansdowne MS 94 f.85
Portrait: National Portrait Gallery, London
38 Hatfield House, Cecil Papers 165/10
Drawing: BL, MS Add.48027 f.850*
39 BL Add. MS 23240 f.65
Portrait: Falkland Palace/Bridgeman Art Library
40 PRO SP 78/18 f.52v
Portrait: National Portrait Gallery, London
41 PRO SP 12/214 f.108
Portrait: National Portrait Gallery, London
42 BL Harley MS 6798 f.87
43 PRO SP 12/215 f.114
Portrait: National Portrait Gallery, London
44 BL Harley MS 6986 f.45
45 BL Lansdowne MS 99 ff.20v & 21r
46 PRO SP 78/25 f.161
47 BL Add. MS 74286 ff.33, 33v
Portrait: National Portrait Gallery, London
48 Hatfield House, Cecil Papers 83/35
Portrait: National Portrait Gallery, London
49 PRO SP12/289 f.48
50 Hatfield House, Cecil Papers 29/9
51 Lambeth Palace MS 936 no 274
52 Shakespeare Birthplace Trust, ER 27/4a
Portrait: BL, G 11631
53 BL Cotton MS Titus B.XIII, pt.2 f.551
54 BL Cotton MS Titus B.XIII, pt.2 f.568
55 BL Loan 34
56 Hatfield House, Cecil Papers 76/97
57 BL Add. MS 18738 f.40v
Portrait: Victoria and Albert Museum/Bridgeman Art Library
58 Hatfield House, Cecil Papers 135/144
59 PRO SP 102/49 f.5
60 Hatfield House, Cecil Papers 144/240v
Portrait: Bridgeman Art Library

# Index

America 45, 47, 75, 85, 87, 103
Anjou, François, Duke of (formerly Alençon), letter to 73;
  67
Arcimboldo, Giuseppe, painting by 69
Armada, Spanish 75, 97, 99, 103, 105
Ascham, Roger, letter by 41;
  17, 19, 138
Assassination and Murder 49, 79, 119

Bacon, Francis, play by 117;
  29
Boethius, 113
Boleyn, Anne, 12, 19, 65, 125
Bothwell, James Hepburn, Earl of 49, 53
British Library 8
Bruno, Giordano, letter by 83;
  69, 115
Burghley, see Cecil, William

Casket Letters 8, 139
Cathay 41, 45, 103
Catherine de' Medici, letter by 67;
  portrait 67;
  73
Cecil, Sir Robert, transcript by 89;
  8, 111, 125, 127, 129, 133
Cecil, Sir William, Lord Burghley, letter by 35;
  letters written for Elizabeth 53, 61, 91;
  letter to 65;
  patent of ennoblement for 59;
  letters docketed by 29, 35, 37, 39, 45, 63, 65;
  portrait 35;
  8, 10, 14, 41, 51, 89, 127
Cely, Thomas, letter by 75
Clouet, François, portrait by 67
Codes and Ciphers 83, 87, 95
Common People, letter by 127;
  105, 115, 119
Condition of manuscripts 9
Cotton, Sir Robert, MSS collection 8, 17

Darnley, Henry, Lord, portrait 49;
  49, 53
De Critz the Elder, John, portrait by 95
Dee, John, letter by 103;
  69, 115
Dickons, Robert, letter by 105
Drake, Sir Francis, letter by 97;
  portrait 97;
  9, 47
Droeshout, Martin, portrait by 119

Edward VI, letter to 23;
  portrait 23;
  14
Egerton, Sir Thomas, warrant to 125
Elizabeth I
  autograph letters by 17, 19, 21, 23, 25, 65, 73, 129;
  letters signed by 41, 53, 121;
  speeches by 43, 89, 99;
  poetry by 113;
  translations and letters in foreign languages by 17, 19, 41, 73, 113;
  documents signed by 61, 85, 125;
  documents in the name of 59, 91, 119;
  literary compositions by 17, 19;
  letters and petitions to 27, 29, 31, 33, 35, 37, 39, 45, 47, 49, 51, 55, 57, 63, 67, 69, 71, 75, 77, 79, 81, 83, 87, 93, 95, 97, 101, 103, 105, 107, 109, 111, 115, 123, 127, 131, 133;
  plays for 117;
  poems for 135
  portraits: 'Pelican', frontispiece;
    as a girl 17;
    in coronation robes 29;
    in 1572 43;
    'Darnley' 89;
    Oliver pattern 129;
    'Rainbow' 135
  embroidery by 16
  admirers, suitors and favourites 21, 31, 35, 55, 57, 67, 73, 101, 107, 109, 111, 123;
  bastardy 23;
  cult of Accession Day 29, 117;
  education 17;
  handwriting 10-11, 19, 41, 129, 133, 137;
  imprisonment 25;
  income 33;
  languages 17, 113;
  marriage and succession 31, 35, 43, 55, 57, 67, 71, 73, 129, 129, 131, 131;
  religion 29;
  signature 7, 12-14
Essex, Robert Devereaux, Earl of, letter by 109;
  letter to 121;
  death warrant 125;
  portrait 109;
  8, 11, 63, 99, 107, 117, 123, 127
Executions, warrants for 65, 91, 125;
  8, 11, 63, 89, 93, 115
Eworth, Hans, portrait by 25;
  139

'Fagot, Henry', letter by 83;
  41
France 17, 35, 67, 73, 83, 95, 107, 109

Galley Slaves 75
Germany and Hanseatic League 41, 47
Godunov, Tsar Boris, letter by 133
Gresham, Sir Thomas, letter by 33
Grey, Lady Jane, 12, 23
Grey de Wilton, Arthur Grey, Baron, letter by 77

Hamburg, letter to 41
Hardwick, Bess of, letter by 71;
  129
Hatfield House 8
Hawkins John, letter by 47;
  9
Henri III (formerly Anjou) 67, 95
Henri IV, letter by 107;
  109, 129
Henry VIII, letter to 19;
  portrait 19;
  14, 17, 29, 71, 131
Herle, William 41, 63

Hilliard, Nicholas, second Great Seal 12;
portraits by frontispiece, 43, 109, 111
Holbein, Hans, portrait of Henry VIII 19
Holy Roman Empire 69, 103

Ink, manufacture of 9-10
Inquisition, Spanish 75
Ireland 77, 121, 123
Italic hand 10-11
Ivan the Terrible, letters by 55, 57;
portrait 55;
11, 41, 45, 139
James VI, letter by 93;
letter to 129;
portrait 93;
131
Jenkinson Anthony, letter by 45;
55, 57

Key, Adriaen Thomasz., portrait by 79
Knox, John, letter by 37;
29

Lansdowne MSS 8
Leicester, Robert Dudley, Earl of, letter by 101;
portrait 101;
9, 35, 41, 71, 87, 93, 99
Luther, Martin 27, 29

Malta 39
Mary I, letter to 25;
portrait 25;
12, 14, 23, 27, 37, 71
Mary Queen of Scots, letters by 49, 51, 81;
letter to 53;
death warrant 91;
portrait 81;
drawing of execution 91;
35, 37, 63, 65, 73, 89, 93, 131
Melanchthon, Philip, letter by 29
Mountjoy, Charles Blount, Baron, letter by 123
Naval and Maritime 45, 47, 75, 85, 97, 103
Netherlands 79, 87
Norfolk, Duke of, letter by 63;
warrant of deferral 65;
9, 61

Occult Magic and Witchcraft 83, 103, 105, 115
Oliver, Isaac, portraits by 129, 135

Paper 9
Parchment 9
Parliament, speeches to 43, 89;
111
Parr, Katherine, letter to 17;
19
Paulet, Sir Amyas, letter to 91
Pens 10
Pepys Library 9
Philip II, letter by 31;
27, 79
Plays and Playwrights 89, 117, 119
Poetry and Poets 77, 87, 111, 113, 119, 135, 141
Pole, Cardinal, letter by 27;
Public Record Office 8

Ralegh, Sir Walter, letter by 111;
poem by 135;
portrait 111;
seal 85;
warrant for 85;
7, 8, 103, 127
Religion 19, 25, 27, 29, 31, 37, 39, 63, 67, 69, 75, 77, 79, 83, 95, 105, 115
Riccio, David 49
Ridolfi Plot 61, 63
Rudolf II, letter by 69;
portrait as Vertumnus 69
Russia 41, 45, 55, 57, 133

Scotland 35, 37, 49, 51, 53, 81, 89, 91, 93, 129
Seals 11-12, 57, 59, 61, 85, 91, 119, 121, 125
Secretaries and Scribes 14, 49, 61, 77, 89, 97, 105, 133
Secretary hand 10
Seymour, Edward, Protector Somerset, letter to 21
Seymour, Thomas, Lord 21
Shakespeare, William, exemplification for 119;
portrait 109;
10, 117, 121
Sharpe, Lionel, transcript by 99, 140
Sidney, Sir Philip, letter by 87;
portrait 87;
69
Slavery, 47, 75
Smith, Sir Thomas, letter to 61
Spain 31, 75, 83, 97, 99
Spanish Inquisition 75
Spenser, Edmund, letter by 77;
7, 101
Spies and Spying 75, 83, 95, 115
Stafford, Sir Edward, letter by 95
Stamped signatures 14, 49, 137
Stuart, Lady Arabella, letter by 131;
portrait 71;
71

Teerlinc, Levina, document illuminated by 59;
portrait by 49, 139
Tilbury Speech, 42, 45
Tobacco 47, 85
Torture 57, 61, 115, 139
Tower of London 25, 61, 63, 65, 125
Trade and Finance 33, 55, 57, 133
Treachery 95
Tyrone, Hugh O'Neill, Earl of 121, 123

Unicorns 45, 138

Valette, Jean de la, letter by 39

Walsingham, Sir Francis, decipherment by 95;
letters forwarded to 77, 83;
portrait 95;
7, 41, 81
Warwick, Ambrose Dudley, Earl of, warrant to 85;
87
Watermarks 9
William the Silent, letter by 79;
portrait 79
Wilson, Dr Thomas, letter to 61;
8

Young, Richard, letter by 115